DRUMBEAT

DRUMBEAT

Anger and Renewal in
Indian Country

Edited by

Boyce Richardson

Summerhill Press

The Assembly of First Nations

© 1989 Assembly of First Nations

Published by Summerhill Press Ltd.
52 Shaftesbury Avenue, Toronto, Ontario M4T 1A2

Distributed by University of Toronto Press
5201 Dufferin Street, Downsview, Ontario M3H 5T8

Cover design by Images Art Direction Inc.
Cover photo courtesy of The Ottawa Citizen
Text design by Michelle Maynes
Printed and bound in Canada

Canadian Cataloguing in Publication Data
Main entry under title:
Drumbeat: anger and renewal in Indian country
ISBN 0–929091–03–5
1. Indians of North America – Canada – Political activity.
2. Indians of North America – Canada –
Government relations – 1951 – .
* 3. Indians, Treatment of – Canada.
4. Indians of North America – Canada – Civil rights.
5. Assembly of First Nations. I. Richardson, Boyce.

E92.D78 1989   323.1'197'071   C89-095184-5

Contents

Acknowledgements

We wish to thank the following:

Peter Digangi, Daniel Christmas, Marie Battiste,

Elizabeth Thunder, Richard Overstall, Mary Wadden,

Paul Williams, Dave Nahwegahbow, Russ Diabo,

James Morrison, Mary Laronge,

Heritary Chiefs of the Gitksan Wet'Suwet'en,

Marvin George.

Twenty Years of Disappointed Hopes

Georges Erasmus
National Chief, Assembly of First Nations

As people of the First Nations of Canada we have a vision of the sort of country we want to live in and to build in collaboration with other Canadians. It is certainly not the sort of country we have now, one in which our people have been relegated to the lowest rung on the ladder of Canadian society; suffer the worst conditions of life, the lowest incomes, the poorest education and health; and can envision only the most depressing of futures for our children.

We do believe, however, that our situation can be turned around. We believe not only that we can rescue ourselves from these depressing conditions, but that, in the process, we can contribute enormously to the health, effectiveness, and decency of Canada, benefiting every person who lives in this country.

To do so we have to go back to the agreement made in the Two-Row Wampum Treaty signed between First Nations and the newly arrived Europeans in 1664.

All across North America today First Nations share a common perception of what was then agreed: we would allow Europeans to stay among us and use a certain amount of our land, while in our own lands we would continue to exercise our own laws and maintain our own institutions and systems of government.

We all believe that that vision is still very possible today, that as First Nations we should have our own governments with jurisdiction over our own lands and people.

We should decide about and benefit from the type of development we want in our own territories, not have such development forced on us to serve outside interests.

We should have tribal courts run by our own people. We should administer our own child-care and social services. We should take control over our own education, as we have already begun to do.

In this visionary Canada we would be free to express in our actions our tremendous concern for the environment, to undertake our traditional role as protectors of Mother Earth. Once our jurisdiction was recognized we would clear up pollution and prevent further degradation in our own territories, and we would establish sustainable economies that would consider the long-term future of our children and grandchildren.

In this Canada our treaties would be recognized as the sacred documents they are supposed to be and would be properly implemented in accordance with the full spirit and intention of the original terms and conditions. In effect, then, we would be participants in a bilateral arrangement with the federal government. Provinces would no longer have authority over us in our own lands, and whenever federal-provincial agreements were negotiated, we would be included, accorded a role similar to that of the provinces today.

We realize that what we are asking for requires new perceptions among Canadians of the characteristics of our country. But we believe that the changes we propose can be easily accommodated in the Canadian confederation as it exists now. Within that structure of different orders of government and distinct founding peoples, we would be regarded as a third participant, a separate founding nation, exercising control over its own territories.

Under such a system, we would not, of course, make laws for other territories, any more than, say, Quebec makes laws for Alberta. But our relationship with the federal government would be different. The honour of the Crown was pledged to preserve the best interests of the aborigines, and in 1867 a section was included in the British North America Act intended to enable the federal government to act as a buffer between the First Nations and the provinces, which were emerging as the new power-brokers.

In our vision of a better Canada, the federal government would continue to act as trustee, safeguarding the spirit and intent of the treaties and of past undertakings. Our problem has been that the federal government has largely abrogated that role. Yet, the continuing validity of that original Royal Proclamation has recently been reaffirmed in the justice system, and the proclamation itself included in the new Canadian constitution.

Aboriginal Self-Government in the United States

We have been pressing for this model of a revised government structure for a long time, but so far without success. Perhaps most Canadians do not realize that it already exists in the United States, where some eighty cases involving aboriginal-sovereignty issues arising out of the treaties have been fought up to the level of the Supreme Court. To a large degree these treaties were similar to those we signed in Canada: in the U.S. cases, First Nations have argued that sovereign nations entered into treaties, and that in doing so those nations did not relinquish sovereignty.

In deciding these cases, the U.S. courts have more or less recognized that First Nations' sovereignty survived the treaty-making process, and they have granted to First Nations a large degree of internal self-determination within what they call "Indian country." This country has been identified as the reserve lands set out in the treaties, whether or not those reserves were later broken into residential plots and sold to non-natives. In fact, there are reserves in the United States where the majority of residents are non-natives, but the tribal governments have their own courts, environmental-protection laws, police forces, child and educational legislation, and powers of taxation over everyone who lives within their jurisdiction. In short, in recent decades, the tribal governments in the United States have come to be recognized as having virtual parity of powers with the fifty state governments, and are included whenever a new federal-state relationship is being formulated.

While we do not wish to duplicate the U.S. system completely, we look to it as proof that the self-government proposals we have been trying to persuade Canadians to accept can, and do, work without detriment to the national governmental fabric, an absurd claim made often by our detractors.

We are keenly aware that the system we propose is not without the potential for problems; however, we believe that our interests and those of the people we live among are similar. We know that, in the modern world, no man, no race, no group or nation, is an island. Our vision of a better Canada rests on a foundation of co-operation among peoples.

Most of our people live in the Canadian hinterland, part of the country that has long been held hostage by the metropolitan centres. We know that non-Indians in the hinterland — whether special-interest groups, school districts, hospital boards, or municipal councils — need more resources, just as we do. And we understand that when we manage to win recognition of our right to self-government, with jurisdiction over non-Indian residents within the boundaries of our areas, it will be our mandate to ensure the equitable distribution of all benefits and responsibilities. One group of our people has vivid experience of this.

A year or two ago the Gitanmax, Kispiox, Kitwanga, and Moricetown bands of the Gitksan Wet'suwet'en Nation in British Columbia, 8,000 in number, passed a set of by-laws that gave them a great deal of power over the fishery in their reserves. As these by-laws were not disallowed by the federal government, they became, in fact, the law. The 25,000 non-native population of the area, especially those downstream, perceived that they were affected by our by-laws. An alliance was formed between the provincial government and local sport and commercial fishermen (with heavy lobbying in their favour from the Department of Fisheries and Oceans) that sought and won a court injunction, placing the by-laws in abeyance. So the victory of our people in winning more power over activities within our own lands was short-lived, temporarily nullified by actions of the surrounding majority.

Yet, these possible future difficulties are not insurmountable, merely obstacles to be overcome.

Enough of Outside Control and Manipulation

One thing we do know for sure is that control and manipulation from outside our communities have been the rule for many decades, and such a system of governance has certainly not worked; in fact, it has created an intolerable level of social and economic disorder among us. What we want is self-reliance, self-control, internal growth. We want to start a process of healing. We want to contribute to North American society, through better education, higher rates of employment and literacy, less dependence on welfare, and finally through a determined attack on the youth suicides, family abuse, alcoholism, and social dissolution that blight so many of our communities today.

We believe that to confront all these problems is not only in our interest, but in the interests of all Canadians. In fact, demographics indicate that as the national birthrate in Canada falls, and ours remains high, we are destined to become an ever-larger percentage of the Canadian work-force, estimated in at least one province to reach 40 per cent within a decade or so. This fact alone is one good reason why it is necessary to improve the educational levels of our people, and why there was such an immediate and strong reaction from young aboriginal people early in 1989 when the full impact of the funding cuts for our post-secondary education became fully understood throughout the country.

We cannot believe that our vision of a Canada in which we play a special and constructive role is so far removed from the wishes of ordinary Canadians as to be unattainable. Yet, in our struggle to achieve this goal, we have, in recent years, met with nothing but set-backs. It would not be an exaggeration to say that governments have exhibited a certain paranoia in response to our proposals. This paranoia seems to stem partly from economics: governments are afraid of what our proposals might cost. However, the hidden costs of ignoring them — welfare payments, health charges, unemployment insurance, not to mention the fact that so many of our people are unable to contribute as they should to the economy and cultures of Canada — are already immense.

Even more threatening to governments than the perceived monetary costs of our proposals is what they see as a loss of power. That is where a sort of paranoia is evident: governments cannot contemplate anything that might lead to a reduction in their powers, even when the application of that power over First Nations communities across the country has appalling results.

For us, this lack of response has become a crisis. Indeed, in June 1987, in face of the shocking indifference to our needs exhibited throughout the 1980s by Canadian governments at all levels, we held a First Nations assembly to consider what we could do next.

We considered four devastating facts:

- The process for recognizing and dealing with our claims to lands and resources had been deliberately stalled.

- We had been given a contemptuous brush-off by the First Ministers as we attempted to define with them the aboriginal rights entrenched in the constitution and had been completely shut out of and ignored in the Meech Lake agreement for constitutional amendment.

- Most of our efforts to stimulate economic, social, and educational change in our communities had been stymied by an unimaginative bureaucracy whose determination to hang on to its powers was matched only by the frequency with which it claimed readiness to transfer these powers to First Nations.

- In spite of favourable court rulings, Canada still refused to implement fully the terms of existing treaties.

Frustrated by the racist double-standards being applied to our people across Canada, our assembly decided that the time had come to move to direct action. This was not an idle threat, but a solemn decision to create the kind of pressures that we hope will bring Canadian governments back to the negotiating table.

Since that time we have had a series of confrontations between First Nations and the political and law-enforcement authorities of the dominant society. In these confrontations our people have discovered that non-violent actions of civil disobedience not only generate enthusiasm and solidarity among our own people, not only bring more attention to our grievances and attract considerable public support outside our own communities, but also have the desired effect of forcing governments, under pressure of public opinion, to take us more seriously, and even to resume negotiations.

This book is about some of the more prominent of these confrontations. Our people have not undertaken these extreme measures lightly. They have faced hostility from competing interests, arrest, imprisonment, and hardship. They would much rather be engaged in honest negotiations with governments than be standing for weeks and months at road blockades at great hardship to themselves and inconvenience to the public. But their patience is exhausted.

In almost every case described in this book, the disputed rights of First Nations have been denied for many decades, sometimes for hundreds of years. This is Canadian history as we have lived it, not the version of it that finds its way into Canadian textbooks or schoolrooms.

This book is about what aboriginal people have endured, and continue to endure in this country as we grapple with the colonizers voracious appetite for land and resources, and their increasingly omnipotent industry and technology.

Our Expectations Dashed

Sadly, as we head towards the 1990s, we, the people of the First Nations, have to admit that our relations with Canadian governments have never been worse. Our rising expectations of recent decades, our hopes for a better future, have unfortunately turned out to be illusory, shattered by the grim reality that governments, whether Liberal or Tory or NDP, are still not ready to work honestly with us to resolve issues that have been outstanding for centuries.

For the last few decades we have been riding a roller-coaster of political hopes and promises — our hopes often lifted in response to apparently serious commitments by governments to deal decently with us, and as often dashed as governments have failed to live up to these commitments.

We were encouraged in the 1970s as the Trudeau government retreated from its strange view that "the treaties cannot go on forever" (to quote one of Mr. Trudeau's infamous statements). In 1973 that government undertook to deal with our many land claims, which had been so often ignored, neglected, or violated in the two centuries since they had been written into law by the Royal Proclamation of 1763.

We could scarcely have expected that the claims process then established would move at such a snail's pace. At the present rate of progress, it could take hundreds of years to resolve our claims.

We were encouraged again in the early 1980s when we

succeeded in persuading government to entrench aboriginal rights, with specific mention of the Royal Proclamation in the Canadian Charter of Rights and Freedoms, and to lay down a formal negotiating process by which these rights would be defined in agreement with First Nations.

We certainly did not anticipate that Canada's First Ministers would make such a perfunctory effort to work with us on a definition of the meaning of our rights.

The result has been that our heightened expectations have given way to a pervasive sense of frustration as the promise for resolution of our concerns through the various forums offered — negotiation, self-government (as outlined in the Penner report of the Parliamentary Committee on Indian Self-Government), and the constitution — have each, in turn, proved meaningless.

The direct actions engaged in by our people have taken many forms:

- the Haida of British Columbia stand in the path of logging machines that are preparing to clear-cut their ancient forests;

- the Lubicon of northern Alberta and the Teme-Augama Anishnabai of Northern Ontario block the roads into their ancient lands in an effort to force governments to listen to them;

- the Mohawks of Akwasasne continue to affirm their sovereign right to cross the international border freely, as they have done since time immemorial;

- the Mi'kmaq and Malaseet of Nova Scotia defy provincial-government efforts to restrict ancient hunting and fishing rights that have recently been confirmed by the Supreme Court of Canada;

- the Gitksan-Wet'suwet'en of northern British Columbia enter a precedent-setting court battle to affirm their ownership of and jurisdiction over lands they have always occupied;

- the Innu of Labrador invade a NATO airbase as part of a brave and lonely battle against low-level flights by jet fighters that threaten to decimate the animal populations on which they depend and to bring to an end a hunting culture that has lasted for thousands of years;

- the Algonquins of the Ottawa Valley, frustrated by the refusal of federal and provincial governments to discuss with them the sustainable development of their traditional lands, pitch their tents on Parliament Hill, which is built on Algonquin land, are arrested and charged with committing a nuisance in a public place, and later block logging roads in their traditional lands.

Many of these struggles have galvanized other Canadians, who have quickly understood that the best interests of the nation of Canada lies in a just and honourable settlement with the First Nations. Indeed, thousands of Canadians, especially those in environmental and human-rights groups, churches, and some unions, have perceived the struggle of the First Nations as an effort to moderate the blind power of the industrial machine as it smashes its way through the Canadian hinterland. They have supported First Nations on those grounds, among others. But, of course, there is much more to the case made by First Nations than simply a defence of the environment.

The evidence shows that since the rise of the modern Indian political movement, governments have consistently underrated the seriousness of the claims for land, resources, and self-government that could be mounted by the people of First Nations in all parts of Canada. So little attention was paid to these claims in the first half of this century that a cabinet document of the late 1960s suggested the Canadian government could settle all aboriginal land claims in the country for $11 million. A more recent estimate has put the figure at $4.8 billion. Though there is far more involved than money, the difference between the two figures is a measure of the unreality of the traditional response of Canadian society to aboriginal claims. And it is, perhaps, an explanation of the panic that seems to seize contemporary Canadian politicians in face of our demand for just treatment.

The fact is that, for generations, Canadian governments have treated us as a disappearing race, and have administered us accordingly. "I want to get rid of the Indian problem," Deputy Superintendent of Indian Affairs Duncan Campbell Scott told the House of Commons in the early 1920s. "Our object is to continue until there is not a single Indian in Canada that has not been absorbed into the body politic, and there is no Indian question, and no Indian department." Nothing could have been clearer than that.

"Before a quarter of a century is gone, perhaps, the savages will be no more than a memory!" wrote a Quebec civil servant in 1897. "Is it wise to sacrifice, for needs that are more fictional than real of this race that is leaving, the interests of the majority of the state?" His argument was repeated, virtually verbatim, by a judgment of the Quebec Court of Appeal in 1974 in the case brought by the James Bay Cree against the Quebec government's hydro-electric project.

We native people have been subject to such reasoning throughout our history. Yet, we have not disappeared; we have survived, as we have done since long before the appearance of Europeans, against no matter what odds. Unfortunately, to the present day, governments have been unconscionably slow in coming to terms with the fact that we will always be here, and that our claims for justice, land, resources, and control over our own affairs will never go away and must be fairly and honourably dealt with.

My purpose in this introduction is to provide the political background against which the events described in this book have been played out. Let us take them in order: First, the comprehensive claims process that was initiated by the Liberal government in 1973; second, the constitutional process by which we succeeded in having our aboriginal rights entrenched but not defined; third, a brief account of the social, educational, and economic dilemma in which our people find themselves.

Comprehensive Claims: Discriminatory, Dilatory, and Unjust

The Royal Proclamation of 1763 stated clearly that the Crown should be the only body to deal with First Nations' land, and this had to be done before such land could be used by others. In many parts of the country this issue was never dealt with: in violation of the proclamation, in large parts of the Maritimes, all of Quebec and British Columbia, and many other parts of Canada as well, land was occupied by settlers without any prior negotiation with the First Nations who had always occupied it.

In theory, the comprehensive claims policy promised a solution to this problem; in practice, the way the policy has been administered has been not only unjust, but discriminatory towards and burdensome for our people.

Only three comprehensive claims were negotiated in the first ten years of the policy: the James Bay Agreement (1975) and the Northeastern Quebec Agreement (1978), both negotiated somewhat independently of the claims process, and that of the Inuvialuit of the Mackenzie River delta (1984).

Six other claims (the maximum that the government will negotiate at any one time) remain unresolved at time of writing, and it may be noted that none of them has been on the table for less than ten years. Another nineteen claims have been accepted for negotiation, eight are under review, and another twenty are expected to be submitted. So, with fifty-three claims either submitted or awaiting access to the process, at the present rate it will take 160 years to resolve these problems.

A fundamental problem is that First Nations and the federal government have approached negotiations with different viewpoints and objectives. The government, in its search for finality in all agreements, has viewed the process as one in which an aboriginal group fully cedes, surrenders, and extinguishes all of its rights flowing from its aboriginal title and ownership of the land, in return for which the government returns to aboriginal people some small portion of rights within the land-claims agreement.

As First Nations, however, we believe that our aboriginal title includes ownership and jurisdiction over all lands and resources within our traditional areas. For us, claims resolution is a process of determining what land, resources, and jurisdiction will be shared with the governments of Canada. For us, the process is not one of negotiating extinguishment of our aboriginal rights, but of arriving at an equitable agreement on sharing.

Our people find it fundamentally unjust that we should be required as a condition of entering negotiations to surrender the very rights on which our entire case is based. Such is required of no other group in Canadian society. A second stumbling-block has been the refusal of government to deal, as part of the claims process, with the governing powers that First Nations will have over their lands when the negotiations are completed.

Not Only Land, but Jurisdiction over It

Land, and jurisdiction over land, go hand and hand. We have been pressing for fair land settlement to provide the basis for an economically viable life for our people, but we have also insisted on our right to aboriginal self-government over that land. By this we mean our right to exercise jurisdiction over our traditional lands, resources, and people. We must share in the benefits that come from the resources of the land, and we must make decisions in the best interests of our people, the land, and its resources. Government has accepted such jurisdiction as a goal, but has given it a much more restricted interpretation than we know is necessary.

We have also found it inequitable, to say the least, that, in the claims process, the federal government has taken it upon itself to act as judge, jury, advocate, prosecutor, and defendant — a totally unprecedented move, as far as I know, in Canadian negotiation.

The first thing that happens to a claim when it is submitted by a First Nation is that it is evaluated by the Department of Justice as to its acceptability on legal grounds. This judgment is made before any negotiation is entered into, and without any forum for appeal. Indeed, four claims have been rejected at this stage, some of which ran up against an extraordinary concept invented by Justice department lawyers, namely, "superseded by law." According to this idea, if laws of general application have been passed that do not make explicit reference to aboriginal people, but have an indirect effect on a First Nation's rights, then, in the opinion of the federal government, such laws extinguish that First Nation's rights. In Nova Scotia, for example. Even though no effort was ever made to deal with aboriginal title, when the Nova Scotia First Nations entered a comprehensive land claim, federal lawyers decided the claim was invalid because First Nation rights had been "superseded by law." The same effect results when a province gives out land patents or makes regulations covering hunting. In this case, rights are held to be extinguished, even if such was not the purpose of the action. This concept has never been tested in the courts, and lawyers who conceived it have never been able to define it satisfactorily. It is tantamount to declaring that an act of trespass in a person's house gives the trespasser rights over that property.

Another classic notion by which the federal government has denied First Nations access to the claims process is called "acquiescence." According to this doctrine, aboriginal people lose their rights by acquiescence when they do not resist the appropriation of their lands and resources by settlement. This is a Catch-22, as the reader will see later in this book. In a case where a First Nations people — the Lubicon of Alberta — have resisted in modern times by putting up road blocks to restrict access to their lands, the full power of the law was brought to bear on them by the provincial government; they were arrested and

their road blocks dismantled. Clearly, the law demands acquiescence, then uses it as an escape clause to avoid dispensing justice.

The comprehensive claims process generally applies to First
Nations that have never signed a treaty; but, the experience of
First Nations that have signed treaties has been equally frustrat-
ing. Many treaty provisions have not been implemented, and the
federal government has interpreted treaties in the narrowest of
terms and has tried to change treaties arbitrarily, without the
consent of the First Nation concerned. I doubt if there is a single
treaty First Nation that believes its rights are being properly
protected. There is no effective forum for redress of grievances,
and no way has been found to get Canada to sit down and
modernize, renovate, or fully implement existing treaties. In the
Prairies, where the government has agreed that the First Nations
are entitled to lands they were promised but never received
under treaty, there have been endless arguments about which
population figures should be used in assessing the land entitlement: should it be figures from the date of first survey, or the
current population? When was the first survey? Was there ever a
first survey?

When agreements to resolve treaty-land entitlement were
finally reached in Saskatchewan and Manitoba, the current
government saw fit to repudiate them unilaterally. In this context the utility of even negotiating with the Crown is called into
question. Although "certainty" is a concept that preoccupies the
government lawyers, there is no certainty that the Crown will
fulfil its commitments.

In these and many other ways, the federal government has
blocked progress at the negotiating table, and in a bullying and
defiant way has challenged First Nations to go to court if we do
not like what we are offered, even though they know that
aboriginal people do not have the resources to fight long legal
battles. The Gitksan Wet'suwet'en court case, documented in
this book, illustrates the difficulties of this route. Two other
examples are pertinent: after the Teme-Augama Anishnabai

managed, in 1973, to impose a land caution over 110 townships in Northern Ontario, asserting aboriginal ownership, the Ontario government changed the legislation to preclude other First Nations from using the same tactic. Ten years later, when the Lubicon went to court to try for the same thing, the Alberta government retroactively changed the legislation to ensure that the band's action would fail. (These same tactics have been used by the South African apartheid government to deny the rights of Africans.)

Similarly, in 1985, the Supreme Court of Canada confirmed the right of Mi'kmaq Indians to hunt under a treaty of 1752, which the court declared to be in effect. Yet, in 1988, in defiance of that ruling, provincial game officers arrested and charged thirteen Mi'kmaq who were hunting outside the provincial hunting season, and have vowed to continue to prosecute Mi'kmaq citizens who exercise their rights.

In our view the Mi'kmaq case should have provided an opportunity for the federal government to begin bilateral negotiations with our people to redefine the terms of many of the old treaties. Instead, the government has chosen to ignore it. Even more absurdly, the minister has acted as if the treaty was with J.M. Simon (the Mi'kmaq who won the case) and not with all Mi'kmaqs. According to this reasoning, every Mi'kmaq would have to go to court to prove that he is descended from those who signed the 1752 treaty. This is the attitude of a federal government that is supposed to be there to protect the rights of aboriginal people.

These are only a few of the anomalies that have made the claims process unworkable.

The Conservative Government Reneges on Its Promises

We conducted intense lobbying on these issues during the 1984 election and after it; at first, we had some hope that the new Mulroney government would honestly try to improve matters, and meet us half-way. Their first minister of Indian Affairs, David

Crombie, had a task force make a thorough study of the comprehensive claims policy. The recommendations of this task force, released in March 1986, met a number of our objections to the present process, and was broadly acceptable to us and to other Canadians who keep close watch over these matters. It suggested, for example, that aboriginal rights should be recognized and affirmed as a matter of principle in every agreement, and the policy of extinguishing aboriginal rights in agreements should be abandoned.

The task force said the government's aim to reach "finality" in each agreement (which, incidentally, is shared by First Nations, who do not want to have to go back to square-one every time they need to affirm their rights) should be met by "balancing the need for certainty in the orderly development of land and resources, with the need for flexibility in the evolving relationship between aboriginal groups and governments in Canada." Such "balancing" could be done, the task force suggested, by having agreements reviewed on a periodic basis to determine whether they continue to meet the objectives of the parties.

Finally, since land and jurisdiction are so intimately connected, the task force agreed with us that First Nations' self-government should be negotiated as part of the claims process: such practice would be consistent with the constitutional recognition and affirmation of aboriginal rights and with the government's commitment to self-government.

Our hope that these recommendations would improve matters was dashed with the precipitate removal of Mr. Crombie from the Indian Affairs portfolio. Within months the new minister, Bill McKnight, had issued a revised comprehensive-claims policy, which virtually ignored the task force recommendations and was even more reactionary than what we had before. At the Assembly of First Nations, we described it at the time as yet another government invitation to aboriginal people to commit suicide.

The new policy further restricts the claims process by requiring the active participation of the provinces south of the sixtieth parallel. This is part of an obvious effort to expand the bilateral federal-aboriginal relationship confirmed in 1763 into a tripartite federal-provincial-aboriginal relationship. The policy is seen by First Nations as an effort to set up a good guy–bad guy scenario, where the provinces play the bad guy (as at First Ministers' meetings), with the federal government as the good guy encouraging First Nations to take what they can get because of the regressive provincial stand. It is also in direct conflict with the letter and intent of the Proclamation, which explicitly acknowledged that the interests of the colonies (now provinces) were diametrically opposed to those of First Nations.

Also, the new federal policy imposes a "municipal model" of self-government, avoiding any discussion of self-government powers for First Nations that encroach on federal or provincial powers, even though it is clear that our communities need many of the powers exercised by these two levels of government if we are to function effectively and succeed in the immense task of revivifying the life of our people.

Furthermore, throughout the new policy document, First Nations are characterized, not as "Nations or Tribes," as recognized by the Royal Proclamation, but as just another interest group in Canadian society, whose interests are recognized, but whose rights are not protected.

Finally, in an extraordinary misuse of language, the government policy admits the need for an alternative to extinguishment of land rights, but both of its suggestions involve "cession and surrender" of aboriginal title, either throughout the settlement area or in non-reserve areas. This new terminology seems to have the same old meaning. Posing cession and surrender of aboriginal lands as an alternative to extinguishment is like making suicide mandatory as an alternative to capital punishment.

Our Objections to Extinguishment

We have opposed extinguishment on many grounds: our aboriginal rights flow from the ownership of the land; extinguishment severs our links with the past, and ensures that our future rights will flow from the government's granting of rights. This converts our rights into privileges. In addition, extinguishment prevents revival of our aboriginal rights when the government does not honour its agreement. And finally, we oppose it because it is unnecessary.

The government's own task force said that, if extinguishment is not abandoned, "there will be no possibility of achieving land claims agreements based on common objectives"; it also said that there are other viable methods of dealing with this problem. We agree. The policy of extinguishment was not introduced until after confederation. In the early British treaties, aboriginal title was never surrendered in the lands that remained in aboriginal hands, and the task force suggested this older method could be used as a model for future treaties.

Virtually every First Nation has put forward alternatives to extinguishment in its negotiations, but they have not been listened to. For example, we have suggested that our jurisdiction, flowing from our ownership of the land, continue, but that we could relinquish our aboriginal rights over areas agreed to be left open for development. However, such development would be subject to specific terms and conditions, which, if breached, would result in re-examination of the agreement. We also feel that, as a first priority, aboriginal title should confer continuing benefits to First Nations — such as royalties and employment benefits — before other priorities (federal, provincial, and corporate) are considered, and that within the area covered by any agreement First Nations jurisdiction be retained over certain decisions.

These, then, are our many objections to the comprehensive claims policy as it is now implemented. I think readers will agree that this list of problems is a formidable one. Our frustrations have arisen from the fact that, from our point of view, the government's approach in the last few years has become much more restrictive, and less accommodating to our needs (and hopes) than it has ever been. We certainly cannot report progress, or even the prospect of progress in the immediate future.

Regrettably, we have to report that the Mulroney government from the first has apparently been pulled two ways: at the same time as Indian Affairs minister David Crombie was holding out the promise of change for the better, the deputy prime minister, Erik Nielsen, as part of his review of government spending, was recommending Draconian cuts that would entirely change the relations of First Nations with the federal government.

Nielsen's report suggested that the federal government should reduce the cost of its obligations to us, and eventually end delivery of programs and services; in other words, the federal government should hand over the First Nations of Canada to the provinces, being careful to do it gradually to avoid resistance. This was also suggested in 1969, in Jean Chrétien's White Paper, which was withdrawn in face of the massive resistance of the aboriginal people. But, just as our people have always felt that the Chrétien prescription for our future has since been implemented by stealth, so, more recently, we have seen Nielsen's strategy implemented.

I will say more about the effects of this later, particularly in relation to education. Here, it is enough to remark that Crombie's tentative moves towards resolving the difficulties in the claims process were out of sync with the ideologies emanating from Nielsen and the right-wing of the Conservative party in Parliament. His successor, McKnight, was put there to lower our expectations and cut services, and he has certainly succeeded in doing both.

The Constitutional Process: A Dead-End

Native people in Canada will not soon forget the contempt with which we were treated in the long negotiations leading up to the patriation of the Canadian constitution in 1982; or the equally contemptuous treatment we have received since negotiations to define our rights broke down in 1987.

We watched with mixed feelings as the national debate on the constitution proceeded in the first years of this decade. On the one hand, we were very much aware that any constitutional change might adversely affect the treaties that our forbears had signed with Great Britain before Canadian confederation; on the other hand, we were hoping that the inclusion of aboriginal and treaty rights in the constitution would, for the first time, signal our place in confederation.

We held many meetings to discuss what might happen, and the consensus was that we should conduct a determined lobby, both here and in Great Britain, in an effort to ensure that our rights would be protected when the constitution was "brought home." In particular, we did not want our link to the Crown to be affected. Our nervousness arose, in part, from the fact that the meaning of our rights written in these pre-confederation treaties had not been tested in Canadian courts, but, more perhaps, because of our memory of the callous way in which we have been treated by Canadian legislatures and courts in the past.

We embarked on a significant plan to generate publicity, organized considerable lobbying in Canada and (surprising, I think, to many Canadians) in Britain, aimed directly at the Crown, and at the British Parliament, which still held custody, as it were, over our constitution. At one point, we gathered together more than five hundred chiefs for a major assembly in London. We held tours throughout the country, and even sent teams and information packages to Europe to educate the public there about what was at stake.

The result was that we became a constitutional issue. In the course of all this work, the First Nations of Alberta, New Brunswick, and Nova Scotia asked the English Court of Appeal for a declaration that responsibility for Indians be left with the British Crown. That may have seemed to many Canadians a somewhat bizarre procedure; yet, though we lost that case, we did obtain, in the judgment issued by the English Court of Appeal, a remarkable statement of the responsibilities that the Canadian government has undertaken by repatriating the constitution, and a ringing declaration of the continuing validity of all the ancient undertakings given to us by the British Crown.

In this judgment, the distinguished jurist Lord Denning described the Royal Proclamation of 1763 as "equivalent to an entrenched provision in the constitution of the colonies of North America" and held that it is binding on the Crown "so long as the sun rises and the river flows." Its force as a statute, said Lord Denning, is analogous to the status of Magna Carta, which has always been considered to be the law throughout the Empire. That is a remarkable confirmation of the views our people have never ceased to espouse since Canada was colonized.

Lord Denning said the obligations of the British Crown under the Royal Proclamation, and under the pre-confederation treaties signed with native people, were undertaken by Canada with the passing of the British North America Act of 1867, and he went out of his way to reaffirm their continuing meaning. He said the proposed Canadian constitution "does all that can be done to protect the rights and freedoms of the aboriginal peoples of Canada," but if there should in future be any reason for distrust, then "the discussion in this case will strengthen their hand so as to enable them to withstand any onslaught....They will be able to say that their rights and freedoms have been guaranteed to them by the Crown, originally by the Crown in respect of the United Kingdom, now by the Crown in respect of Canada, but, in any case, by the Crown. No Parliament should do anything to lessen the worth of these guarantees. They should be honoured by the Crown in respect of Canada 'so long as the sun rises and the river flows.' That promise must never be broken."

When this splendid statement of our case was made in 1982 we could be excused for hoping that its spirit would infuse the law-makers and justice-givers of Canada. Indeed, as far as the courts are concerned, the spirit of Lord Denning appears to have had some effect, because Chief Justice Brian Dickson has since held in one case that "treaties and statutes relating to Indians should be liberally construed, and doubtful expressions resolved in favour of the Indians"; in another case, he has held that there rests upon the federal Crown a fiduciary duty or trust-like responsibility when it deals with reserve lands.

This finding of a fiduciary duty of the federal government raised many fundamental questions that the government has shown no inclination to address. This is another illustration of the difficult position we find ourselves in. Ever since confederation we have been in a kind of strait-jacket in that the same government that is supposed to protect our rights is our chief antagonist in many issues that are vital to our future. For example, the very lawyers who dreamed up the concept of our rights having been "superseded by law" and "surrendered by acquiescence" are in flagrant conflict of interest because they are, at one and the same time, supposed to be fulfilling their fiduciary or trust obligation to First Nations while also protecting the interests of the Crown.

There is little doubt in our mind as to which of these tasks they take more seriously. Indeed, it is not too much to say that there are government lawyers who have made a life's work of finding ways to diminish the rights of aboriginal people. They expend enormous energy on this, including trying to dismantle what has been recognized and affirmed by the constitution. I can give an example: one advance made in the constitution was the recognition and affirmation of rights and freedoms acquired through future land-claims settlements. Justice department officials have recently set out to make a concerted effort to call this into question. The approach is to suggest, little by little, that some parts of comprehensive agreements may not, after all, be protected by the constitution. For example, they now hold that self-government may not be constitutionally protected, unless there is a clause that very clearly states the contrary. Recently the Nisga'a of northern British Columbia tried to include in their prospective agreement a clause that said that everything in the final agreement would have constitutional protection, but they could not get the government to agree to the wording they wanted. Finally, they wrote asking for a definitive statement by the government as to what was included and what was not. What they received in reply was a convoluted legal statement that seems to say that some sections might be protected, and some might not, and only the courts would know.

Our People Treated As an After-Thought

Our high hopes — and, if one may say so, Lord Denning's high hopes — for a just and honourable resolution of our problems have been sorely betrayed in the seven years since the Constitution Act was passed recognizing and affirming our aboriginal rights.

Indeed, even before the act was passed, we had a striking demonstration of how expendable we apparently are in the eyes of the nation's provincial premiers.

First, we were included in the proposed deal but then, when Trudeau finally did get nine of the premiers on board (without Quebec), the proposed constitution that they would agree to no longer included aboriginal rights. We had been dropped as if we were no more than an after-thought.

When this happened we renewed our lobbying — in fact, what we had done previously was nothing compared with the work we now did. We formed coalitions across the country such as we had never known before, and organized tremendous effort to put pressure on the premiers and prime minister. Eventually they agreed to put the clause recognizing and affirming aboriginal rights back into the charter, but with the word "existing" added— "the existing aboriginal and treaty rights of the aboriginal peoples of Canada are hereby recognized and affirmed" — in an obvious effort to limit the meaning of the clause. Included also was an amendment that was intended to shut us up — that the details and definition of our rights would be resolved through a conference.

Now began a phase, lasting about five years, in which we did seem to be included in the constitution. The conference we held with the First Ministers, in March 1983, was an occasion of immense symbolic significance for our people. Almost 450 years after the arrival of the first Europeans, we at last had the opportunity to discuss our future face to face with them, nation to nation. For the last 150 years we had seen our cultures and languages suppressed and our economy undermined. We had been impoverished while the newcomers became enriched. Through all this time, though absent from the country's political agenda, we had never ceased to believe in, and stubbornly to affirm, our ancient rights.

So, our people turned up for this meeting in Ottawa with a proper sense of its solemnity and significance. Our leaders were in full regalia; we opened each day with public prayers arising from traditional ceremonies; we handed the traditional pipe of peace around the table. We believed we were gathered to do something that First Nations have always done — to discuss great issues with the objective of arriving at a consensus satisfactory to both sides.

It was clear from the first that the European side did not share our leaders' attitudes. But, in that first meeting, we did manage to get agreement on a constitutional amendment requiring a five-year negotiating process in which three further meetings would be held between First Nations and First Ministers. The agenda proposed for these meetings included four items: equality rights; aboriginal title and aboriginal rights, treaties and treaty rights land and resources; and aboriginal or self-government.

But, by the time the last of these three meetings was held, in March 1987 — they began under the Liberals and ended under the Conservatives, who were firmly pledged to resolve outstanding issues — we had not succeeded in dealing with any of the agenda items.

What happened in that last meeting was shocking to all native people in Canada. When negotiations arrived at a stalemate, Prime Minister Mulroney, who, along with most of the premiers, insisted that self-government could not be enshrined in the constitution until it was clear what self-government meant, had a number of choices. He could have extended the process without amendment of the constitution by announcing a continuing series of meetings, as an act of political will; or, he could have adjourned the meeting for a couple of years, to grapple with the problem of Quebec's position in relation to the constitution, and then come back to us.

But what he chose to do instead was to come back into the conference in the middle of the day, throw up his hands, and announce there was nothing further he could do. He told the country it was all over, even before our allotted time for the conference had run out.

Within less than a month he played a totally different role when he gathered the same First Ministers at Meech Lake to consider the place of Quebec. He said he was locking the door; they'd work all night long, if necessary; they weren't getting out of the lodge, would have to stay two or three days, until they agreed to resolve the question of Quebec.

First Nations' leaders were astounded to see that, at Meech Lake, Mulroney and the same premiers signed a vague and imprecise accord, the details of which were to be worked out by 1990. There are obviously two standards that the prime minister and premiers follow: one for themselves, and another for aboriginal peoples.

It seems to us in retrospect that the Meech Lake accord was already in the works when they decided to give up so easily on defining our rights: they didn't want any agreement among the nine premiers that might conceivably prejudice their coming agreement with Quebec.

Since then, all we have been able to get out of the federal government is a promise that, if and when the day comes that there are enough provincial governments in favour of amendments covering aboriginal rights, then the process will be renewed. But that process, with its countless meetings with officials and ministers from all across the country, could not produce consensus.

So, what we have run into is a complete dead-end: in our view the prime minister has adopted a hypocritical approach. He takes the view that, for aboriginal people, constitutional amendments will somehow come out of the air. We will all, simultaneously across the country, at some magical future time, arrive at a meeting of minds without putting any work into it. But, at the same time, he has no similar illusions on any other subject. The Meech Lake accord constitutionally entrenches two First Ministers' meetings every year on other subjects.

A Racist Double-Standard

So, we believe — heavy-heartedly, I may say — that his position is extremely racist, and reveals a double-standard. Our only hope is that we can somehow force Mulroney to move. And the only present hope for that seems to lie with the political leaders in Manitoba and New Brunswick who are insisting that the Meech Lake accord be amended to include, among other changes, a renewal of First Ministers' meetings with the First Nations. We have tried to change the government's mind: we have met with the various leaders, have made presentations to whatever parliamentary committees have considered Meech Lake.

But, I have to say that when we realized the immense concessions the prime minister made to the provinces in the

Meech Lake accord, and compared them with his refusal even to consider such concessions towards aboriginal people, the level of frustration among our people rose considerably. Quebec could be recognized as a distinct society, but not, apparently, the First Nations, who were here long before any Quebeckers or any other European set foot on the continent. We, too, have our own languages, our own cultures, our own ways of life. How, one might ask, could we be more distinct than we are? The whole process was not only a negation of our high hopes when we entered negotiations, but a caricature of our traditional methods for resolving conflict and reaching consensus.

We held a meeting in June 1987, where we decided to go out and generate the pressure needed to force the Canadian governments back to the negotiating table. We would begin to implement ideas we had about self-government and our land; and, in places where our people's patience had run out, we would get involved in direct action. That is why we have had, since then, the many confrontations described in this book.

At the same time we realized that, in face of the government's apparent decision not to negotiate with us, court cases will become much more important in our future than they have been in the past, when, in Canada as distinct from the United States, we have tended to rely on the political rather than the legal route towards resolution of conflicts. Unfortunately, it seems that the political route is now being closed to us.

We have taken a hard look at U.S. case law, have tried to assess how it might apply to our Canadian situation, and have concluded that we need to create a native legal agency to help bring important cases to court and carry the fight all the way up to the Supreme Court where necessary. Legal costs have become so high that, for example, the case being fought by the Gitksan Wet'suwet'en could eventually cost them $10 million. In such circumstances it becomes impossible for many groups even to contemplate going to court. Our intention is to create this agency, and to have lawyers on salary who can fight the court cases needed to affirm our rights.

This, then, is the political background to the actions taken in various parts of the country by aboriginal people in defence of our lands, our communities, and our rights.

An Effort to Educate the Public

Our people have tried in every case to explain the facts clearly to non-native people and to persuade them that the positions we have taken are in the long-term best interests of the whole community. For example, Chief Gary Potts, of the Teme-Augama Anishnabai who live in the Temagami area of Ontario, has repeatedly brought it to public attention that, at the present rate of cutting, there are only five years' worth of logging left in the forests his people are trying to defend, even if the government should permit the companies access to them. The native purpose is not to shut down the economy of the area, as their opponents claim. Rather, the long-term public interest lies in saving the remaining trees and collaborating on a forestry regime that is sustainable over the long term. These educational efforts have had a great deal of success: every environmental group in Ontario is opposing the extension of logging roads into this last remaining stand of timber. Yet, the Ontario government continues to bow down before the four hundred jobs that are at stake. If they would take a longer view they would realize it would be far cheaper to compensate the loggers for the few years of work they have left, and get on with re-creating the economy of the area on a more viable basis.

Similarly with road blockades undertaken in various parts of the country. The Haida who blocked the way to forests that were about to be clear-cut on the Queen Charlotte Islands attracted nation-wide support, not only on human-rights grounds, but because they were also battling for a more sustainable approach to the economy of their lands. The Lubicon of northern Alberta attracted support not only throughout Canada, but all over the Western world. In their effort to boycott the Olympic art show, "The Spirit Sings," they conducted an educational campaign that affected the outlook of hundreds of museum curators, anthropologists, and archaeologists, not to mention members of the public.

In Barriere Lake, Quebec, the Algonquins, one summer day in 1988, slowed traffic near their reserve and held what they called an "information toll": in six hours they obtained 1,400 signatures from passing motorists who supported the Algonquin aim to replace the present destructive forest- and water-exploitation of their lands with a more sustainable economy that will benefit all sectors of society into the far-distant future. In each case our people have tried to organize well for non-violent, effective action, and at the same time to educate the public about what they are doing and why.

We have pointed out to representatives of the Canadian government that, if they are really serious about protecting the Canadian environment, and want to so something to stop future destruction of the ecological balance, the best way to do it would be to recognize as quickly as possible the legitimate claims to aboriginal title that First Nations are making across the country. Given control of our own territories, we would immediately instil project-by-project decision-making, and there is no way in the world that our people would be making the kinds of decisions that are now destroying wildlife habitat, decimating forests and off-shore resources, and degrading soil, air, and water. We have proven that this is so by the programs that we are trying to have accepted in many parts of the country. In almost every case these ideas have been rejected by governments, almost without serious consideration. Given a choice between dealing with aboriginal ideas of conservation and sustainability, and the exploitive ideas of huge corporations, the government never shows any hesitation in choosing the latter.

In the face of all these discouragements, in a speech in 1988 I warned about the dangers that lie ahead if our people are to be continually frustrated in their efforts to resolve their problems. If a serious attempt is not soon made to resolve a wide range of problems such as those outlined in these pages; if educational, housing, and economic difficulties in so many of our communities are not overcome, we can certainly expect a more aggressive response, especially from younger people. They will begin to take a critical attitude to leaders such as me who have been trying for years to resolve our problems through negotiation, but have been getting nowhere.

Our populations are increasing rapidly. As well, some 100,000 to 150,000 people who had lost their Indian status through the policy of "enfranchisement" have been reinstated and are now able to return to their reserves.

I warned in my speech that Canadians could not expect our people to remain peaceful for ever. In reaction, some said I was encouraging violence, though that was the farthest thing from my mind. I was trying to get the Canadian public and government to become aware that conditions among aboriginal people, already by far the most disadvantaged group in Canada, are not improving, and that this situation is leading to frustration. Many people, however, have said I was correct, and they have restated my warning from one end of the country to the other; still others have said that I understated the case, and that we may already have run out of time.

The Struggle for Social, Educational, and Economic Revival

The dead-end we have run into in trying to get constitutional recognition of our ancient rights, and resolution of our just claims to land and self-government, is having a severe impact on the struggle for social, cultural, and economic revival in First Nations' communities from one end of the country to another.

For it is not only at the negotiating table with First Ministers that aboriginal people are not really being taken seriously; we encounter these same attitudes, too, in our day-to-day dealings, as we try to gain control over education, economy, culture, and indeed every other aspect of our lives from the agencies established by government that still consider themselves to be the guardians of our interests. This attitude — that we are wards, and they our guardians — is so pervasive that we have learned to be wary when such agencies declare their readiness to hand over control of affairs to people in the reserves; what they really mean, we have discovered, is that they will maintain control of the purse-strings and policies, while enlisting our people in the task of administering their system.

Education is a good example. In the last fifteen years a great deal of the most innovative approaches to educational reform in Canada have been carried out by First Nations who have tried to seize community control over the way, and the things, their children are taught. Some 243 First Nations communities in Canada have established some form of jurisdiction over the education of their children, but a major study carried out last year by the Assembly of First Nations has shown that, even when jurisdiction is transferred to First Nations communities, there are a thousand mechanisms that government departments — ranging from Indian Affairs down through provincial education departments to municipal school boards — are able to use to restrict the scope and quality of our innovations. Even the most independent and experimental of First Nations–controlled schools remain to a large extent in thrall to the funding mechanisms established by the Department of Indian Affairs and the educational strait-jackets erected by provincial departments.

The movement for First Nations' control of education came from the fact that provincial schools have so utterly failed to meet the educational needs of their many First Nations' students. This situation became so obvious that, in the 1970s and 1980s, our people in many parts of the country decided to take matters into their own hands. Angrily in some cases, often ill-prepared for the responsibility, and sometimes blissfully unaware of the difficulty of what they were trying to do, they set up their own schools, opening them in trailers or old buildings, working with untrained teachers, with too little money, with inadequate materials, and sometimes ill-defined goals. And yet out of this have come some remarkable schools, obtaining extraordinary results.

Almost all of these schools have been based on traditional First Nations' values — self-reliance; generosity; and respect for personal freedom, nature, and wisdom — and they have attempted to return to the holistic qualities of education as it was traditionally practised by the aboriginal people of North America. In our view the serious conditions of alcohol and drug dependency, family violence, child abuse, unemployment, incarceration, housing and educational deficiencies, disease, and violent death that are found today in so many First Nations communities are a measure of the extent to which government-defined and -imposed programs have undermined our values. The aims of the schools that have been taken over by our communities are to develop among students (in contrast to what they have been getting from the state-run schools): strong moral character; an appreciation of spiritual and cultural values; a respect for sound traditions; concern for the rights of others, regardless of race or creed; and a willingness and capacity to act in the best interests of one's family and community.

To quote the program of one of the most successful native-controlled schools, in Manitoba: "The school program uses the Medicine Wheel, an aboriginal symbol, as the model for school discipline. The main values taught are caring, sharing, honesty, and determination. The school rules are: respect for the Creator, respect for life, respect for elders, respect for parents, and respect for self."

Naturally, these values require a type of school that is very different from those established by the dominant society, and it has been difficult to fit such schools into the educational framework established by the provinces.

First Nations parents are just as concerned as other parents that their children have a sound formal education that will enable them to function successfully, and studies that have been done of children whose formal education has been started in native languages indicate that, in the early grades, they perform just as well in mathematics, social studies, and science as do other Canadian students, and they quickly catch up in English when that subject enters the curriculum in grade four. But, in addition, they have learned their native languages, and have a new pride in themselves, their community, and their nation.

Some of these schools have even produced children who are much more fluent in the native languages than are their parents, and they have had a positive effect on the cultural atmosphere in their communities.

Of course, plenty of mistakes have been made, but the experience has convinced us that we must have jurisdiction over our own education if we are to meet the goals that, according to our study, First Nations parents demand: that is, a curriculum that teaches cultural heritage and traditional skills, eliminates stereotypes, and promotes self-worth (in other words a curriculum of culturally relevant content), along with the academic subjects, particularly in language, reading, maths, science, and computer skills.

Our study records some remarkable achievements: in some cases, whole curricula and the materials to teach them have been developed by the people in the community, in spite of their lack of resources and their apparent lack of the skills needed for this kind of work. This confirms us in our belief that First Nations communities possess talents and capacities that need only the opportunity and encouragement to come to fruition.

The Main Problem: A Lack of Resources

The single greatest problem is the lack of resources, and here we have discovered a sort of triple-standard. The federal government is responsible in law for the education of First Nations children, but when such children are transferred from federal schools to community-run schools, the per-capita expenditure for their education is reduced, and when they are transferred to provincial schools, the expenditure increases. Our study discovered some amazing examples of discrimination. In one Manitoba community, for example, $4,300 per student was allocated by the federal government to a school taken over by the chief and councillors, while they paid $8,000 for every native student who would attend a new provincial school that was being built right across the road. The federal government signs long-term master tuition agreements with the provinces that cover the funding of native students for the next twenty years. Needless to say, our people are never consulted when these arrangements are made.

Yet, in general, our schools have reduced drop-out rates, improved success rates, and have increased immensely the involvement of parents in the educational process.

Unfortunately, Erik Nielsen's strategy of putting a lid on spending is having a baleful effect, especially on the funding of post-secondary education for native students. In spite of all the difficulties I have mentioned, the numbers of native students who qualified for post-secondary education rose from 2,500 in 1973 to 15,000 in 1988. This was possible because every student was eligible for assistance from the Department of Indian Affairs for tuition costs, books and instructional materials, living expenses, transportation, and special tutorial assistance. This assistance program was one of the government's most successful; it raised the participation rate of native students to 3 per cent of the age group, compared with 4.3 per cent of the Canadian population as a whole. But, just as this approach to equity with other Canadians was in sight, the government decided that the Treasury Board should decide how much money would be allocated to the program, regardless of the number of eligible students.

So, from the school year 1987–88, the assistance was no longer available to everyone of our people who qualify for it. The Treasury Board established a priority list: first, those who were receiving funding before 1987–88; second, those who applied for funding before that year but were deferred because of applying too late for the school year; third, eligible high-school graduates or mature students enrolling in undergraduate programs for the first time; fourth, students entering college-preparatory or postgraduate courses; and, fifth, students who previously dropped out of a college or university.

According to this list, it seems, those who needed the assistance most were the least likely to get it.

We expected these cuts to lead to a reduction in participation rates among First Nations students in post-secondary schooling, and this year we estimate that some 2,000 students were not admitted who would have been under the old system. Also being reduced are the numbers of older students (over twenty-five years of age); this reduction is serious for our people, because such students comprise a larger portion of post-secondary aboriginal students than the national average. The program-funding reduction has increased inequities based on locations of our communities, their past usage of the program, and their relative wealth. And the new policy represents a decision, basically, to leave out the newly eligible students who have regained their status under Bill C-31. With 50 per cent of our people under age twenty, we have a pool of some 250,000 who could conceivably aspire to go to university or post-secondary institutions of one kind or another. So, even the present number, 15,000, although a big advance on a few years ago, does not by any means represent the potential numbers of our post-secondary students.

On March 29, 1989, the government added a new twist to its native-education policy, by capping funding for post-secondary schooling at $130 million. This stimulated one of the biggest movements of opposition to government policy, especially among our young people, that we have seen in Canada in recent years. We held a special chiefs assembly and decided on a National Day of Protest. Within a few months, six such National Days of Protest had been held. Native students undertook fasts, marches, sit-ins, demonstrations, information sessions, and so on, all across the country. Thousands of people were involved, and we received much support from the Canadian public, including churches, labour organizations, students' associations, university professors, and human-rights groups.

We were battling for three objectives: first, the suspension of the new policy, and lifting of the funding cap; second, the return to the pre-1987 guidelines governing the students to be funded; and third, a one-year moratorium during which consultations would be held in a manner acceptable to First Nations and students.

We attained some of our objectives. After a month of this insane activity, the government moved away from the proposed cap on funding, virtually stating that there was no cap, but that funding levels would be decided in yearly budgets. Second, they more or less guaranteed that every eligible aboriginal student would go to university, and that waiting lists would delay their entry by no more than six months. We did not gain our third point, the moratorium on implementation of the policy.

What this whole incident pointed out was that policies can be dictated, whether we like them or not, without consultation: this characterizes the basic relationship between ourselves and the federal government, and it must change.

The unfortunate result is that the government is saying to our people: you've gone far enough up the education ladder. And to many of them, government is saying: you may continue to be eligible for welfare, but you are no longer eligible for post-secondary education. The decision has been taken in spite of the amazingly high level of employment obtained by our First Nations graduates. Some eight or nine out of every ten aboriginal students who attend post-secondary institutions are hired as soon as they enter the work-force. We have figured out that, within two decades, the result of our post-secondary successes would have been to reduce our unemployment rates to a level comparable with that of the general population — something we could not even have dreamed about five years ago.

So, what kind of sense does this new policy make? Certainly

First Nations students were outraged when the full impact of the funding cuts became evident during the winter of 1988–89. All over the country they gathered to demonstrate against the policy, and in some places they moved into government offices, occupied them, conducted fasts, and took other desperate measures to persuade the government of the urgency of their needs.

In response, cynical government spokesmen talked about us getting "free" education to which we were not entitled. Our treaties make it clear that one of the prices paid us for our gift of immense lands, from which the newcomers have drawn colossal wealth, was the promise of education.

This education issue is a good example of the problems our people confront, where a policy that makes no sense is introduced. Many First Nations communities today have 80 to 90 per cent unemployment rates, and government spends enormous sums on maintaining these people through the payment of social assistance that is a right for all Canadians. Our great hope for climbing out of this state of dependency is to produce a highly educated generation that can put its knowledge and skills to work in improving life on the reserves. In fact, it costs more to keep people uneducated and unemployable, either in the reserves or in the cities, than to put them through university. This is, for us, a definition of frustration.

There is already a drastic shortage of schoolrooms on our reserves. We estimate there are 85,000 students on reserves who, at minimum standards, should occupy 3,400 classrooms. There are, however, only 2,300 classrooms, according to official figures. To make up this shortage would cost $237 million in 1986 dollars. We could have between 5,000 and 26,000 more students on reserves when those restored to Indian status arrive, which will increase the present shortage by anything from 200 to 1,000 classrooms. Our figures indicate, then, that at the lowest figure $411 million and at the highest $552 million are needed in capital expenditures just to overcome the present shortage of classrooms in First Nations. These figures indicate how very far our people are from enjoying equal treatment with other Canadians.

In this field, as in some others, the federal government seems to be pulling in conflicting directions: on the one hand, they appear to want to hand us over to the provincial education authorities; on the other, they espouse the idea that we should be masters in our own house. Sooner or later they will have to make a decision on this matter. We want them to get out of education, to vacate the field, to recognize that First Nations have the right to govern themselves, which includes running their own schools. The federal government should cease to hand over to the provinces the huge amounts — nearly $200 million a year — that they now get for the education of native students.

Housing: Still a Desperate Situation

In housing our people still face a desperately critical situation, as they have done for generations. Statistics Canada in 1985 acknowledged a backlog of 12,000 housing units needed on reserves. Some 2,000 units are being built every year, not enough even to keep up with new family formation.

We believe 12,000 is an underestimate. But this severe shortage will be worsened by the return to the reserves of people who have been restored to status. If only half of them return, we could need an extra 25,000 houses. There is no First Nations community in Canada that does not have a housing shortage; the building of the one, two, or half a dozen houses allotted by Indian Affairs, regardless of how great the need is, is not the answer. Neither Indian Affairs nor the Canada Mortgage and Housing Corporation has a long-term projection of our future needs. We tried twice to get the minister to join with us in a housing study, but both efforts were vetoed by his senior officials. Now we are doing our own study.

Economic Development: A Spotty Record

As in housing and education, so in economic development we meet constant set-backs in our efforts to get new initiatives going. Though there have been some successes in different parts of the country, they are not yet sufficient to eliminate the chronic poverty that grips so many of our communities. We placed great hopes in the Native Economic Development Program that was launched in 1983. We hoped it would enable us to bypass the bureaucratic delays we always faced in getting approval (or even refusal!) of projects from Indian Affairs. Yet, the new agency turned out to be even slower than the department. Two new levels of bureaucracy were added, a Native Advisory Board and the Ministry of Small Business, which often rejected projects for no particular reason that we could discover. We had hoped the agency would try to create major national institutions — a bank, for example — that could help develop native enterprises, encourage local businesses, educate native people in business methods, show them where to get money, arrange for needed services, and so on. But, when the Conservative government came to power, they did not like that type of institution. The program could have been very useful if it had ever been implemented properly, but it never was, and it has just withered away. That is only one example among many I could mention.

We had great hopes when, a few years ago, a businessman came to Indian Affairs as an assistant deputy-minister. He had travelled the country, talking to native people, and had produced a report full of challenging ideas for development, many of which came from native people. But not a single one of these ideas was ever implemented. With the amount of money spent on economic development actually going down as a percentage of the total spending on native people, it is little wonder that this man became completely discouraged and went back to private business.

I would not want to leave the impression that native people are making no progress at all. It remains true, however, that every step forward must be made in face of enormous discouragement. In comprehensive-claims negotiations, First Nations have been seeking ways to enhance their land-based activities based on traditional patterns of life. The most successful part of the James Bay Agreement has been the guaranteed income for trappers, but we have found that the government does not want to institute such a guarantee elsewhere, presumably because one of the objectives of government still is to get our people off the land so that it can be used for other purposes.

In many of our communities isolation from the centres of economic activity has been a major problem. Yet, in some places, the people have learned to take advantage of this isolation. The people of Winisk, in Northern Ontario, for instance, have relocated to a new community twenty miles up-river. They have no roads into the new community, where they are practising a land- and water-based economy, hunting, fishing, trapping, gathering berries and firewood, living with the land and with the seasons, and they are finding themselves better able to protect the integrity of their community than if they were living on a highway that would bring the world to their doorstep.

There is some encouragement for land-based activities in the two territories — programs for winter cabins, assistance for community hunts, and so on — but, on the whole, in spite of some successes, we have to admit that nothing has yet made a real dent in our poverty.

We can report that there is underway a quiet cultural renaissance. Many native artists are active, and have become well known throughout the nation, the languages are being taught on a larger scale than ever before, the elders are coming back as an important element in our culture, more and more young people looking to them for their wisdom to point the way to a solution to our many problems.

This cultural revival will eventually have its effect on the appalling social conditions under which so many of our people suffer. But we know only too well that a cultural awakening by itself is not enough. We also have to win the war against poverty, bad housing, poor health, and an education system that is hostile to the very values we hold so dear.

We want other Canadians to understand our dilemma and work with us to overcome our problems.

THE INNU OF
UNGAVA

THE CONFRONTATION

Word spread quickly around the village. The Pasteens lost no time. Hurriedly Sheshatshit's oldest couple put on their coats and rainboots. A daughter tried to dissuade them from going. It was cold and wet, the eighty-year-olds might get sick. But Mary and Michel Pasteen would not listen. Time was running out for their people.

Within a few hours Mary Pasteen was shuffling beside her nearly blind husband, clutching him for support. The Pasteens, and seventy other residents of Sheshatshit, boldly walked past a startled security guard at an entrance to the air-force base at Goose Bay. Before the guard could close the gates, the Innu were inside. Some sat down when police tried to move them. Others, like the Pasteens, stood firmly on the runway, refusing to leave until they met the NATO officials who were deciding whether to establish an $800-million Tactical Fighter Weapons Training Centre in the Innu homeland. The protestors had come to tell NATO their land is not for sale, and Canada has no right to give it away.

Hundreds of Innu have since been arrested for civil disobedience. Six times security at the base was breached.

Throughout fall 1988, tents were set up at the end of the runway and on a bombing range in western Labrador. Innu families cooked caribou, trapped, and tried to live as normally as possible as the jet bombers screamed overhead.

This did little to move the hearts and minds of government and military officials, but it increased public awareness of the issue. Canadians and people elsewhere who'd never heard of the Innu are learning how determined they are to hold on to their land and way of life. Suddenly, a people who want only to live in peace, who, until the 1950s, were living a nomadic, hunter-gatherer existence, have found themselves in the limelight, at the centre of such issues as war and peace and the rights of minority peoples to retain their cultures in the face of the military-industrial complex.

David Confronts Goliath:
The Innu of Ungava versus
the NATO Alliance

Daniel Ashini

"*I*NNU" MEANS "human being." Perhaps at one time, many, many years ago, we thought we were the only human beings. We lived in a world dominated by animals and their spirits. The animals fed and clothed us, and we showed our gratitude by treating them with respect and honour.

Many confuse us with the Inuit; because the name is similar. It's just a coincidence that their name for "the people" is so much like ours. We are not Inuit, we are a different people, even a different race.

We are called "Montagnais-Naskapi" by French and English speakers. We were first called "Montagnais" by the French explorers because we hunted in the mountains (*les montagnes*). The word "Naskapi," which conveys the meaning "uncivilized," has been incorrectly applied to those "Montagnais" who had less-frequent contact with European society.

Today there are 10,000 Innu living in thirteen villages in northeastern Quebec and Labrador. It is hard to know how many of us there were before the Europeans came. Many of our people died from diseases brought from Europe, such as measles, tuberculosis, and smallpox. Our numbers are increasing now, but collectively we are far less healthy and well-off than most

Canadians, and much worse off than we were when we were running our own affairs.

"Nitassinan" is the word for "our land." It is a vast territory, stretching from the mouth of the Saguenay River to the Strait of Belle Isle, from Lac St-Jean to Ungava Bay, as far as the Atlantic coast. Our villages are called Utshimassit (Davis Inlet), Sheshatshit, Pakuat-shipu (St-Augustin), Uanaman-shipu (La Romaine), Nutashkuan, Ekuanitshu (Mingan), Pessamiu (Betsiamites), Maliotenam, Uashat (Sept-Iles), Matimekush (near Schefferville), Kawawachekamach (10 km/6 miles from Schefferville), Les Escoumins, and Quiatchouan (Pointe Bleue), near Lac St-Jean.

We are one of the last hunting-gathering cultures in North America, and just thirty years ago industrial developments on our land dealt the final blow to our nomadic way of life.

Despite hundreds of years of contact with the European newcomers who came to our land, we did not try to live like they did. We adapted those aspects of European society that were compatible with our own. The fur trade, for example, brought new tools to our culture, but it did not significantly change the way we lived on the land. We adopted different religions and have learned new languages, but we did not give up our valued travelling ways until our land was seized for industrial use.

For hundreds of years after the Europeans came to Nitassinan we continued to spend most of the year hunting, travelling long distances on foot and by canoe throughout the interior of our homeland. The pattern changed slightly when we started coming out to the coast each summer to visit the priests and to trade. Like clockwork, however, every fall we went back to the interior of our homeland, where southern society generally left us alone, showing little interest in our hunting way of life until they wanted our land.

Thirty years ago Nitassinan was suddenly in high demand for logging, mining, and hydroelectric development. Paper mills destroyed much of our forests. Iron-ore mining, hydroelectric projects on our rivers in Quebec, and the huge development of Churchill Falls displaced many of us from our hunting and fishing territories.

A railway was constructed at Sept-Iles to ship out the iron ore, and many airports were built, without consulting us, much less with our consent. The more territory we lost, the more difficult it was to continue hunting and fishing in the interior of Nitassinan. The only compensation we received for the theft of our land was welfare cheques and government allowances, both of which impoverished us materially and spiritually, while the Canadians who handed out these "social assistance" pittances profited greatly from our natural resources.

Dr. Hugh Grant, a political economist from the University of Toronto, estimates that, between 1975 and 1987, $14 billion was made from resource development in Nitassinan. The Innu have paid the human costs.

Our rivers are now dammed, fish-spawning grounds have been destroyed, caribou and other animals have drowned or moved away because their feeding grounds are now under water.

We are no longer nomads, but we are still Innu and continue to hunt and camp in Nitassinan's interior. We retain our language, our identity, and the values that are so dear to us. Many of us are happy only when we are living in the interior of Nitassinan, which we call "nutshimit." Our villages are plagued with social problems that vanish when we regain contact with the land.

Divided by a Stroke of the Pen

There are some who think there are two Innu territories, one in Quebec and one in Labrador. That's because, in 1927, Britain carved up its administration of Nitassinan and gave Newfoundland control of the eastern part, while Quebec got control of the rest. This imposed settlement had nothing to do with us; we are one people. With the stroke of pen on paper in England we were suddenly, and without our knowledge, administratively separated. Today our people are jailed if they stray across this border to hunt on the "other" side. The other side of what? We are one nation and will never recognize a line drawn by foreigners across our country.

The caribou, so central to our way of life, recognize no boundaries in Nitassinan. Caribou meat is the staple of our diet, the staff of our life. The other animals are important, too, but not as important as the caribou.

The caribou hunt is of immense social significance to us. Caribou brought into an Innu camp carries much prestige to the successful hunter. The meat is distributed communally, and the bone-marrow grease is eaten in a ritual during the mukushan (feast) that follows a particularly successful hunt. The caribou hunt and the rituals surrounding it reaffirm Innu values and reinvigorate the Innu spirit. Our life as a hunting people cannot be lived in the static boundaries of the village.

Every lake, river, and mountain in Nitassinan has a name in Innu-aimun, our language, but you will see few of these names on most maps. The maps have been made by the European newcomers who ignore our ownership of this land. It is heart-breaking to hear our children refer to places by these European names — foreign words plastered recently on places that have had Innu names for thousands of years. It is as if we have become strangers in our own land. We have become the foreigners. Our children learn the new names in school, and are taught to forget they are Innu. They grow up without pride in who they are, and more sadly, confused about who they should be.

You would not have to go back many years to see how happy and proud our people were in their homeland. We travelled freely to the beautiful lakes, rivers, and mountains of Nitassinan. Now, we feel like prisoners kept captive by a foreign government.

There are those who call our way of life "savage" and "primitive." These people know nothing about Innu culture. Is it "primitive" to place one's family above everything else, to show respect for the elderly, to raise children to be generous towards and considerate of others?

Is it "savage" to work hard for your livelihood, chopping wood, walking long distances to set traps, hunting, gathering boughs, and picking berries? Our tents are not considered fit homes by those who have never been inside them. This is how the Jesuit priest Pierre Biard described our homes in 1616, and they are just as comfortable today: "Over the fir floor are often thrown some mats, or sealskin as soft as velvet; upon this they stretch themselves around the fire with their heads resting upon their baggage. And, what no one would believe, they are very warm in there around that little fire, even in the greatest rigors of the winter."

Our tents are now heated with woodstoves, and the floors still covered with fragrant boughs. We enjoy the close contact with our families in hunting camps where we are free from many of the encumbrances of village life. There are no bills to pay, we are far from television sets, telephones, the need for cash and are far more able to renew our important spiritual ties to the land and to nature. Most of us moved into houses for the first time just thirty years ago, but we have never given up our attachment to living in tents in the interior of Nitassinan, where we are able to provide for our families in the best way we know how, through trapping and hunting. Let me describe in more detail the "uncivilized" life from which the newcomers would save us.

One of the most important rules in our society is to share. An Innu hunter's prestige comes not from the wealth he accumulates but from what he gives away. When a hunter kills caribou or other game, he shares with everyone else in the camp. Guy Bellefleur, an Innu from Unaman-shipu, explained this in September 1986 when he appeared before Canada's Federal Environmental Assessment Review Office (FEARO), which is investigating the effects of military low-level flying in Nitassinan: "The older men, the wise men, used to tell them [the young] old legends....The legends say that he who does not respect nature will find it very difficult to find food. All we caught we used to share with the other families that accompanied us on our hunt, and this was something that was respected day after day...and that is the principle that still guides us today."

We share work as well. No Innu will ever walk past another busily engaged in a task that can be shared. It is this cultural emphasis on co-operation that makes standard capitalist development incompatible with our society. A reporter once asked a resident of Sheshatshit why the only store and the taxi service in the village are run by non-Innu.

"No Innu could take money from another for a service," Mani Pia Benuen replied.

This ethic is slowly changing as Innu communities move more in the direction of the wage-based economy. In the bush, however, it will never change because it is so deeply rooted in our culture.

We are proud of the way we have taken care of Nitassinan. Our religion teaches us that the land has been loaned to us by Tshishe-Manitu, the Great Spirit. We are the caretakers of this beautiful territory that we have been given to live on. It is our duty to pass it on, undamaged, to future generations until eternity. We have done our best to protect this land.

There are few other places in the world where the lake and river water is unpolluted. We have always treated the animals with respect as well. It is customary, for example, to dispose ceremoniously of certain animal bones. It is forbidden to over-hunt or to waste meat. We believe Nitassinan is watched over by the spirits of animals, and we are the human caretakers. According to our religion the hunter must have a good relationship with the animals or he will not be rewarded with a successful hunt. This is why we have treated the animals and the land with such respect. We have conserved our wildlife and find it hypocritical when we are told to buy government licences and obey non-Innu hunting laws to promote "conservation." This regulation comes from the same people who have slaughtered thousands of animals and rendered huge tracts of land useless, for their industrial development. They want to extend this kind of "conservation" throughout our land.

In the past, Innu hunters wore their best clothes to go hunting. Much care was taken to embroider the hunter's tunic, which was made from caribou hide as soft as the most expensive suede you can buy in southern stores. Innu women made warm pants and vests for their families, and beautiful moccasins, which are light on the feet and very warm. We still wear these moccasins today, and they are superior for their warmth and comfort to anything you can buy in stores. Our snowshoes are also made with great care and expertise. Their netting varies for different snow conditions. In the spring, for example, the snow is heavier and the weave of the snowshoe must be looser than for snowshoes worn on the light, deep snow of January and February. Survival and comfort in the north is our expertise, as it is for the other northern indigenous people.

The White People Come among Us

To understand the rapid changes in our lives it is helpful to look back at what has been written by visitors to Nitassinan.

We were among one of the first people the early European explorers met in North America. In 1534, Jacques Cartier made a voyage along the Gulf of the St. Lawrence, and among the native people he encountered were the Montagnais, or Innu, whom he noted were already familiar with Europeans because they boarded his vessels as easily "as if they had been Frenchmen."

Three hundred years later, a Hudson's Bay trader, John McLean, wrote this of Innu who traded at Fort Chimo, the so-called Naskapi: "They are at present the most independent of the whites of any other Indians on this continent, the Esquimaux excepted. The few fur-bearing animals their barren country affords are so highly prized that the least exertion enables them to procure their very limited wants; and the skin of the reindeer [caribou] affords them the most comfortable clothing they could possess."

William Brooks Cabot, an adventurer from Boston, made several voyages into the interior of our country in the early 1800s and wrote this of the Innu he encountered: "In 1911 the Indian country was unvexed by any white person, so far as I can learn....The people are lords over their fine country, asking little favor err save that the deer may come in their time....Their country is still theirs, and the deer, and long may they so remain."

From Cartier's time to Cabot's time, four hundred years of contact with Europeans, and we were still nomads with sovereignty over our homeland. It is only since our land and our sovereignty has been lost that the life that Cabot hoped we could maintain has been taken from us, and our existence made into a pain to be endured, or not.

We had little complaint with the early European newcomers who came to our homeland because it is vast and we spent much of our time in areas that were inaccessible to the Europeans. We thought they were civilized people, our "guests," and we were generous to them, as is our duty; we shared our land and its animals. We did not suspect they would one day seize everything from us as they have done. We continued our nomadic way of life, untroubled, until the middle of this century. That's when the descendants of the newcomers insisted on establishing their sovereignty over our homeland.

Now we are arrested for doing things we have done in Nitassinan for thousands of years. We are arrested if we hunt out of the seasons established by provincial laws. We are arrested for trespassing on land the settlers claim as their own. In some parts of Nitassinan, our people are even arrested if they cut firewood without permits. There is no end to the harassment we meet at the hands of those who now claim to govern Nitassinan.

When the settlers first came to our land, we helped them. We taught them about the animals, and where they could find the great rivers and lakes of Nitassinan. We showed them how to live and survive in this country, one of the coldest on earth. Canada was built by the fur trade in which the Innu were active participants. We traded animal furs for flour, cotton, rifles, alcohol, and other products. How could we have foreseen the tragic effects that alcohol, for instance, would have on our people? How could we have foreseen the industrial developments that would drive us off our land? When it began we didn't know how to fight against the giant companies that flooded and ravaged our land for hydroelectric power, mines, pulp and paper. This is how we were repaid for our generosity to the newcomers.

Many Innu are bitter that today's descendants of the first Europeans in our country treat us so ungratefully and with such little regard. Antoine Malec spoke of his hurt to the FEARO inquiry in 1986: "We, the Indians, just as the Africans and whatever race you are talking about, must be respected and informed and consulted when anybody wants to use something that we own, something that is ours....Maybe we were too generous. Our hearts are that big. There is room for everybody in our hearts."

The Innu: A Classically Colonized People

What has been done to the Innu is a typical act of colonization, repeated on every continent on earth when an industrially developed society decides it has an interest in bringing "civilization" to a different culture. Sometimes the colonizers have benign goals, sometimes otherwise, but the effects are much the same.

The dictionary definition of "to colonize" is "to take possession of a relatively undeveloped country and settle one's surplus population there." We have shared our land with Europe's surplus population and were happy to do so, but we never gave them control over it. That has been taken, without treaty or land-rights agreement.

We Innu are a distinct people with a single language, a single indivisible national homeland, a single culture and national identity. This is how the United Nations defines a "people." The United Nations Covenant on Civil and Political Rights states: "All Peoples have the right to self-determination. By virtue of that right they freely determine their political status and freely pursue their economic, social and cultural development."

Canada, a signatory to this covenant, nevertheless refuses to recognize the Innu right to self-determination. It is as though Canadians don't think we are capable of running our own economic, social, and cultural institutions. This is an arrogant and racist assumption. It was well articulated by Labrador official Walter Rockwood in his 1950s report on the terms of Newfoundland's union with Canada: "Civilization is on the northward march, and for the Eskimo and Indian there is no escape...the only course now open...is to fit him as soon as may be to take his full place as a citizen in our society. The Indians of Labrador are still more primitive than the Eskimos...because of less intimate contact with our civilization." He wrote this in a royal commission report about the terms of Newfoundland's union with Canada. Rockwood's arrogance indicates how little attention the rights of native people got in the transfer of Newfoundland from colony to province.

Rockwood's "northern march of civilization" has had devastating consequences for the Innu. The suicide rate for our people in Labrador and their Inuit neighbours is five times higher than that of Canadians (non-natives), and twice as high as that of other native people in Canada. The suicide rate is even higher among our young people, aged fifteen to twenty-four. The rate in northern Labrador is seventeen times the national average, and seven times higher than for native youth elsewhere. We have an exceptionally high accident rate, and many of these accidents, often fatal, are linked to alcohol addiction. We have no statistics for Innu communities on the north shore of the St. Lawrence, but we suspect they are similar.

This kind of self-destructive behaviour was unknown to the Innu until the middle of this century, when we lost control of our land and our lives. Dr. Kay Wotten presented the above figures to the Canadian Public Health Association in 1983 after two years of study on the northeast coast of Nitassinan. She concluded: "It is the plight of a people whose social framework has been gravely damaged and its fragile economy ruined leaving the young with a stultifying sense of worthlessness; a culture whose customs and traditions have been mocked."

Our customs and traditions are mocked by the colonizers, so much so that many of our own people have been convinced they are inferior. Such psychological and emotional suffering will end only when we regain our independence.

One of the greatest psychological blows to our people came when we settled into the poorly constructed houses built for us by the colonial governments in the 1950s. The Innu at Pukuatshipu hung on to their cherished tents and nomadic life-style longer than did the rest of us. They didn't move into houses until 1971, and that year all of their newborns died. Dr. Wotten says we found the transition difficult because we were "forced to live on reservations or settlements with inadequate sanitation and housing; left without [our] traditional medicine which was scorned and rejected by Whites and provided with a diet poorly suited to [our] needs."

Since we abandoned our nomadic way of life the colonial governments in Nitassinan have relentlessly worked to assimilate the Innu, and that is what is destroying us. We cannot be turned into clones of the European settlers. This is how assimilation was explained in the government's 1959–60 annual report on Labrador: "Indians must be taught the three R's, and will also need vocational training, but it would be naive to think that this will automatically solve all the problems overnight. As with Indians elsewhere there are deeply rooted psychological problems to be overcome before the process of integration is complete."

Yes, we have something deeply rooted in our psychology — we are Innu hunters and gatherers, and are proud of it. Hunting is the form of living that lies at the core of our identity as a people, that animates our social relationships, and that, for thousands of years, has breathed life into our people. We are offended by those who have categorized our hunting existence as primitive. The policies of the European newcomers in North America are racist in that they consider themselves superior to us.

Assimilation Begins at School

Our children are taught in a foreign language by non-Innu instructors. The schools are controlled and run by non-Innu and systematically alienate our children from Innu society. The result is that the pupils come to feel contempt for their parents and their national identity. The school program creates feelings of inadequacy, inferiority, and shame among our children. We are aware of what is happening each day our children leave for school, but feel powerless to stop it. If Innu parents keep their children out of school, they are cut off from the welfare benefits we have come to depend on since our land was taken from us. A Norwegian anthropologist, Georg Henriksen, lived among our people in Utshimassit (Davis Inlet) in the late 1960s. About the school system he wrote: "Today the Nascaupi [Innu] struggle through the first grades in school until they are 15 or 16 years old, trying to learn what is supposed to be good for white city dwellers. White middle-class values are forced upon the young through an education that is largely irrelevant to their social and cultural background and to the natural environment which they must later exploit to make a living."

Is it any wonder, then, that the Innu, like other indigenous people, want to run their own schools? We want our children to learn skills that will be useful for a life in our homeland. Instead, we are forced to send our children to schools that teach them European history, geography, social values, religion, and language. Innu students must adopt a view of the world that treats their own nation as invisible or non-existent if they are to pass their grades. Innu children seeking to understand their own history, or who challenge what they are being taught, are considered subversive, or at least, misguided. Recently a group of Innu teenagers in Sheshatshit attended an unauthorized seminar on Innu history and geography and were reprimanded by the school principal. He told them they were being "brainwashed."

Why such a reaction? Are the colonial authorities worried this will interfere with their plans to assimilate our children? We know assimilation will never work; instead, our social problems will just get worse. Assimilation is ethnocide and, indirectly, genocide. Violence directed inwards, adult and juvenile delinquency, and generalized social collapse are all symptoms of extreme alienation.

The parade of Innu and Inuit who come before the colonial courts almost on a daily basis is taken as evidence of our innate savagery, rather than as part of the damage caused by an assault on our societies, our social structures, our languages, our self-respect, and, above all, our lands. Thirty years ago we lived in a society where crime was virtually unheard of.

The Prejudice of a Labrador Mayor

If the mayor of Goose Bay, Henry Shouse, is to be believed, we are too lazy to run our own affairs. He made this "eloquent" speech in Montreal to the FEARO panel in 1986:

> They are capable of doing many things, and not only capable but these downtrodden Indians...have opportunites for education that none of your children have unless you're mighty rich. In Newfoundland and Labrador they can go to school free. They get their airfare free. They get their books free. Their tuition, their travel, their board, everything free. They have the capability of becoming anything they want to be, but they have to want to be that....They have the opportunity since Goose Bay

started, having lived only about 25 miles away, to have every opportunity in the past 42 years to work, to become steadily employed. No one has taken advantage of it.

You would think our children are flying off to "finishing school" in Switzerland at the expense of Canadian taxpayers! The Innu are getting no frills from Canadian taxpayers. And it is not because we get our education free that it becomes more accessible or even attractive to us. We are denied the most basic right to study in our own language, and to study a curriculum rich with our own values and customs. French Canadians have this right, but the indigenous people have not.

As for competing for work with whites, we are not the only people of colour who complain about the discriminatory practices within the Canadian work-force. Mayor Shouse's attitude towards the Innu is typical of that of many of our neighbours who shun and belittle us. They do not hire us even though their wealth was gained at our expense. Our young people trained in technical skills will want to take their place in that world, just as others will want to continue hunting as a way of life.

None of our young people wants to be forced to leave his or her birthplace for a job in the south. It is only when we have control once again of our resources in Nitassinan that the two ways of life can be merged, and we Innu will rediscover peace.

In the bush, where many Innu families spend up to half the year, our values and traditions are re-established. The beauty of Nitassinan is a source of great joy. In the autumn the country is ablaze in beautiful colours, and berries grow in profusion on the ground. The warmth of our tents and closeness of our families provides a happy refuge from the cold. We watch the spring come in all its glory, and await the honking sounds of geese returning from the south.

This is why our life in "nutshimit," the interior of our homeland, is so special to the Innu, why we have such a deep attachment to Nitassinan. This is how I expressed our aspirations to the FEARO panel on October 13, 1986: "We want to keep the door open to our children, our grandchildren, for them to be able to pursue the traditions of our ancestors in the interior of Nitassinan. The great many Innu who continue to go into the country each fall and spring will be our lifeline to the past and to the future, a lifeline that will be one of the greatest importance to us all in permitting us to pass on to future generations the great wealth of knowledge about the animals and the land that is our heritage."

The Terrifying Militarization of Nitassinan

The militarization of our homeland for jet-bomber training by NATO air forces threatens to cut us off forever from our vital lifeline. What has been done to our homeland in the past is all bad enough. This development threatens to wipe us out.

For the past eight years Innu land has been used by an increasing number of European air forces to practise low-level flying. Jet bombers, weighing 27 tonnes (30 tons), travel 900 km/h (540 mph) just 30 m (100 feet) above the ground.

When they pass overhead, the canvas of our tents ripples, the trees sway, and animals flee in fright. The jets travel faster than the speed of sound.

Sometimes we see the huge war machines a fraction of a second before the sound roars over us. We then suffer what is known as the "startle" effect. The suddenness of the jet's arrival, and the deafening noise, take us by surprise and our hearts race as our bodies react in panic. The children cry; our elders clutch their chests in fear. This is how the colonizers now attack our peaceful life in the interior.

The Americans built the air-force base at Goose Bay in 1942 but used it as a stopover point for flights headed overseas. Their aircraft didn't fly over Innu in the bush. The British used Vulcan bombers to practise low-level flying in the 1950s, but those jets didn't fly as low or as fast as the new ones do. Few Innu families hunting in the bush ever heard or saw the Vulcans. Since 1980, however, almost every Innu family who has camped and hunted in the interior has been terrorized by British, Dutch, and German Phantoms, Tornados, and Alpha jets. The number of flights increases every year, from 3,000 sorties in 1984 to 7,000 in 1988, and a projected 40,000 in 1992.

It is hard to imagine what it is like to be overflown by one of these bombers unless you have experienced it. Here are just a few of the comments made by Innu to the FEARO panel that visited our communities in 1986. Ambroise Lalo's comment may make you smile, but try to imagine the terror he describes: "Some of our brothers from Natashquan get so afraid, in fact, that they run away. In fact, one of them was so terrified that he lost his false teeth while he was running away…and when a man comes back from a hunting trip, he often tells us that he almost killed a caribou, but that caribou was scared by a plane flying over, and the Indian is very sad since he cannot feed his family."

Mrs. Wapistan, La Romaine: "I cannot express what I felt the first time I heard such a tremendous noise. I was so shaken up that I even forgot about my children and my husband."

George Gabriel, Schefferville: "To see them so low means that we cannot go on the water with our canoes anymore. We are afraid that they will capsize."

George Gregoire, Davis Inlet: "We do not even hear them once they are coming and suddenly a big noise hits when they are over the camp."

If you think we are overreacting because we are not used to noise, perhaps you will more readily believe a former Canadian member of parliament, Keith Penner, who was flown over by a jet bomber in Wales. His comments were quoted by Bernard Cleary at the Schefferville hearing of FEARO: "I had no warning….I was pinned to the ground, shaking all over. It is not the sort of experience that one would like to have twice in one's lifetime."

A journalist, Marie Wadden, wrote in the *Montreal Gazette* that she was overflown while on assignment in Nitassinan: "Five minutes after the plane passed over, I was still aware of the painful pounding in my chest. I was inside a tent when the jet came."

We fear Innu families will stop going into the bush if this flight training continues. They will stop going out of fear, but also, because the animals and plant life they depend on will disappear. This is already happening, as Guy Bellefleur told FEARO: "Over the last few years the game we can catch has decreased because of the military manoeuvres of NATO....Since these manoeuvres began the Indians have been disturbed. Their game and wildlife has been disturbed, and many other Indians will come and give testimony...we are all faced with the same problems."

James Pasteen of Davis Inlet said: "All wildlife will be driven away, lakes will be polluted, fresh-water fish will not be any good to eat, there will be increased health problems."

If the Innu stop going into the bush our skills and knowledge, built up over thousands of years, will be lost.

Dr. David Suzuki, scientist and television personality, has expressed his solidarity with the Innu, and warned us at a meeting in Sheshatshit in December 1988: "If you lose your land and way of life, you will disappear. You may live in towns but you won't be Innu anymore." Many of us listened to his warning with sinking hearts. How true this is. Every day since these military activities began we have felt our land and way of life slipping farther and farther away.

Canadian Government Committed to Our Destruction

NATO's proposed $800-million Tactical Fighter Weapons Training Centre will go either to Goose Bay or to a site in Turkey. We would prefer the training site goes nowhere, for we have no wish for the Turks to suffer as we are suffering. Indeed, even if NATO chooses Turkey, Canada plans to increase the number of fighter jets training in Nitassinan through the signing of bilateral agreements with its European allies. Regardless, therefore, of the NATO decision, Canada is committed to a policy that will destroy Innu culture and lead to the death of many of our people. The military users have already carved out two large flying zones in Nitassinan, totalling 100,000 sq. km (38,000 square miles. Three-quarters of the southern zone is on the Quebec side of the colonial border, while most of the northern zone is in Newfoundland jurisdiction. We reiterate, both zones are in Nitassinan, and all Innu who camp and hunt within these flying zones are affected by this activity.

We have great concern for the health of the animals under our care in Nitassinan, especially the caribou herds that we depend on so much. We and our Inuit neighbours have been the caretakers of the largest caribou herd in the world, the George River herd, and we are afraid that low-level flying may destroy it. A workshop on caribou held in Alaska, in November 1987, was presented with evidence that the herd has been declining at a rate of 5 per cent a year since 1984, and attributes this to decline in the females' physical condition, deterioration of the calving-ground habitat, delay in births, and several other factors. What was once thought to be a healthy herd of 600,000 animals is now estimated to be just half that.

Biologists and Innu hunters have found caribou that appear to have starved to death. We know that, when caribou are frightened, they will not stop to eat, but will continue to move, day after day, until they feel safe.

At the FEARO hearings in Montreal, Alain Methot, speaking on behalf of L'Association des Pourvoyeurs du Nouveau Quebec (commercial harvesters of caribou), said the George River herd has changed its migrating habits since the low-level jets came. He says the caribou are thinner and less healthy than they used to be. Methot told the commission the caribou used to travel 8 to 15 km (5 to 10 miles) per day. Now he says they are travelling 50 and 65 km (30 and 40 miles) a day, without stopping to eat.

We are not satisfied with the scientific studies that have been carried out for governments and the Department of Defence. They have concentrated on a sedentary herd in the Red Wine Mountains, rather than on the great migratory George River herd. No cardio-vascular studies have been done to determine the physical effects low-flying jets have on the caribou. We can see, however, that serious damage is being done.

Biologists say the caribou are starving because they are too numerous and have eaten out their grazing grounds. We disagree. We believe there are other areas where the animals can graze, but they are afraid to go. Here is the testimony of a hunter, James Pasteen, in Utshimassit (Davis Inlet): "There is a good place for feeding grounds in southern Labrador but caribou will not migrate there because of the noise of the jets and the gas that has dropped on the ground."

The military says it can avoid flying over the caribou when they are mating and calving. This promise cannot be met. How can inexperienced young pilots recognize and avoid mating caribou from the cockpits of jets travelling 900 km/h? Even if certain zones are off-limits at certain times, occasionally pilots will surely stray off course.

The military also claims it can avoid Innu hunting camps. This too is impossible, since the Innu don't stay in one place when they are hunting. Innu hunter Guy Bellefleur explained this to members of the FEARO panel: "The Montagnais territory is a land without limits, without borders, so in order to survive we have to be nomads. We always have to wander and seek our subsistence and that is why we must disperse. We cannot be too numerous at a given lake or next to a given river."

The prospects of Nitassinan being turned into a theatre of war causes great anguish to our people. Father Alexis Jouveneau, a priest in La Romaine, told the FEARO panel his Innu parishioners are very concerned: "They are upset and there is a collective psychosis which is undermining the heart and way of life of Indians here on the lower north shore...you might as well build a psychiatric clinic right here and it will soon be overfilled."

Guy Bellefleur told the panel: "The Indians cannot change their mental set-up....Even though they have set down close to the river, they keep their mentality...of ages past where they have travelled throughout their territory."

And Cajetan Rich of Davis Inlet told FEARO: "We were taught how to survive and live in any kind of threatening weather. We have been taught where to find food, and when to expect caribou....We were also taught what to do in cases of emergency....Now we see our land as a possible place where war practices are going on and that is a threat to our way of life and our culture."

Innu Land to Be Bombed

NATO planners want to establish six bombing ranges in Nitassinan, in addition to one that already exists. Four of the bombing ranges would enable NATO jets to use non-explosive concrete missiles for target practice. These kinds of missiles have already caused environmental damage on the existing bombing range in western Labrador. A young Innu hunter, Bart Penashue, and his cousin went to the bombing range in fall 1988 to see first hand what was happening to the land there and said: "Some of those bombs weigh over a thousand pounds, and they make huge craters in the ground, one we saw was over seven feet deep. They drop into rivers, and destroy beaver dams."

Three additional bombing ranges would be required by NATO for live weapons training. The bombing range at Primrose Lake in northern Alberta and Saskatchewan is 1.2 million hectares (3 million acres) in size and native people are not allowed to hunt, trap, and fish inside its boundaries.

The low-level jet flights are terrifying enough; we oppose all of the other activities that would accompany a NATO combat centre. We demand the land already seized for the existing bombing range be returned to us.

Enormous pressures will be brought to bear on the resources of Nitassinan by the visiting military personnel. It is estimated 30,000 European airforce personnel will pass through Goose Bay each year that the NATO centre is open. Already the visiting Europeans are hunting and fishing in Nitassinan, and even the residents of Goose Bay are complaining about this. What wildlife survives the low-level flying will quickly be destroyed by over-hunting and -fishing. We are also concerned about the impact 30,000 single male transients will have on the community closest to the base. Some young women in Sheshatshit are already complaining of sexual abuse from personnel at the military base.

The purpose of low-level flight training is to teach NATO pilots how to avoid enemy radar detection in wartime. More than 97 of these NATO jets (which cost an estimated $40 million each) crashed in the countries where they were training in 1988, and 100 people in West Germany lost their lives as a result of some of these accidents. In West Germany the jets are not allowed to fly below 75 metres (250 feet); yet over our land they are permitted to fly much lower. The Germans want to export the noise and danger here, and Canada has opened her arms.

Since jet training started in Nitassinan several jets have already crashed. We fear a forest fire may be started by one of these accidents. This would be ecologically disastrous since it takes 90 years for trees to grow in our scant subarctic forests.

The bombing exercises planned for the proposed NATO centre will use laser technology. The Canadian Public Health Association (CPHA), which studied the problem of fighter jet training over Nitassinan in 1987, says this is dangerous: "The output of a laser is often invisible to the eye, making accidental exposure more difficult to control. Exposure to living tissue can result in temporary or permanent damage to the tissue."

We oppose the use of lasers in our homeland, just as we oppose air-to-air combat training. During air-to-air combat, jets launched from one airport in Nitassinan play the "enemy" role, as other jets fight them at medium and high altitudes, using laser and other sophisticated technology to simulate combat and to show those on the ground which side is "winning." Nitassinan will be bombarded with sonic booms while this supersonic gamesmanship is carried out.

The CPHA concluded that sonic booms could be dangerous to animal and human health in Nitassinan as well, and recommended they be avoided until a full environmental review is completed.

The government has ignored this recommendation and supersonic air-to-air combat training, which produces sonic booms, has been permitted since February 1988.

The CPHA says the health of the Innu and Inuit in northern Quebec and Labrador has been overlooked in the planning of this development: "The Government of Canada did not adequately consider the rights and welfare of the aboriginal people of the Labrador area in any significant way when the air base was established at Goose Bay nor in its subsequent development. The aboriginal rights and welfares should have been considered in this process....It should be recognized that it is the native people who may be at the greatest risk for bearing the costs of the development. Their cultural identity is linked to the use or abuse of the land. "

Our Security Threatened by Defence Policies

Canada justifies its action under the guise of doing its part for world peace. In fact, many believe the kind of training that takes place in Nitassinan will harm the cause of peaceful relations in the world. If Canada and NATO persist in this policy, let them train over some of Canada's large national parks. We don't understand why we should be sacrificed for Canada's defence policy. We had nothing to do with any of the world's wars, and want nothing to do with any future wars. It is our security that is being threatened by the defence policies of other nations. This is unjust and immoral.

The International Federation for Human Rights sent a mission to Nitassinan and concluded in 1988 that the Innu are being denied certain internationally recognized collective and individual human rights.

We have been totally left out of the planning and decision-making surrounding the militarization of our ancestral homeland even though it threatens irrevocably to change our lives. To be ignored in this way is nothing new, but this development is too far-reaching, too destructive, to go unchallenged. We can't think of a worse desecration of our homeland than to have it used for war games.

We are also told the jet-bomber training will help stimulate the economy of Goose Bay, an airport town that didn't exist before the 1940s. A short visit to Goose Bay and then to any of our villages will demonstrate the hypocrisy of this argument.

The 10,000 Innu in Labrador and northern Quebec live in far greater poverty than the average Canadian or resident of Goose Bay. We are to be sacrificed for the "economic stimulation" of others, and forced to pay the high human costs that will come from this military activity. It would appear that the concerns of 10,000 Innu people merit less attention in Canada than the economic needs of a single-industry town like Goose Bay.

We have been given no other choice but to use civil disobedience. When we are arrested for trespassing on military property we plead "not guilty." We are breaking no laws since this is our land and we are free to walk about on it. It is Canada that is acting illegally by stealing our land from us.

We are mocked for our concerns. At the FEARO hearings in Montreal, Herb Brett, a Goose Bay town councillor, described Innu life in the bush this way: "Their lifestyle is they have a paid charter into the country to come out after three months with very few skins with maybe half a case of toilet paper and a few cases of canned goods, if you want to be facetious about it."

This is the depth of understanding our neighbours have of our way of life in the interior. We do not go into the bush to "bring out skins," rather we go there to provide for our families with the best food available — the meat of our animals. University of Laval anthropologist Paul Charest reports that, in 1983, 500 of the 650 residents of Uanaman-Shipu (La Romaine) spent several months hunting in Nitassinan, and together with Innu from two neighbouring villages they provided their communities with 109 tonnes (120 tons) of meat and fish that year.

Nutshimit is our grocery store, the place we go to get our food, and it is the most nourishing food we can eat. The hard work of hunting and keeping warm in the bush is healthy for us, physically and psychologically. An Oblate priest, Father Jim Roche, described life in an Innu hunting camp to the *Montreal Gazette* on June 25, 1988: "In the bush, life is full of real struggle. It's hard to get wood and meat, but after a day of walking in snow that is soft and up to your knees, you appreciate more the simple things, like heat from the tent stove, tea, and a hot meal. In the village, that struggle is gone."

The mayor of Goose Bay, Henry Shouse, showed his contempt for our efforts to defend our way of life, when, at a FEARO hearing in Montreal, he compared our struggle to the "productive" work of his own son: "I have a son who went to university in St. John's and studied wildlife biology, and came back with a degree. At the same time a young Indian was in St. John's going to the same university. Where is my son now? He is off up in the country trapping. Where is the Indian? He is part of the protest group."

These public attacks show the level to which the debate has descended. The effects are devastating. Broken down by the policies of the colonial government, some of our people have stopped fighting against the lies and have stopped respecting our traditions because they have come to believe these practices are "primitive."

Gain for Others — Suffering for Us

The military use of our homeland cannot be justified. The people who will benefit economically are the descendants of European newcomers, and a small assimilated Métis population, who look forward to making their fortunes by serving the pilots-in-training and their military support staff.

Those who will suffer, and are already suffering the negative effects, are the 10,000 Innu and several thousand Inuit who depend on the resources of their homelands. Whose concerns are the most legitimate? At FEARO hearings in Sheshatshit, Lyla

MacEachern, the wife of an Innu hunter, put it simply and eloquently:

> Whose lifestyles are more valued; who as a people are more valued? In the past, it has been quite clear that, as a people, the Innu have been the least important. My father-in-law, Matthew Ben Andrew, died several years ago. His land, his place in Nitassinan, which he considered the heritage for his children and grandchildren, was in the area flooded over and today still underwater because of the Churchill Falls hydro project. Other Innu who shared this area in Nitassinan lost canoes, traps, and other supplies because they were never even informed that this so-called development was going to happen, much less invited to take part in a process like this one [FEARO] to discuss what the outcome and mitigative measures of such a project might be.

Sixty-four-year-old Manian Michel, an Innu mother of twelve, could barely contain her anger when she spoke to the FEARO panel:

> Do you have any shame that you should come to our land and face us like you are now, requesting that we give up our land to you? You never, never stop what you are doing now, sitting in front of us trying to get our land. We will never give it up. I am very angry when I see white people, such as yourselves, looking for us to give up our birthright. I am very angry today. How many times have the Innu come to you to look for land, to look for anything?
>
> Even the Innu, in its despicable condition, in its wretched condition, never come to you for anything. Do you hate the Innu, do you want to kill the Innu?
>
> You have killed us in many respects. We have nothing. No animals, there are no animals near us, and we cannot even drink our water, we cannot get wood without a permit.

We have been accused of using this military issue to push for a generous land-claim settlement. The day a land-claim deal is signed between our people and the Canadian government will be one of the saddest days of our lives. Many Canadians think the land-claims process is a fair and just one. It is not. We will be forced to relinquish our claim to Nitassinan forever if we accept compensation for the seizure of our lands. The most we can hope for is to receive an adequate land base to continue our hunting way of life, and money to develop the few resources that will come with such a land base. We must depend on the charity of Canada, that is what it amounts to. We must go cap in hand to see what crumbs will be given to us. This reliance on charity was created by their policies and ambitions, not ours.

A lot has been said about the James Bay settlement. It has been called "just." Much of the homeland of the Cree has been flooded and more flooding will take place when other hydro projects are developed. Only time will tell if the Cree people have enough land and resources to defend and maintain their way of life. The James Bay settlement has proven, however, that we are quite capable of running our own economic and social systems.

Many of our people, the elders especially, oppose relinquishing title to Nitassinan and are highly skeptical about Canada's intention of offering us a fair settlement.

Some of our young feel we have no choice. Canada is going ahead with development on our homeland, whether or not our grievances are addressed. We have been told it will take ten to fifteen years of negotiations to resolve our land claims. What will be left of Nitassinan in ten to fifteen years' time? Will the majestic George River caribou herd be intact? Will our language and culture survive another decade of colonial domination? Will the spirit of the Innu endure that long, or will it be broken? Maybe this is what Canada is waiting for.

The Innu will continue to use civil disobedience and will continue the fight for our rights in Nitassinan. We will continue to appeal to Canadians' sense of justice. We will not simply disappear off the cultural face of this world without a fight.

THE MI'KMAQ

THE CONFRONTATION

Ironically, the morning of September 17, 1988, was a calm and beautiful day on Hunter's Mountain in Nova Scotia. Soon, however, over 100 of our Mi'kmaq Harvesters and their supporters arrived to mark the beginning of what would be a most controversial two-week Treaty Moose Harvest.

Grand Chief Donald Marshall, Sr., stepped forward and led the hushed group in a brief Mi'kmaq prayer to guide our harvesters.

Hidden from view, a short distance up the mountain road, scores of provincial game wardens and support RCMP officers were waiting. Just three days earlier the Nova Scotia minister of Lands and Forests cavalierly declared that the Treaty Moose Harvest was "unauthorized." Orders were issued by the government of Nova Scotia to stop Mi'kmaq Harvesters from carrying out our planned harvest of moose.

Despite public announcements that the Mi'kmaq would be charged, the harvesters proceeded up the mountain. At the centre of the controversy was the 1985 Simon decision of the Supreme Court of Canada, which unanimously ruled that the 1752 treaty between the British Crown and the Mi'kmaq Nation was valid.

In a few minutes, the harvesters' vehicles were stopped and searched. A government helicopter circled the area, reporters and film media mingled between officers and harvesters. The line of vehicles with harvesters stretched as far back as the eye could see down the mountain road. The day would be a long one. One by one the cars were searched and weapons seized. The officers even seized the harvesters' identification and sanction cards issued by the Grand Council.

Six of our harvesters were charged under a provincial law. Despite the tension, the armed confrontation provoked no retaliation, and was peaceful.

This day marked the beginning of another long struggle for the Mi'kmaq to exercise a right. But the story does not begin with that day; the story goes back far into our history — a time when a chain of covenants was made.

The Covenant Chain

Grand Chief Donald Marshall, Sr.,
Grand Captain Alexander Denny,
Putus Simon Marshall,
of the Executive of the Grand Council of the
Mi'kmaw Nation

Protection and allegiance are fastened together by links, if a link is broken the chain will be loose. You must preserve this chain entire on your part by fidelity and obedience to the great King George the Third, and then you will have the security of this royal arm to defend you.

I meet you now as His Majesty's graciously honoured servant in government and in his royal name to receive at this pillar, your public vows of obedience to build a covenant of peace with you, as upon the immovable rock of sincerity and truth, to free you from the chains of bondage, and to place you in the wide and fruitful field of English liberty.

The laws will be like a great hedge about your rights and properties. If any break this hedge to hurt or injure you, the heavy weight of the laws will fall upon them and punish their disobedience.

— Nova Scotia Governor Jonathan Belcher addressing the Mi'kmaq at Halifax, 1761, at ceremonies renewing the Treaty of 1752.

Freedom and liberty...confrontation...subjugation...resistance —all of these words describe the current situation in Nova Scotia as it relates to relations between the Mi'kmaq people and our settler neighbours. Despite protections afforded by international and domestic law, a people are forcibly dispossessed of their land and resources, their governmental institutions are intentionally destabilized, their children condemned to a bleak future based on poverty and dependency—all so that others can reap a profit. Some backwater Third World dictatorship? No, Canada (Nova Scotia). Such has been the history of the Mi'kmaq people.

A youth is convicted of murder and sent to prison. After serving eleven years of his term, it is found that he has been wrongly convicted. Could this have anything to do with the fact that he was a Mi'kmaq?

It took this event to spark the public outcry that led to the establishment of a royal commission to study the Nova Scotia justice system. Although at time of writing, the Royal Commission's final conclusions have not been made public, much of the testimony given during the course of the proceedings pointed to consistent and racist discrimination against Mi'kmaq citizens on the part of the state's police forces, provincial politicians, and the judiciary.

Solemn and binding treaties are signed between nations. These treaties are recognized and affirmed in the Royal Proclamation of 1763, the Constitution Act, 1982, and upheld in a landmark 1985 Supreme Court of Canada judgment. But when the citizens of one of those nations attempt to exercise their rights according to the terms of the treaties, they are arrested and harassed. Could this have anything to do with the fact that they are Mi'kmaqs?

The treatment of the Mi'kmaq has only recently been the subject of media and public scrutiny, but that is not to say that previously all was well. It just goes to show how little Canadians know about what actually goes on in their own country. It also explains why Canadians have traditionally let their politicians and governments get away with so much. In this chapter, we intend to introduce you to our history and to our current struggles, as a way of shedding some light on this dark corner of the public's consciousness. To understand how things got to be this way, we will have to take you back a few hundred years, to the times when there were no great numbers of non-Mi'kmaq in our traditional territories. It is only by taking the journey back that one can really get a balanced understanding of what is happening now and where things are going.

Self-Reliance and Self-Determination

The Mi'kmaq are used to dealing with other peoples. Prior to the arrival of the Europeans, we carried on relations with other indigenous peoples throughout North America, among other things for the purposes of trade, alliance, and friendship. All such dealings were based on mutual respect and co-operation, and formalized through the treaty-making process. The Mi'kmaq called this international law, the law of Nikamanen. Treaties are spiritual as well as political compacts that confer solemn and binding obligations on the signatories. The spiritual basis of the treaties is crucial to an understanding of their meaning, since it represents an effort to elevate the treaties, and relations among peoples, beyond the vagaries of political opportunism and expediency. They are intended to develop through time to keep pace with events, while still preserving the original intentions and rights of the parties.

About six hundred years ago, the Mi'kmaq people were invaded from the west by the Haudenosaunee (the Iroquois). After a number of fierce battles, the invaders were beaten back, and a treaty of peace was concluded. With peace restored, the nation reorganized itself: all of Mikmakik, our traditional lands, was divided into seven sakamowti (districts), and each of these in turn was subdivided among many wikamow (clans). Each clan was led by a sakamow (chief); a sa'ya (spiritual leader); and a keptin (war chief). [see map]

Together, the sakamow and keptin from each district formed one national council, the Sante' Mawi'omi (grand council or "holy gathering"), whose purpose was to advise the people and defend the country. This national confederation was first created in the tenth century. It was called Awitkativitik ("many families in one house"). The ancient symbol of this union, which can still be seen carved into the rocks around Kejimikujik Lake, is a ring of seven hills (the seven districts) and seven crosses (the seven chiefs), surrounding the sun and the moon (who together represent Niskam, the Creator).

The Mikmaw Nation is an alliance of many aboriginal peoples who inhabited Mikmakik. The meaning of *"Mi'kmaq"* is "the allied people"; "Mikmaw" is singular. "Mikmakik" means "the land of friendship," and covers present-day Newfoundland, St. Pierre et Miquelon, Nova Scotia, New Brunswick, the Magdalen archipelago, and the Gaspé peninsula of Quebec.

The leadership of the Grand Council is made up of three positions: the Kjisakamow (grand chief) is the ceremonial head of state; the Kjikeptin (grand captain) is the executive of the council; and the Putus (wisdom) is the keeper of the constitution and the rememberer of the treaties.

Mi'kmaq economy was based upon hunting, fishing, gathering, and farming, as well as trading surplus resources with other nations. This economic regime was founded upon the overriding principle of sustainable, responsible development to ensure long-term self-reliance and prosperity for our people. Through economic self-reliance we were assured social and political self-determination: the freedom and liberty to decide for ourselves the future of our people. We were also great travellers, having learned the art of sailing centuries before the arrival of the Europeans. In our boats we explored the North American seacoast from the frozen ocean beyond Newfoundland down to the Gulf of Mexico and what is now known as Florida.

The Norsemen may have ventured onto Mi'kmaq lands a millennium ago, but it was not until the 1600s that we experienced any sustained contact with European peoples. This was when the French established tiny settlements within our territories to engage us in the fur trade.

The relationship that developed between our people and the French was based on mutual co-operation and respect, and we had no reason to perceive any threat to our lands or our sovereignty. However, there was one very serious consequence of this contact: disease. It is estimated that at our peak, there were 100,000 Mi'kmaq. Once the new diseases and sickness brought to North America by the Europeans took their toll, however, our numbers on the coast were substantially reduced, and we began to move inland.

One other important change that came out of our contact with the French was in the spiritual realm. On June 24, 1610, our Kjisakamow, Membertou, was baptized as a Catholic, and a covenant was made to protect the priests of the church and the Frenchmen who brought the priests among us. A great wampum belt 2 metres (2 yards) in length records this concordat. On the left are the symbols of Catholicism: the crossed keys of the Holy See, a church, and a line of text from the gospels written in our own language. On the right are symbols of the power of the Grand Council: crossed lances, an armed keptin, a pipe and arrow, and seven hills representing the seven districts. At the centre, a priest and a chief hold a cross, and in the hand of the chief is the holy book. Over the course of the seventeenth century, the whole of the Mi'kmaq people became Catholics, and took St. Ann as their patron.

Perhaps it was inevitable that we would be drawn into the imperial competition between the English and the French that took place throughout Europe and North America during the seventeenth and eighteenth centuries. In any event, the Mi'kmaq did become key players in this struggle as it affected our territories: because of our strength, we could not be ignored.

In their haste to destroy French settlements, British forces crossed and devastated our country, and the lands of our allies of the Wabanaki Confederacy (the Penobscots and Passamaquoddies of what is now northern New England, and the Malecites of the St. John River valley in New Brunswick were the core of this confederacy; from time to time the Mi'kmaq Nation co-ordinated foreign policy with its members). As a response, we permitted the King of France to erect fortifications on our soil, and for a number of years we harassed British shipping from north of Casco Bay to the Grand Banks.

The tug of war began as early as 1621, when King James I of England "granted" part of the eastern seaboard to a Scotsman, Sir William Alexander, and it was dubbed "Nova Scotia." However, this action met with stiff resistance from the Mi'kmaq: we refused to enter into any treaty relationship through Alexander. The French convinced England to relinquish its claim soon afterward. In 1689, war was declared between Great Britain and France, and the following year the French at Port Royal in Mikmakik surrendered to English forces.

Neither the Mi'kmaq nor France's other indigenous allies recognized British sovereignty, however, and we continued the war until 1699. We believed that it was a matter of religious as well as political freedom, because at that time we were of the understanding that the English were "pagans." It was many years later, in 1761, that Kjisakamow Toma Denny told the British: "I long doubted whether you was of this [Christian] faith....I declare moreover that I did not believe you was baptized; but at present I know you much better than I did formerly."

By 1713, with the Treaty of Utrecht, France was compelled to give up its claims to the Acadian peninsula in favour of the British, but it retained claims over Cape Breton, Prince Edward Island, and Newfoundland until 1763. Despite a drastic decline in our population during the previous century, the Mi'kmaq still had superior numbers to the Europeans that were present in our territories in 1713. At that time, there were maybe three thousand Acadians, a few hundred British and French soldiers, and almost no British settlers in Mikmakik. As a result, our loyalty was sought by the French, who depended on our help to harass the British, and by the British, who needed our co-operation to protect themselves from French attacks.

The Treaties: Formalizing the Relationship

Because Anglo settlement began in earnest on the eastern seaboard of what is now the United States, relations between the British and the Mi'kmaq were profoundly affected by earlier developments in New England. Around 1640, the Massachusetts Bay settlers, who perhaps numbered in the thousands, began to expand into present-day New Hampshire and Maine. These lands were the traditional homeland of the Wabanaki Confederacy and the Mi'kmaq Nation.

Britain's professed policy was that it had to formally purchase tribal lands before settlers could take up legal estates. But repeated encroachments by growing numbers of settlers disrupted tribal land-use patterns, ownership, and economies.

It appeared that the colonists and the colonial governments were attempting to ignore the imperial instructions relating to the protection of indigenous land and resource rights. As a result, hostilities broke out during the 1670s. The Imperial Crown was forced to step in and provide assurances to the affected indigenous nations that their rights, under the stated imperial policy, would be respected. These assurances were formalized in treaties of peace, eleven of which were concluded with the southeastern Wabanaki tribes by 1717.

These arrangements, however, did not bind the Mi'kmaq, or respond to their concerns regarding their territories in Mikmakik. In 1719, Great Britain appointed a governor for Acadia ("Nova Scotia"), and instructed him to engage our "friendship and good correspondence" through treaty. He was governor in name only, though, since he kept his office in Boston, 100 km (600 miles) away. In any event, at this time, the Grand Council refused to enter into any treaties with the Crown.

But the ongoing problem still existed: the Imperial government and its laws could not maintain discipline among the land-hungry colonies. By 1722, armed confrontation once again flared up with the Wabanaki Confederacy. The Mi'kmaq joined in the battle and, in that year alone, our warriors took twenty-two British ships. England clearly had to focus its efforts on securing a more lasting arrangement. This was accomplished in 1725, when the leaders of the Wabanaki Confederacy, the Penobscots, Malecites, and Passamaquoddies, signed a treaty of peace with the British in Boston.

While they accepted nominal British sovereignty, they refused to surrender any more of their lands, and only agreed to cease and desist from disturbing "existing" Anglo settlements that had been created in the 1690s. Subsequently, the members of the confederacy ratified this compact, including a distinct treaty of the Mi'kmaq district, Gespogoitg (identified in the 1725 Treaty as the "Cape Sable Indians"). However, having made no former treaties with Britain, and wishing to remain non-aligned, the Grand Council of the Mi'kmaq Nation did not formally adhere to the Treaty of 1725.

The terms of the Treaty of 1725 conform to a pattern that had been established earlier. It was built on the law of Nikamanen. But it was the first formal treaty between the Wabanaki and the British Crown. For us, it served as a fundamental agreement on the nature of our relations, and it was to be renewed at appropriate intervals.

Parallel to this development, we continued to maintain our relationship with the French. Annual meetings with their representatives took place on Ile St. Jean (now Prince Edward Island), and France retained its naval base at Louisbourg, in Cape Breton, which had been constructed after the "loss" of Acadia in 1713. In 1743, hostilities were renewed between the imperial powers once again, ending with the defeat of the French at

Louisbourg two years later. By that time, Louisbourg had become a vital French military and commercial base, with a population of about 3,000 souls. With the Treaty of Aix-la-Chapelle in 1748, England was required to return Louisbourg to France, and, as a result, the British began to build Halifax at Chebucto Bay on the Atlantic coast.

The Crown appointed Lord Cornwallis to "govern" Nova Scotia in 1749, and directed him to make peace with us. That same year, a Royal Commission of Inquiry into the legal rights of the indigenous nations in North America established the legal principle that the "Indians, though living amongst the King's subjects in these countries, are a separate and distinct people from them, they are treated as such, they have a policy of their own, [and] they make peace and war with any nations of Indians when they think fit, without control from the English."

Apart from the stationing of a few hundred soldiers at Annapolis Royal and Canso, almost no British settlement had occurred in Atlantic Canada prior to the establishment of Halifax. But this initiative, as well as British designs on other Nova Scotia locations, made it clear that they were intending to do in Mikmakik what they had already done in Maine and New Hampshire. On September 24, 1749, the Grand Chief of the Mi'kmaq declared war on the British, stating: "It is God who has given me my country in perpetuity."

By October of that same year, repeated attacks on British ships led Governor Cornwallis to issue a general order to "annoy, distress, take or destroy the Savages commonly called Micmacks, wherever they are found." But the Lords of Trade, Cornwallis's bosses, thought "gentler Methods and Offers of Peace" held greater promise, providing that "the Sword is held over their Heads." In August 1751, Malecite, Passamaquoddy, and Penobscot representatives met with British commissioners at Fort St. George, objecting to unlawful settlements on their lands. The commissioners stated that the governor's "intention" all along had been to renew the Treaty of 1725, and went on to invite the tribes to meet in Halifax with Cornwallis.

Grand Chief Jean Baptiste Cope and his delegation came to Halifax in November 1752 to meet with Governor Cornwallis's replacement, Peregrine Thomas Hopson. After long discussion, it was agreed that the Treaty of 1725 would be renewed. Grand Chief Cope also said that he desired a new compact between England and the Mi'kmaq Nation. Hopson agreed. The Elika-wake ("in the King's house") Treaty acknowledges the Mi'kmaq as British subjects, and confirms their separate national identity within the United Kingdom. It also guarantees the Mi'kmaq the freedom and liberty to hunt, fish, and trade under the explicit protection of His Majesty's Civil Courts.

The Mi'kmaq agreed not to "molest" any existing British settlements, but did not consent to any new ones. The symbol of this treaty, in our traditions, is an eight-pointed star representing the original seven sakamowti and the British Crown, with the Union Jack at its centre.

In the Mi'kmaq view, the Mi'kmaq Compact, 1752, affirmed Mikmakik and Britain as two states sharing one Crown — the Crown pledging to preserve and defend Mi'kmaq rights against settlers as much as against foreign nations.

During the course of the next few years, various of the districts in Mikmakik ratified the treaty of peace, but things were far from over. The French continued to be in conflict with the English over commerce and settlement in North America, and Halifax was under siege by the Mi'kmaq and Wabanaki. Fort Beausejour, a French fortress on the Chignecto isthmus, was taken by the British in 1755. At the same time, French Acadians who did not swear allegiance to the English Queen were deported, and many Mi'kmaq rose up in arms to protect the rights of their francophone neighbours. As a result, in 1756, Lieutenant-Governor Lawrence offered rewards for Indian scalps and prisoners.

The imperialist struggle between France and England over North America, however, was in its last phase. The French fort at Louisbourg fell to the British in 1758. The capture of Quebec in 1759, and Montreal in 1760, put an end to France's designs in North America. With a view to consolidating their "winnings," the British acknowledged that relations with the indigenous peoples would have to be normalized. In Article 40 of the French Capitulation, Britain formally promised to protect the Indian property and rights in the New Prerogative Order. The Lords of Trade in London were keenly aware that the safety and future of English settlement in North America depended on the friendly disposition of the Indians. In 1760 they stated that settlement must "be done with a proper regard to our engagements with the Indians" (i.e., the treaties).

With European tensions resolved, the accessions to the Mi'kmaq Compact, 1752, began. Many of the Mi'kmaq districts again reconfirmed their commitment to the 1725 and 1752 treaties. By royal instructions issued to colonial governors in December 1761, British settlers were required by the Crown to remove themselves from any and all lands not lawfully obtained.

The new governor of Nova Scotia, Jonathan Belcher, announced in a 1762 accession meeting with the Mi'kmaq district chiefs who resided in areas that had been occupied by France that the King was determined "to support and protect Indians in their just Rights and Possessions and to keep inviolable the treaties and Compacts which have been entered into with them." Belcher's proclamation explicitly identified and reserved the territories still occupied and claimed by the Mi'kmaq, including the sea-coasts of the Unamaki, Epikoitik, Piktokiok, Sikiniktiok, and Gaspekiok sakamowti — altogether about two-thirds of the province as it was at that time.

Through the Royal Proclamation of 1763, King George III consolidated all previous policies related to the settling of Indian lands and settler conduct with the Indian Nations. The proclamation stated unequivocally that the tribes were not to be disturbed in their use and possession of their traditional lands, and that the only way in which such lands could be acquired was through treaty with the Crown. This statement was an early articulation of the Crown's trust responsibility to ensure that the Indian Nations' rights and interests were safeguarded in the face of increasing settlement and competition for lands and resources.

Despite all of these commitments and guarantees, the settlers did not necessarily possess the willingness or the ability to ensure that the New Prerogative Order was implemented by the colonial governments and settlers. The reality that Britain was intent on settling North America, and reaping profits from its resources, undermined its stated policy of protecting the integrity of our nation. To this day we have been faced with the same schizophrenic approach to our rights as a people: in law, and at the level of rhetoric, our rights are recognized and protected; but in practice, because of immigrant self-interest, we are treated as if we do not even possess the most basic of human rights.

Treaties Broken: Distorting the Relationship

The appropriation of our land and resources continued. While France had come among us primarily to trade, the British planned colonization. There were no permanent French settlements in Mikmakik before 1605, and as late as 1686 the European population of Acadia was scarcely 900. Britain established its first major colony in our territory in 1749, and within a century Europeans outnumbered us in Nova Scotia. Many Mi'kmaq migrated to their ancient islands of Cape Breton, St. Pierre, Prince Edward Island, and Newfoundland to maintain their way of life. France had been, to a large degree, a guest who had never asserted any overt control over our affairs; Britain at once set about seizing our lands.

The commitment to let us retain the Catholic religion was also broken. All of our priests were expelled, and we were forced to rely on the French at the island of St. Pierre, off Newfoundland, for religious books. Our own keptins assumed the role of priests for many years after.

At the outbreak of hostilities between the American colonies and Great Britain, General George Washington, commander-in-chief of the revolutionary army, wrote to the chiefs and captains of Mi'kmaq Nation requesting military assistance.

On July 17, 1776, a mutual defence treaty was concluded at Watertown, and the Mi'kmaq became the first nation to formally recognize the United States, which had proclaimed its independence just two weeks earlier at Philadelphia. By 1779, relations with Britain were restored and reaffirmed with the Crown at a meeting of the Grand Council that took place at Piktokiok.

But the peace between America and Britain left the English with only one naval base in North America, Halifax. To strengthen their strategic position, and to accommodate the many loyalists who moved north from the thirteen colonies, the British intensified their colonization of Mikmakik. This activity disrupted our economies, and began to severely restrict our people's access to the land and resources that were so essential to their survival. By the 1790s, many of our communities were starving, and the commitments made by the Imperial Crown that settlement would only take place after lands had been formally surrendered by us seemed to be forgotten by the settlers.

At the same time, however, both Britain and the United States continued to recognize the special status of the indigenous nations, including Mikmakik. The first commercial treaty between the two states, known today as the Jay Treaty (1794), guaranteed our continuing rights to pass across the new border and engage in trade, as we had always done. This element was of particular relevance to us and to other nations such as the Haudenosaunee, whose traditional territories were split by the imposition of the international border.

Again, in 1814, when Britain and the United States concluded a treaty of peace to end the War of 1812, they guaranteed the restoration of all the rights and privileges previously enjoyed by the indigenous nations.

In the nineteenth century, the confiscation of protected Mi'kmaq hunting grounds began in earnest. Squatters, tolerated if not actively aided and abetted by local authorities, took up large tracts of our traditional territories without our consent or any form of compensation. Repeated representations to the Crown regarding these ongoing breaches of the terms of our treaties were either stalled or ignored.

Finally, in 1841, Kjisakamow Peminawit submitted a petition to the Colonial Office in London, and as a result, they reminded provincial officials that the Mi'kmaq had "an undeniable claim to the Protection of the Government as British subjects," and that we should be compensated for any losses. The province of Nova Scotia responded by agreeing to set aside 50,000 hectares (125,000 acres) of land as "Indian Reservations" for our use in 1842. Most of these lands were already recognized Mi'kmaq family estates.

We are still uncertain as to how this amount of land was decided upon, but it is clear that it had little to do with the actual areas of land that we were using and occupying at that time, and nothing to do with our economic and social needs as a people. In any event, well aware that it had no authority to force us into abandoning our existing settlements, the province told London that it would "invite" the Mi'kmaq chiefs "to cooperate in the permanent resettlement and instruction of their people." We continued to live where we had resided and where we could, refusing to be confined to areas that we had not participated in selecting.

Soon it became clear that even this attempt at fulfilling the Crown's obligations of political and legal protection was inadequate. Only half of the 50,000 hectares were ever set aside and, by the 1850s, even this small remainder of our homeland was being settled illegally by Europeans. This had a catastrophic effect on our economies, since without adequate access to land and resources, there was little chance of putting food on the table or of generating surplus with which to trade.

Instead of expelling the squatters, as was required by the 1762 and 1763 proclamations, and by its own 1842 legislation, the province in 1859 required some of them to pay for the land they had illegally taken up. Few ever did. The Grand Council of the Mi'kmaq Nation wrote to the governor in Nova Scotia, challenging the constitutionality of "this extraordinary proposal to deprive them of th[eir] rights by entering into compromise with the violators of them," but it was not heard.

The wildlife resources that were the basis of our economy were hunted and fished out by settlers, our few farms were stolen, and we were reduced to living as itinerant woodcutters and peddlars of handicrafts. We suffered the same fate in Prince Edward Island and New Brunswick, which became separate provinces in 1769 and 1784, respectively, and in Newfoundland. New Brunswick began selling lands that we still reserved or occupied in 1844; in Prince Edward Island only one tiny island was left for our use by 1838. None of these actions was undertaken with our consent or formalized through imperial legislation, as was required by the Proclamation of October 7, 1763.

In fact, the imposition of borders and new administrative regimes had the effect of separating our people and undermining the Grand Council's ability to act as a cohesive unit. Our nation found itself confined within boundaries that had nothing to do with the way we had organized ourselves historically. But, despite the problems that this situation posed, we retained our tribal authority, and continued to maintain the political structure of the Grand Council.

We retained our language and religion in the face of an overwhelming Anglo-Protestant majority, and continued to meet as a whole people at Potoloteq (Chapel Island on Cape Breton) on St. Ann's day each year. On the whole, we maintained our traditional communities, although their number decreased as our lands were seized by settlers or sold outright by local government officials.

The British North America Act, 1867, united most of Britain's North American provinces under a single federal government, and entrusted Canada with responsibility for "Indians, and land reserved for Indians," as well as "treaty obligations." However, it also appeared to give the provinces authority over the lands and resources within their boundaries that had been properly ceded by the relevant tribes.

In our case, this had a prejudicial effect on the matter of our traditional territories, since, from that time onwards, although Canada had the responsibility for upholding the treaties and protecting our rights and interests, it was the provinces (the successors to the land-grabbing colonies) who asserted that they held "title" to the land. To this day, the division of powers established by the BNA Act has been used as an excuse for non-fulfillment of the Crown's treaty commitments and as a pretext for preventing serious discussion on the land question.

Political Repression

The remainder of the nineteenth century was a very difficult period for the Mi'kmaq people. Our collective attention was focused on day-to-day survival, with little time for anything else. During this time, the federal government began using its "powers" under the BNA Act not to protect our rights and interests, but to destabilize our nation and to make it over in the image of the European. The twentieth century has proven to be a continuation of this trend, at least in terms of federal government policy.

"Elected councils" were introduced, in spite of the authority and jurisdiction of the Grand Council in New Brunswick, PEI, Quebec, and Newfoundland, and a host of administrative procedures, which were intended to complete the destabilization program, were imposed. Although the government intended to undermine the Grand Council's authority with this initiative, we have adapted and developed a co-operative approach along with the elected councils. However, interference by outside agencies in Mi'kmaq internal affairs became even more pronounced than it once was, particularly on the part of the federal Department of Indian Affairs. Bureaucrats at the local, regional, and headquarters levels took it upon themselves to determine who was and who was not a Mi'kmaq; when houses would be built; how meagre reserve resources were to be utilized; how elections would be conducted.

This attempt at imposing an irresponsible and irrelevant form of indirect rule upon our people has proven to be an unmitigated disaster, made the worse because the unelected bureaucrats who continue to wield these powers are not accountable either to the Mi'kmaq or to the Canadian people.

At the same time, outside enforcement agencies began aggressively to restrict Mi'kmaq citizens in the exercise of their economic rights, particularly as they related to hunting, fishing, and commerce. We were told that any treaty rights we "may have had" were extinguished, and that we had no legal basis on which to pin them. No recognition was given to the many and positive assurances we had received from the Crown regarding our rights, or even to our economic needs as a society.

From 1941 until 1953, a "centralization" program was initiated in which our citizens were coerced into moving onto two "recognized" reserves in Nova Scotia: Eskasoni and Shubenacadie. The intent of this program was ostensibly to make "administration" easier for the non-Mi'kmaq bureaucracy, but its effect was to take more Mi'kmaq citizens off the land, and to further undermine their self-sufficiency. The school at Wycocomagh and many Mi'kmaq farms were burned down by Indian Affairs as a means of ensuring that our people would relocate to Eskasoni. In the end, over 1,000 Mi'kmaq were displaced from their farms in various parts of the province, and compelled to reside on what had become two acutely overcrowded containment centres.

Our youth were taken away from their families and forced to attend residential schools, where they were beaten to prevent them from speaking their own languages or practising their culture. The aim of the residential school system was to wipe out any sense of national identity on the part of youth, and replace it with European values and culture. It did not succeed in completely fulfilling these objectives, but it did serve to disorient and demoralize three generations of our people.

These efforts at dismantling our nation accelerated in 1960 when the federal cabinet decreed that the Mi'kmaq in Nova Scotia were to be divided into twelve separate "Indian Bands," to be dealt with as individual entities instead of a collectivity.

The ill-conceived and unconscionable strategy to destabilize our traditional forms of government, eliminate our culture, and ravage our economies has clearly been intended to terminate our rights, and our existence, as a people. But it has been met with ongoing resistance on the part of the Mi'kmaq. We have, of necessity, adapted to the new forces with which we must contend in our traditional territories, but always within the context of our collective aboriginal and treaty rights. Beginning in the mid-1960s, our people began to mobilize in new ways to defend the nation.

The unilateral imposition of policies and legislation affecting our people had to be dealt with. They needed assistance in coping with the morass of bureaucratic procedures and policies that were being spawned by the federal and provincial governments. In 1969, the Union of Nova Scotia Indians (UNSI) was formed to do just this. Since its inception, UNSI has worked closely with the Grand Council, the Mi'kmaq communities in Nova Scotia, and with other Mi'kmaq institutions to preserve and enhance our collective rights.

Six years later, in 1975, the Native Council of Nova Scotia was established to represent the specific interests of those Mi'kmaq citizens who are not recognized as "Indians" by the federal government. It has always been the position of the Mi'kmaq that we know who we are. However, successive federal governments have seen fit to decide for us who is, and who is not, a Mi'kmaq, and this has had the effect of dividing our communities and creating a "second class" of Mi'kmaq citizens. The Native Council was formed to address the special needs of these people.

The Grand Council, UNSI, and the Native Council of Nova Scotia have developed a close working relationship with the objective of revitalizing the Mi'kmaq Nation and undoing the damage that has resulted from hundreds of years of outside interference and discrimination. It is only by building a strong institutional base that we can hope to renew the prosperity and self-sufficiency that our people once enjoyed.

However, the struggle has also been taken up on a number of other fronts. One of the most important of these is the exercise of our political rights as a people. The United Nations international covenants on Economic, Social, and Cultural Rights, and on Civil and Political Rights, both state very clearly that "in no case may a people be deprived of its own means of subsistence." Yet this is precisely what has been done to us.

Hunting and Fishing Rights

The protection of our rights to engage in hunting, fishing, and commerce as embodied in the Treaty of 1752 is entirely consistent with the intent and the letter of these covenants, and yet, over the years, federal and provincial governments have made a conscious effort to deprive our people of their means of subsistence. The effects of these efforts are visible in all of our communities, where one of the primary sources of income is now welfare, and where many of our citizens continue to be arrested and convicted for engaging in traditional economic pursuits and commerce.

The Treaty of 1752 is unequivocal when it speaks of hunting and fishing: "It is agreed that the said Tribe of Indians shall not be hindered from, but have free liberty of hunting and fishing as usual." We sought protections for our traditional economies so that we could provide for our children as we had always done. Today, we do not hunt and fish for sport; we engage in these activities to put food on the table and to generate revenue for our people. The recurring problem was that federal and provincial legislation was being used to prevent us from exercising our rights, and to wantonly harass the breadwinners of our communities.

Repeated efforts at negotiating this issue with the federal government had failed, and so a decision was taken by our leadership to pursue the matter through the courts. The case that was chosen involved James Matthew Simon, a Mi'kmaq citizen resident at Shubenacadie. In September 1980 he was stopped by members of the federal police, the Royal Canadian Mounted Police, and searched. Mr. Simon had in his possession a type of shotgun and shells that were not "permitted" under the Nova Scotia Lands & Forests Act, and was charged with offences under that legislation. In defence of these charges, Mr. Simon cited the Treaty of 1752, and its hunting provisions.

The attorney-general of Nova Scotia argued that whatever treaty rights "may have" existed had been extinguished. Since settler governments had succeeded in ignoring their treaty obligations to the Mi'kmaq for almost two hundred years, we assume he considered those treaties to be irrelevant. The Nova Scotia provincial court apparently agreed with the attorney-general for the province, since they convicted Mr. Simon. His appeal was dismissed by the Nova Scotia Supreme Court. Ultimately, he sought, and was granted, leave to appeal to the Supreme Court of Canada.

On April 17, 1982, Section 35 of the Constitution Act came into force. It states that "existing aboriginal and treaty rights" are "recognized and affirmed." Although generally the constitutional-amendment process was not satisfactory to the Mi'kmaq, it is acknowledged by us that constitutional recognition of the treaties was a positive step. In fact, it did have a bearing on the outcome of the *Simon* case.

On November 21, 1985, the Supreme Court rendered judgment, and acquitted Mr. Simon on all of the charges laid against him. For the province, it was a significant defeat. For us, it was a vindication of many of the things we had been saying all along. The court found that the Treaty of 1752 is still a binding and enforceable agreement between the Crown and the Mi'kmaq people, and that its protections regarding Mi'kmaq hunting rights override provincial legislation that interferes with these rights.

As important, the court ruled that the treaties must be interpreted in a flexible manner that takes into account changes in technology and practice. For instance, Mi'kmaq hunters could not be limited to using spears and handmade knives, as they once did, and as the attorney-general of Nova Scotia had argued. It was also made clear that this right extended not only to subsistence hunting, but also to hunting for commercial purposes.

As a result of this decision, we knew that we were in a much stronger position to proceed with formalizing the exercise of our rights to the hunt. On Mi'kmaq Treaty Day, October 1, 1986, the majority of our leadership in Nova Scotia ratified a set of interim hunting guidelines as a first step towards this end.

The basis of these guidelines is a Mi'kmaq concept, Netukulimk, which includes the use of the natural bounty provided by the Creator for the self-support and well-being of the individual and the community at large. The guidelines covered safety and conservation considerations, as well as stating clearly that the treaty rights of Mi'kmaq citizens to hunt overrode existing provincial restrictions related to seasons, quotas, licences, and tagging and hunting gear and methods. At the same time, it was made clear that only those Mi'kmaq who followed the guidelines would be protected by the terms of the 1752 treaty.

As a result of these events, attempts were made to negotiate a more formal arrangement with the other levels of government. However, they did not bear fruit, and today, the Mi'kmaq hunting guidelines are still in effect. Recent actions by the province of Nova Scotia do not lead us to believe that they are committed to dealing with this issue in good faith, and recent inaction on the part of the federal government to ensure that our rights are protected leads us to the same conclusion. In 1987, six Mi'kmaq citizens were charged with fishing "violations"; twenty-three were charged for hunting deer and moose; and three were charged in connection with commerce and taxation matters.

In the spring of 1988, Nova Scotia announced that the annual moose hunt would be taking place from October 3 to 7. Licences were to be granted to two hundred hunters by lottery. The Mi'kmaq were excluded from having any input into the development of this approach to the harvest. It totally ignored Mi'kmaq rights to the resource, and in fact, only two Mi'kmaq citizens won the "privilege" to hunt moose under the lottery system.

After much thought and discussion, our leadership decided to stage a separate Mi'kmaq moose harvest, to ensure that our communities had adequate access to the resource, and that the harvest would be carried out according to the interim guidelines that had been developed.

Our moose harvest took place from September 17 to 30, 1988, in Victoria and Inverness counties. It was supervised by the Mi'kmaq, and its focus was to provide Mi'kmaq citizens with the opportunity to harvest the resource for subsistence use.

The government of Nova Scotia took the position that this harvest was "illegal", and promptly initiated a propaganda campaign to discredit and intimidate our citizens. The harvest did proceed, but a total of fourteen Mi'kmaq hunters were charged with violations of the provincial Wildlife Act. Their cases are now before the courts. Subsequently, the province escalated its provocation by unilaterally announcing that *any* Mi'kmaq engaged in hunting anything pursuant to the 1752 treaty would be prosecuted.

This experience calls into question the ability of the courts and the present political system to address the matter of our rights in a meaningful and lasting way. Despite the protections afforded to our treaties as a result of Section 35 of the Canada Act, 1982, and despite the enormous degree of effort that went into vindicating our rights at the Supreme Court level, we still find ourselves confronted by settler governments that refuse to recognize their own laws and their own courts.

The situation raises the question: if they don't play by their own rules, then should we? Although Canada prides itself on being one of the world's leading "democracies" and an advocate of human rights, we do not find much evidence of these things in our dealings with federal and provincial governments. Beyond this, it is clear to us that the problem is far more complex than court decisions or political will. It has to do with systemic discrimination and racism that are deeply rooted in the consciousness of the Canadian public and their institutions.

Justice for Who?

One important element of the 1752 treaty had to do with the matter of justice. We knew that something had to be done to regulate relations between our citizens and settlers, but we also knew that the traditional Mi'kmaq justice system had to play a continued role in our own internal affairs. This called for a "two-legged" justice system based on the concept of co-habitation.

For incidents involving Mi'kmaq citizens on Mi'kmaq territory, the traditional Mi'kmaq justice system would apply. For situations involving settlers, the English justice system would be used. And finally, for matters that involved both Mi'kmaq citizens and settlers, the English civil-justice system, with input from the Mi'kmaq, would come into play.

The Mi'kmaq refused to be administered under the political authority of the local settlers or under criminal law in connection with the administration of justice. Instead, the Civil Law of England — the fundamental principles of contract, property, and torts—was understood to be the appropriate basis on which to measure the conduct between Mi'kmaq and British people in Nova Scotia. This understanding is reflected in the relevant section of the 1752 compact and in the accession treaties that were ratified by the various districts of Mikmakik.

As with other understandings reached that had been confirmed by the terms of the treaty, this arrangement was implemented, but proved ineffective. In fact, with centralization in the 1940s, our traditional justice system was usurped by outside institutions and law-enforcement agencies, and even in the settler courts we found that we were not permitted to enjoy "the same benefits, advantages, and privileges" as others, even though they had been guaranteed in the 1752 treaty. This situation is most graphically illustrated by the experience of Donald Marshall, Jr., at the hands of the Nova Scotia "justice" system.

Late one evening in 1971, in a Sydney, Nova Scotia, park, Sandy Seale, a black youth, was fatally stabbed. At the time, the incident aroused emotions throughout the local Mi'kmaq, black, and white communities. But it was only much later that the real implications of what followed would come to light.

Donald Marshall, Jr., was eventually charged in connection with Sandy Seale's death. But, from the beginning, the conduct of the investigation into the killing was questionable. The two "eyewitnesses" to the crime gave testimony that appeared to be *too* consistent, and questions were raised about whether or not they had been coached on what to say. After the "eyewitnesses" had testified, other individuals came forward to the authorities, stating that one of them, John Pratico, was nowhere near the scene of the crime on the evening it occurred. These concerns were dismissed, not only by the Sydney police department, but even by one of Donald Marshall's own defence lawyers. However, in the end it was indeed confirmed that both of the "eyewitnesses" had been coached by the Sydney police, and that they had given false testimony.

It later turned out that the two lawyers initially engaged in Marshall's defence did not make all reasonable efforts to fully investigate the possibility of his innocence: they did not carry out their own investigation, and did not even conduct interviews with the alleged witnesses. No one seemed to doubt the fact that, since Donald Marshall was an "Indian," it was probable that he had committed the crime. He was finally convicted of manslaughter, and sentenced to life imprisonment. Despite his insistence, even after his conviction, that he was innocent, no appeal was allowed, because of the two "eyewitness" accounts.

Meanwhile, there were some people who were not satisfied with the outcome of the investigation or the trial. For instance, there were many unanswered questions about one Roy Ebsary, an old, eccentric character known to many residents of Sydney and its environs. He had been in the vicinity of the crime the night it occurred, and had told then chief detective John McIntyre not only that he had been with Sandy Seale and Donald Marshall night of the incident, but that he had taken a swipe at Seale with a knife. John McIntyre did nothing to follow up on this admission.

Three years later, in 1974, Donna Ebsary, the old man's daughter, approached Sydney police with information that her father had indeed killed Sandy Seale. She spoke to McIntyre, who refused to even listen. The same information was provided to the RCMP, who, apparently, did not follow up either.

The attitude of many of the officials who were handling this case is perhaps most succinctly illustrated by comments that were made by Robert Anderson, who was the director of criminal matters in the Nova Scotia Attorney General's department at the time of Marshall's trial. Eleven or twelve years after the conviction, and after being appointed a county court judge, he was approached by Felix Cacchione, who at the time was working as Marshall's lawyer.

Cacchione was concerned about some aspects of the investigation, and was seeking information from Judge Robertson concerning the 1971 investigation. His response to Cacchione's presentation was: "Don't put your balls in a vise over an Indian." The implication was that Cacchione stood to compromise his future career prospects in Nova Scotia if he became known as an advocate of Indian rights and interests (Mr. Cacchione is himself now a judge in the province).

Ironically, Cacchione's experience and Robertson's comments were consistent with a pattern that had been observed way back in 1849. At that time, the Indian commissioner reported to the Nova Scotia Legislative Assembly that the justice system and the political process in the province could not be counted on to "protect" Indian interests and rights: "Under present circumstances, no adequate protection can be obtained for Indian property. It would be vain to seek a verdict from any jury in this island against the trespassers on the reserves; nor perhaps would a member of the Bar be found willingly and effectually to advocate the cause of the Indians, inasmuch as he would thereby injure his own prospect, by damaging his popularity."

The striking similarity between these events, separated as they are by over a century, demonstrates a certain insidious continuity in settler culture and attitudes, and the degree to which discrimination and racism are part and parcel of the day-to-day reality in this province.

The criminal-justice system is made up of a number of institutions and players, each a part of a system of checks and balances that is supposed to ensure that justice is served. All of these checks and balances failed Donald Marshall, Jr. Some of this malfunctioning might be seen to be bad luck, but the consistent failure of the system in this case cannot be dismissed as merely coincidence. The fact that the system performed so miserably in this instance stems from one common thread: Donald Marshall, Jr., was an Indian.

It was not until eleven years after Donald Marshall's incarceration that things began to change. At that time, Steven Aronson, Jim Carroll, and Harry Wheaton became involved in the case on his behalf, and began uncovering the evidence that finally led to his release and to Roy Ebsary's arrest and conviction.

Even with this turn of events, the system still did not serve Marshall well. Compensation for the eleven years spent behind bars on a wrongful conviction was, at first, refused, then later granted after public opinion was brought to bear on the Nova Scotia government. Early calls for a royal commission into the whole matter were at first rebuffed as well, until finally the public outcry was so great, among Mi'kmaq and non-Mi'kmaq alike, that the province had to comply.

The evidence that came out during the course of the Royal Commission on the Donald Marshall, Jr., prosecution damned not only the individuals involved in the case at all levels, but the Nova Scotia "justice" system generally. It appeared that latently racist sentiments among the principals involved in the investigation and the prosecution played a large part in Marshall's wrongful conviction.

It also appeared that no one cared whether he was guilty or not, because he was a Mi'kmaq: certainly the evidence showed that many officials did not take the care in his case that they normally did in the course of their duties. The fact that he was an "Indian" made it easy for all to accept the likelihood of guilt, and to slough off his personal situation as if it was of little importance, since after all, in the scheme of things, he was "just another Indian."

In effect, the cumulative body of evidence presented to the Royal Commission became an indictment of the whole Nova Scotia justice system. This is borne out by much of what emerged during the course of the commission's work, but in particular by the statements made by Judge Felix Cacchione.

He testified that the province did not display a sense of sympathy or responsiveness to Donald Marshall's plight, but instead, played "hard ball." No one involved in the administration of justice came to his assistance. Cacchione testified that one of the factors that led to this malaise on the part of the system was Marshall's race. He said that if Donald Marshall had been a prominent non-Mi'kmaq Nova Scotian, he would have been treated differently, and the whole matter would have been handled differently.

Eleven years after Donald Marshall, Jr., had been convicted of manslaughter in the death of Sandy Seale, authorities were forced to admit what many had known and stated from the beginning: that he was innocent, and moreover, that he had been cruelly victimized. The so-called justice system failed him miserably, and his experience typifies what we, as a people, have been subjected to over the past few generations.

We trust that the outcome of this exercise will be a complete overhaul of the Nova Scotia justice system, and a return to the arrangements originally contemplated in the Treaty of 1752. Tentative recommendations have been made to the Royal Commission regarding the ways and means of developing and implementing a Mi'kmaq justice system, and how it would interface with the non-Mi'kmaq system. Our next steps will be determined by the Royal Commission's final recommendations, which are still in the process of being completed.

Unresolved Land Rights for Mikmakik

A final word on the deviate nature of the justice system, as it affects the Mi'kmaq, has to do with the federal and the provincial governments, and their approach to the land rights of our people. Earlier in this chapter mention was made of the guarantees that were obtained from the Crown regarding the maintenance of our land base, with particular reference to the effect of increased settlement on our territorial integrity and traditional economies.

Since almost immediately after the signing of the 1752 treaty, the Mi'kmaq have been seeking to resolve the matter of the ongoing theft of our land and resources. We met with little success, since clearly any steps that would lead to a more equitable sharing of land and resources in the Maritimes would be costly to those who now take for granted the benefits of their ill-gotten gains.

As recently as 1973, the government of then prime minister Pierre Trudeau insisted that there was no such thing as "aboriginal title" — after all, who could conceive that non-whites would have land and resource rights to the territories they had inhabited since time immemorial?

But this position changed in the wake of an aboriginal-rights case that originated in the Nass River Valley of British Columbia, with respect to the traditional territories of the Nisga'a people.

The Supreme Court of Canada considered the matter of aboriginal title in the *Calder* case, as it was called, and although the final judgment was inconclusive regarding that matter, it did become clear that the prior rights and claims of the indigenous peoples in Canada could no longer be dismissed so lightly, or in a cavalier manner. As a result, the federal government re-thought its position, and, in August 1973, released a policy statement on the "claims" of Indian and Inuit people.

It now appeared that finally we had an opportunity to negotiate the issues that, for so long, no one except us had wanted to deal with. Because of the lack of treaty surrenders in Atlantic Canada and southeastern Quebec, the Mikmakik claims were considered "claims of a different nature" than the common-law aboriginal claims of British Columbia and the North.

In 1977, the Grand Council, through the Union of Nova Scotia Indians, made a formal application for land and compensation under the 1973 policy. This initial statement of claim has led to twelve years of fruitless discussions and countless pages of correspondence and documentation.

The reason is that, although all parties agree that we never surrendered title to our lands and resources, the federal government insists our rights have been somehow indirectly "superseded by law." The application of this nebulous and racist concept to the matter of our aboriginal rights can only be seen as one more example of the systemic and consistent discrimination that we, as Mi'kmaq people, have had to endure for centuries. The continued validity of the treaty and the Royal Proclamation of 1763 deny the possibility that the concept of "superseded by law" can be applied to us.

At the beginning of this chapter, we outlined how the initial relations between the Mi'kmaq and the British Crown developed and the many guarantees that we sought and obtained from colonial authorities regarding our traditional land and resource base. There is no need to repeat them. The point is that, despite these guarantees, the dispossession of our land and resources and the marginalization of our institutions was allowed to proceed.

The province of Nova Scotia passed certain laws regarding the subdivision and sale of our lands, and indeed subdivided and sold our lands, but these actions were contrary to treaty commitments and to constitutional protections (the Royal Proclamation of 1763, for instance, has never been repealed, and is appended to the Constitution Act, 1982).

In fact, "responsible government" did not exist in Nova Scotia until 1867: until then, the province was entirely controlled by prerogative instruments of the Crown, such as letters patent, instructions, and imperial proclamations. Today, Canada tells us that, because Nova Scotia sold off our lands pursuant to various legislation, our rights have been terminated by these actions and these laws. It does not seem to matter to them that the province's actions were outside of its competence and that they were inconsistent with, and contrary to, imperial directives of the time.

The reality of the matter is that our people have been forcibly dispossessed of their land and resources, and had their economic institutions destroyed, without their consent and without any form of compensation. Meanwhile, others have benefited tremendously, and when they are called to account, they insist that because they carried out these acts, the acts themselves must be legitimate. The blatant hypocrisy evident in this kind of reasoning is astounding even to us, who have been compelled to deal with these attitudes for hundreds of years.

It should be of serious concern to Canadians that their elected representatives are so brazenly violating not only the treaty rights, but the *human rights* of the Mi'kmaq people. Canada insists that our rights can be superseded by law. If indeed this is the case, then it must be a law based on genocide and exploitation, not on justice and equity.

This reality has serious consequences, not just for the Mi'kmaq people and other First Nations, but for *all* Canadians. On the one hand, if only aboriginal peoples' rights can be superseded by law, then Canada's public posture as a champion of human rights and equality rights is an exercise in deception, and subject to a cynical and selective application based on race. On the other hand, if it has nothing to do with race, and any government of the day can reserve the right to ignore its own constitution, treaties, and courts, then sooner or later they will do it to *you*.

Either way, the implications should be shocking to any reasonable Canadian. We are glad to have the opportunity to bring these matters to the attention of the public, since, as we mentioned at the beginning of this chapter, for too long the truth has been suppressed.

It is time that these matters be brought out into the open, so that Canadian citizens can gain a clearer understanding of the conduct of their government, and perhaps realize how unaccountable and arbitrary their "democratically elected" leaders really are.

There are many other issues we could mention, issues related to the fisheries, commerce, health, shelter, and education, but suffice it to say that there is much unfinished business between the Mi'kmaq Nation and Canada. After centuries of alternating neglect and oppression, we demand that our rights and interests be dealt with in the spirit of equity and justice. We aren't asking for anything unreasonable, or anything that would be unfamiliar to the average Canadian.

However, regardless of whether or not Canada is ready to deal with us, we will proceed with the renewal of our nation, and we will continue to prepare for what must be done. In March 1989, an historic summit took place between the leaders of twenty-nine Mi'kmaq communities, representing over 18,000 of our citizens in the four Atlantic provinces and Quebec. This was the first time since 1776 that so many of our communities had come together to develop a common approach to land and treaty matters.

What came out of this summit was a Declaration of Mi'kmaq Nation Rights, which reaffirms the Mi'kmaq commitment to the principles of self-determination, sovereignty, and self-government. The declaration also states that our children have the right to be brought up in the knowledge of their language, history, and culture. And finally, it points to the fact that, as Mi'kmaq people, we must have a fair share of the natural, economic, and fiscal resources of this land called Canada. We are renewing the strength of our nation, which has for so long been in bondage, and we will succeed.

What we are seeking is the freedom and liberty to contribute positively to the future of our people and to our common future as neighbours in this great continent. What we require to do this is an equitable share of our traditional lands and resources, and recognition of our inherent right to govern ourselves.

These are not alien concepts, and they are not threatening, as some would argue. They are based on the reality of the historical record, and on the prevailing norms of international law that guide the conduct of nations in their relations with one another. The facts speak for themselves. We will let you draw your own conclusions.

AKWESASNE

THE CONFRONTATION

December 18, 1968, fifty Mohawks from Akwesasne were arrested for blocking the International Bridge near Cornwall, Ontario. The arrests came as a result of Canada's decision not to recognize the border-crossing rights of aboriginal people in Canada. One of the Mohawks who organized the blockade, and one of the first to be arrested, was a National Film Board student named Mike Mitchell. In the ensuing years, confrontations between the Mohawks and Customs officials repeatedly flared up.

In March 1988, Chief Michael Mitchell of the Mohawk Council of Akwesasne was arrested as he attempted to take a truckload of groceries from one part of Akwesasne to another, crossing the international border. He was exercising border-crossing rights confirmed in the Jay Treaty of 1794. He is fighting the case in the Canadian court system.

On October 13, 1988, 250 police officers from Ontario, Canada, and New York State invaded Akwesasne. With vehicles, helicopters, and patrol boats, they searched for duty-free cigarettes alleged to have been brought illegally across the border. It was almost certainly the biggest attack on a First Nation in Canada since the Riel uprising in 1885.

An Unbroken Assertion
of Sovereignty

Grand Chief Michael Mitchell,
Mohawk Council of Akwesasne

Akwesasne is a Mohawk community that has existed from time immemorial, with its own laws and government, and we have consistently been determined to maintain the sovereignty of our Nation.

The Mohawk Nation is part of the Haudenosaunee, or the Iroquois Confederacy. Under our ancient constitution, known to us as the Great Law of Peace, the Confederacy has existed continuously since long before European contact.

Akwesasne territory comprises several islands in the St. Lawrence River and part of the mainland on both the north and the south shore of the river. Akwesasne is not far from Cornwall, Ontario. Geographically our territory is divided by the Canadian and American international boundary and the interprovincial boundary between Ontario and Quebec. The southern portion of Akwesasne, which lies in the United States, is under the authority of the U.S. federal government and the State of New York, who both claim jurisdiction over our territory. We, at Akwesasne, however, do not recognize any of these borders.

Before the arrival of the Europeans, Akwesasne was one of many Mohawk villages throughout this part of the continent. The original capital of the Mohawk Nation was in the Mohawk

Valley, near Albany, New York. There is evidence also that Mohawk settlements were thriving near Quebec City when Cartier came up the river in the 1500s. Our people were transient, hunting and farming in one area for only five or ten years, then moving elsewhere. Their movement depended on the ability of the environment to sustain them — that is, on the potential for conservation or recovery of the land after farming as well as on other economic and cultural considerations.

Akwesasne had all the ingredients of a good settlement. It was on a river-travel route; water was easily accessible, and the site had abundant forests and lands suitable for farming, both on the islands and the mainland. The Mohawk Valley was the capital seat for all Mohawk communities, and it was there that the Wampum Council Fire was located. The area became popular for settlement among many Europeans, including the Germans, Dutch, French, and British, who came into our country and began to fight what we call the "Two-Hundred-Year War."

Everybody wanted use of the Mohawk Valley and Mohawks as their allies. The British eventually convinced most of the Mohawk leaders to fight for their cause. Joseph Brant became a hero for the British because he brought the Mohawk Nation into the war. Until then, most of the member nations of the Iroquois, or Haudenosaunee, Confederacy had stayed neutral. After this, individual members of the Six Nations Confederacy aided the American or the British causes, but never fought each other. As a unified body the Confederacy did not officially take a side. Because of the war in their homeland, many Mohawk families made Akwesasne their permanent home. More families joined them from Kahnawake in 1755, when the Jesuits were establishing a Catholic mission at Akwesasne.

Following the Revolutionary War, Brant's Mohawks went to the Grand River lands (Brantford near Hamilton, Ontario, and Tyendinaga, near Kingston, Ontario). The other member nations of the Confederacy stayed in their homeland. Onondaga was the capital of the Confederacy. By 1888 the Confederacy transferred Takagista (the Mohawk Nation Wampum Council Fire) to Akwesasne and named it the Mohawk Nation seat within the Confederacy. The War of 1812 resulted in a more formal division of the Mohawk land at Akwesasne, as specified in the Treaty of Ghent (1815). The Treaty of Paris (1783), also called the Washington Line, had drawn the first boundary between the Americans and the British. Later Jay's Treaty of Amity and Commerce (1794) made provisions for border crossing for native people across the U.S.–British border. The War of 1812 may have abrogated the preceding agreements, but they were duly reinstated by the Treaty of Ghent.

During the War of 1812, both British and American forces coerced our people to fight as partisans. Akwesasne, despite these urgings, remained basically neutral. We became skilled in diplomacy, as historical documents that are now being brought to light indicate.

Our belief and faith that we are still an independent nation go back to the first treaty signed in North America, in 1664, when the original European settlers came to confer with our people in Albany, New York. What came out of that was the Two Row Wampum Treaty, in which conditions for our collaboration were agreed to by the two sides. The Haudenosaunee Confederacy, in a presentation to the Canadian House of Commons Committee on Indian Self-Government in 1983, described the meaning of this treaty:

> When the Haudenosaunee first came into contact with the European nations, treaties of peace and friendship were made. Each was symbolized by the Gus-Wen-Teh or Two Row Wampum. There is a bed of white wampum which symbolizes the purity of the agreement. There are two rows of purple, and those two rows have the spirit of your ancestors and mine. There are three beads of wampum separating the two rows and they symbolize peace, friendship and respect.

These two rows will symbolize two paths or two vessels, travelling down the same rivers together. One, a birch bark canoe, will be for the Indian people, their laws, their customs and their ways. The other, a ship, will be for the white people and their laws, their customs and their ways. We shall each travel the river together, side by side, but in our own boat. Neither of us will try to steer the other's vessel.

The principles of the Two Row Wampum became the basis for all treaties and agreements that were made with the Europeans and later the Americans. Now that Canada is a fully independent nation, perhaps it will be possible to strike up the Two Row Wampum between us, so that we may go our ways, side by side in friendship and peace.

The committee placed so much importance on this treaty that the above description and a photo of the wampum belt were printed on the cover of the committee's report.

The Europeans at the 1664 conference said that their King would be a father to us, but the Haudenosaunee replied that there is only one father for us, and we call him Sonkwaiatisen, the Creator. The Iroquois said, this is how it will be: You and I are brothers. We will not make laws for you, but we will look after you, help you settle in this land, give you the medicines you will need to survive, and show you what you can plant, what animals you can hunt, and how to use this land. When the white men and their nations were weak with various sicknesses, it was the Native Americans who offered them medicine and food. Staples in our diet, such as "the three sisters" — corn, beans, and squash — were food types introduced to the Europeans at that time that improved their diets and health.

The original Two Row Wampum agreement stipulated that each side would refrain from interference in the other's government. Because we feel that this agreement is still binding, Akwesasne has steadfastly refused to vote in Canada's elections, both federal and provincial. Each time they come to us with their papers, their enumerators, their polling stations, we tell them to leave our territory. Each time the returning officer broaches the issue, we decline and reiterate the reasons for our refusal to participate. In November 1988, we rejected once more the offer of a polling station in Mohawk territory, inviting, instead, the setting up of one in Valleyfield, Quebec, or Cornwall, Ontario, outside of our territory. "In 1988 we are fighting for our very existence," we wrote to the returning officer last year, "for recognition of our aboriginal rights, including the right to cross freely the borders of North America, to work in either country, to educate our children on either side and bring groceries and clothing where it best suits us."

Our people have always held to this as a matter of principle. Only one Akwesasne person has ever voted in a Canadian election, and that was in the 1950s. Our people felt betrayed and incensed by his action, and his house was burned down. He left Akwesasne and never lived in our community again.

Jay Treaty — Canada's Strange Argument

Sovereignty of the Mohawk Nation was a matter of serious concern in the Jay Treaty of 1794, signed between Britain and the United States. The treaty provided that "the Indians dwelling on either side" of the boundary line created by the 1783 Treaty of Paris were not to be dispossessed of their aboriginal right to travel within their territory with their personal goods and effects, despite the borders between the United States and Great Britain. The 1812 War may have annulled this treaty, but these provisions were later confirmed and restored by the Treaty of Ghent, which effectively brought to an end the Two-Hundred-Year European War in North America. The United States has enacted into law those parts of the Jay Treaty dealing with the right of Indian people to enter and reside in the territory. Canada has not. This has long been a problem for us. In a letter to Deputy Minister of Indian Affairs, Harry Swain, of January 16, 1989, I remarked that we do not consider that the Jay Treaty created any provisions for aboriginal nations. The right to use one's territory and to transport one's personal property within that territory are aboriginal rights that have existed since time immemorial. The 1794 and 1815 treaties between Britain and the United States clarified that those rights were to continue.

Our aboriginal rights were tested in Francis *v.* the Queen, 1956. The Supreme Court of Canada established one fact in the *Francis* decision: that the Crown's promises in the Jay Treaty and the Treaty of Ghent have not been ratified or implemented in Canadian legislation. The rights promised by the Crown in those treaties were not part of the laws of Canada in 1956.

As the Ontario Court of Appeal quoted recently in the case of R. *v.* Agawa: "One must distinguish here between a statute that specifically nullifies a treaty right and an enactment that merely fails to implement or observe it. Legislation of the latter kind would not relieve the Crown of its obligations under the treaty." Canada should not confuse its failure to implement the promise with the question of whether the Crown has any obligations.

In the *Francis* decision, the court held that the Jay Treaty and the Treaty of Ghent were not promises in "Indian treaties," but in fact, the Crown did make promises to the Indian nations who were its allies, both before and after the two treaties in question. Formal statements made in council by Crown representatives were recorded and survive today. The courts were unaware of them in 1956. These are the statements in question:

On August 31, 1796, the deputy superintendent general of Indian Affairs, Alexander McKee, told the Ojibways, Ottawas, Pottowatomies, and Hurons at the Chenail Boarte (now known as Walpole Island): "[The King] has notwithstanding taken the greatest care of the rights and independence of all the Indian nations who by the last Treaty with America are to be perfectly free and unmolested in their trade and hunting grounds, and to pass and repass freely undisturbed to trade with whom they please."

On August 28, 1795, Lieutenant-Governor John Graves Simcoe at Fort Erie explained the terms of the Jay Treaty to the Six Nations:

> Brothers:
> By the present Treaty your rights are guarded, and specifically placed on their ancient footing....
> I have the Treaty in my hands, as printed in the U. States it establishes your rights upon the same basis that had been formerly agreed upon between the French and British Nations, and which I repeated in October last to the Western Indians in the following words: "children, in the victory over the French Nation, the common enemy, the interests of your Forefathers, and of you, their children, were not forgotten in the Treaty between the English the Conquerors, and the French. It was stipulated that your rights should be preserved, those rights which you enjoy as an Independent People. It was declared that you had a right to go to the English French fires for the purpose of traffic, and that you had a right inseparable from an independent people to admit the Traders of either Nation to your Fires as suited your interest or inclination....
> Upon these principles the present Treaty is established, you have a right to go to the British Settlements, or to those of the U. States, as shall suit your convenience, nor shall your passing or repassing with your own proper goods and effects of whatever nature, pay for the same any impost whatever....
> You see therefore that by the Treaty a perpetual and constant communication is secured between you and the King's Subjects and our future trade and intercourse, is guaranteed on the most unrestrained and General footing.

As for the Treaty of Ghent, which was the peace treaty that ended the War of 1812–14, William Claus, the Deputy Superintendent General of Indian Affairs, met with the Indian Allies of the Crown on April 24, 1815, at Burlington Bay. Present were the

Six Nations, Hurons, Shawnees, Kickapoos, Delawares, Chippewas, Ottawas, Sauks, Creeks, Munsees, Moravians, Nanticokes and Misquakies. Claus stated:

> Chiefs and Warriors:
>
> ...in making peace with the Government of the United States of America, your interests were not neglected nor would Peace have been made with them had they not consented to include you in the Treaty which they at first refused to listen to. I will now repeat to you one of the Articles of the Treaty of Peace which secures you the Peaceable possession of all the country which you possessed before the late War, and the Road is now open and free for you to pass and repass it without interruption.

Claus then read the entirety of Article III of the Treaty of Ghent and presented strings of wampum with his words as a sign of the sacredness of the Crown's commitments.

The words spoken to our ancestors were those of perpetuity. They were not told: "The King has secured your rights for a time, while it is convenient."

The reasoning for including those particular provisions in the treaty continue to be valid today. Akwesasne is one Mohawk community, and the line that was drawn through our territory creates precisely the problems and tensions today that the treaty provisions of 1794 were designed to avoid. The problems we encounter in Akwesasne are to be found in every Iroquois community and in many other nations across this continent.

The United States has enacted at least part of the provisions guaranteed in the 1794 treaty. It is ironic that Canada, the successor to the British Crown that insisted on those provisions, has enacted none of them.

We are prepared now to discuss practical and reasonable ways to implement the rights guaranteed to us in the provisions of the Jay Treaty. The promises were made and have not been kept. The lack of implementation does not lessen the Crown's obligations; it means we have unfinished business that should be attended to.

On the basis of these treaty promises, the Six Nations ceased hostilities against the United States in 1815, and it is fair to say that, without the military assistance of Mohawk people at such confrontations as Beaver Dam and Chateauguay, Canada might not be here today.

The Supreme Court of Canada in 1956 did not offer any reason why the promises made by the Crown, both to the United States and to the Six Nations, have not been ratified and implemented through legislation, although it was suggested that the conditions leading to the promises no longer existed.

The community of Akwesasne is the living embodiment of why those rights are still essential for our continued vitality as a people. The border was not our idea. We are still one united people, despite the artificial division of our lands.

The insistence that we should vote in Canada's elections, and the formal refusal to ratify our supranational border-crossing rights, are but part of a continuing effort to prove to our people — and, indeed, aboriginal people everywhere in the country — that we are Canadians, subject to Canadian laws. In 1869, only two years after the Canadian Confederation was formed, Canada decided that no Indian could be in lawful possession of any land without a permit from the Minister of Indian Affairs. Our chiefs and the chiefs of all other communities within our Confederacy — predating Canada's — objected to this intrusion. They especially objected to Canada's assumption of law-making powers over us. We did not, and still do not, feel that Canada should control use of our lands. The terms of Akwesasne's treaty with the British made at Kahnawake in September 1760 specify that we should retain our lands.

We also made objections to the Canadian law by which our women lost their Indian status through marriage to those without Canadian Indian status. It took Canada 125 years to agree that this law was morally indefensible, and to change it. Our people were marrying other Mohawks, but they were from the "American" side of the boundary and Canadian law did not consider them "Indians." We had to fight the matter in the courts to have Canada recognize the cultural integrity of our community in this situation of membership entitlement.

A Fruitless Attempt to Impose "Democracy"

The most serious imposition began with the Indian Advancement Act of 1884, passed by the Government of Canada to allow native people to elect chiefs "with a view to training them for the exercise of municipal powers." The wording was peculiar: "The object of the department is to endeavour to promote their [the Indians'] advancement in civilization and intelligence with a view to eventually attaining to an equality in those respects with the white portion of the population." Though we had long governed ourselves under a constitution on which the Americans modelled theirs, we were not, according to this act, intelligent!

Almost immediately in Akwesasne, the Indian agent began to meddle in the election, declaring that he would reserve to himself "the right to allow or disallow" the election of one nominated candidate, who he did not, apparently, approve of. As I will show later, Indian Affairs has been active in "disallowing" our wishes, right up to the present day.

All of the Mohawk people in Canada declared their preference for our traditional system and, in petitions to the government, recalled ancient obligations undertaken by the British Crown that "each side would remain in its own vessel," that the British would not make compulsory laws for us, and that, as promised in the Royal Proclamation of 1763, the land held by us would be secured free from molestation.

"What is your power and authority to rule our people?" asked one petition to the governor general.

Another Akwesasne petition read:

> The Indian Act breeds only sorrow, contention, hatred,
> disrespect of family ties, spite against one another, and

absence of unity among us Indians. It also creates two distinct parties at the elections. The law was never authorized in its adaptation among Indians....There is only one way to recover brotherly feelings, that of substituting the seven lords appointed by each of the seven totems according to the ancient customs which we know gave us peace, prosperity, friendship and brotherly feelings in every cause, either for personal good, or to the benefit of the whole community.

This petition was signed by more than 1,000 people from Akwesasne, Kanesatake (Oka), and Kahnawake. It is as true today as it was a hundred years ago, when it was written.

When all such appeals were rejected, the Clan Mothers of Akwesasne declared their intention to elect their chiefs by traditional methods in a letter to the governor general:

The ancient custom of creating life Chiefs is that they are selected according to the different clans, there being three from each clan, also three women who each selects her special chief from among her clan. Of these chiefs, one is considered the Head Chief, the second is the "big man" and the third is the "crier". As there are four distinct clans, there are twelve life chiefs.

...But if any misdemeanour shall offend their clans, these women first hold Council with the women of their own clan, and if they find his offence of sufficient strength to warrant his resignation, these women will call upon the men members of their clan and they meet and select another member to represent them. They turn the newly selected member to the twelve life chiefs for their confirmation and ratification.

The women councillors each watch over their special charge and inform them of the rules of their chieftainship.

The women went ahead with their own meeting, appointed and confirmed their chiefs, set up their government, and advised Ottawa of the names.

This took place in 1898, and the department's response was predictable: "The department is determined not to allow any of the Indians to set its authority at defiance."

A police force was sent to Akwesasne to enforce the election, but the people forcibly prevented the election from being held. "They [the Indians] might as well look for the falling of the sky," reported a police officer who had tried to impose the new law, "as to expect recognition of their claim to hold the position of a practically independent state." We are still waiting for the sky to fall, but we have not ceased the battle taken up by these Clan Mothers.

Nine months later, the Canadian authorities tried again, but two hundred people surrounded the schoolhouse where the election was to take place, locked up the Indian agent, and drove the police away.

Two months later, at 4:00 A.M. on May 1, 1899, Colonel Sherwood, commissioner of the RCMP, came to Akwesasne, leading a contingent of police across the St. Lawrence River. They occupied the Council Hall, where they sent a message to the chiefs to attend a special meeting regarding the buying of stone to build the collapsed piers at the Cornwall Bridge. As the chiefs walked into the council office, they were thrown to the floor and handcuffed. One of the women notified the Head Chief, Jake Fire, and as he came through the door demanding the release of his fellow chiefs he was shot twice, the second shot being fatal. The police marched their prisoners to the tugboat and left the village. Jake Fire was shot down in cold blood while fighting for Mohawk Indian government.

Later the government issued warrants for the arrest of more of the chiefs. The seven chiefs who went voluntarily were imprisoned. Five of them were kept in jail for more than a year. Fifteen Akwesasne men were eventually charged and then released.

Immediately after this affair, the representatives of the government took fifteen Indians over to Cornwall and provided them with alcohol. The Indian agents told them each to nominate one of the others present. This was how the elective government under the Indian Act system was implemented at Akwesasne.

This is the way Canada introduced our people to the principles of their democracy. It is little wonder that we found the institution meaningless and completely ignored it for many years. For some twenty years the traditional council continued to be our government, but Canada would not recognize or deal with them. Then, when money started coming out of Ottawa, they gave it to members of the elective system. This continued until the late 1940s or early 1950s. People didn't vote in those elections; sometimes only twenty votes would elect a man to the St. Regis Band Council, as it was known then. Naturally, such a system had no moral stature in the community. Moral leadership continued to flow from our traditional chiefs, who have our continued respect. In 1986, "in honour of Jake Fire and his gallant efforts to preserve the Mohawk government, our Chiefs declared a national holiday which we now observe May 1st of each year."

Divide and Conquer: A Classic Case — Akwesasne/U.S. Side
Unfortunately, many years of interference by outside governments have brought us much trouble. When grants were received for education, medicine, and so on, many of our people began to think of themselves as Canadian or American. We were still one people, but we were divided by the lines drawn through our land.

While we have been trying to cope with the imposition of Canadian authority on one side of our territory, and American on the other, our people on the American side have enjoyed what our First Nations leaders in Canada have always wished they could exercise — sovereignty, tested through the courts and protected by the Constitution. They have self-government in its widest meaning. The New York and U.S. federal authorities cannot come in and dictate laws, except for reasons of national security or extreme emergency. But what we have seen in their experience is that if you do not have a judicial structure, a police force, a judge to impose your laws, you can develop an outlaw state. Thus, on the U.S. side of our territory, gambling, bingo, and slot-machine syndicates have developed, and outside investors are making big money, with a few Mohawk merchants taking advantage of the community — because there is no judicial code.

Smuggling is promoted as economic development, and leaders who have worked for unity among the three councils are branded "sell-outs." Mohawk authority is deemed important by the community, but many of the controls and regulations are refused. Sovereignty will slip through our fingers, and it will be only a matter of time before the collective rights of all Mohawks are lost forever. It would take a lot for our people to wake up and see what we are doing to ourselves. Without laws and judicial structure, some of our people have become rich at the expense of the community. We have to decide what is legally and morally acceptable among the types of economic-development ventures that are brought in from the outside.

The two elective governments have gradually changed their role from conducting puppet governments to Mohawk community governments, which really represent our nation. This change has occurred only after many years of friction between U.S. and Canadian councils, between elective and traditional councils, between Christian and traditional authorities.

Over the decades this divided system of control built up much confusion, tension, and finally even hatred among our people. Families were split apart, brothers set against brothers, until, in 1980–2 this rivalry between our traditional system of government and the elective system came to a head. First, on the American side, the elective council called in the New York State Police to arrest the traditional chief. Eventually, guns appeared, offices were occupied, skirmishes took place. Helicopters flew over us. All roads were blocked off. It was like watching the

Vietnam War on television, except that we were living in the middle of it.

Like many others at the time, I wanted nothing to do with such politics. I was attached to the movement for cultural and spiritual renewal, but we finally decided that something had to be done, so we made an effort to be elected to the band council, even though we rejected its legitimacy.

When we first tried in 1982, we were a minority, but by 1984 that situation had changed. We found that our financial affairs were in sad shape. We had a $2-million deficit, we were hampered by our inability to raise credit, had no direct election for chief, and few powers or resources to take action independent of the controls imposed by Canada's Indian Act. Still, there was optimism in our community. Our people were tired of fighting each other and were ready to talk to each other again.

Trying to Reconnect with Our Past

Our first action was to knock on the doors of our traditional chiefs, invite the elective chiefs from the American side and, for the first time, all sit together under one roof to talk about this great change we wanted to make in Akwesasne. We put together a document, which we sent to the Government of Canada, saying that we wanted to negotiate self-government, that we wanted to reconnect ourselves as a people and return to our traditional principles of government.

The Canadian government had a lot of trouble with that proposal, but we set up a meeting with then minister of Indian Affairs, David Crombie, a man to be respected, and who would listen. We asked him to let us come up with a plan to recover our deficit and to work with us in establishing a management plan. For cultural, historical, and practical reasons, we changed the council's name to the Mohawk Council of Akwesasne. The St. Regis Band Council, so long a cause of conflict in our community, thereby ceased to exist. We established our management plan, and our council sought people from our community who were working in the cities for other organizations or governments and who possessed various skills in administration of finances. We asked them to come home and help rebuild our community.

In 1986, we changed our election regulations so that our Head Chief could be elected by the people of the community, instead of by the twelve council members.

Akwesasne was always known for "dirty elections," and it was normal to have people lodge protests after each election. The Indian Act had vague election codes, and Akwesasne, being a border community, was easy prey to election protests on such issues as residency and eligible membership.

In 1986, a reserve resident wanted to run for Grand Chief as well as councillor, in case he didn't succeed in his first choice. The electoral officer from the reserve ruled that he could run for only one position and requested that he make a choice. When he failed to reply, she entered his name in the race for Grand Chief, the position that he was clearly campaigning for. He lost and protested to Indian Affairs, which declared the election of the four chiefs on Cornwall Island void, leaving the positions vacant.

Our community members were very upset that Ottawa was once again interfering, and instructed our council to fight in the courts to support our community view. We discovered that at the same time as Indian Affairs was telling the Mohawks in Ontario that a man could run for both positions, in a reserve in British Columbia they were taking the opposite position.

We settled the issue by establishing our own electoral code, supported by a community vote.

There are two sections in the Indian Act that define elections: elections by code, and elections by custom. And we decided to go back to elections by our customary methods. This created the problem that Indian Affairs did not recognize our traditional chieftainship structure. I will never forget this process. We spent six months trying to find a way around their rules. We invited their lawyers to come to meet with us. We had a meeting with twelve Indian Affairs lawyers, most of whom knew nothing of what we were trying to do, yet they all gave advice. After listening to them, I was not surprised that Indian Affairs was being sued from all sides, if that is the kind of legal advice they are getting. Finally we defined our new code, and Indian Affairs accepted that "from now on it would be the custom to conduct elections in this manner."

That is how they got around accepting our method as an election by custom. Even so, they asked for a letter from the traditional chiefs before they would agree. We said, why would they need a letter when they do not recognize our traditional chiefs? Nevertheless I still got a letter from the traditional council to agree that in future the code we had written would be the method of conducting elections. I have to say this whole thing, their effort to dictate our elections, is a joke. They try to make us dance to their music, but at some point we have to try to stop this.

In 1988 we conducted our own election with a three-year term.

In these ways we tried to make changes within the structure of the Indian Act — we took over education, elections, and decisions about membership, for instance, but we still lacked the tools to really establish our own control over our own community. We are back where Jake Fire was when he was assassinated in 1899, trying to negotiate self-government, but 99 per cent of the by-laws we have passed have been disallowed by the Canadian authorities, exercising the extraordinary powers that Canada has granted itself under the Indian Act. How much progress have we made when the minister is still able to exercise arbitrary or discretionary power over our decisions, just as he was able to do over our elections a century ago?

When our by-laws were rejected, we went ahead, as far as possible, and implemented them anyway. When, for example, Canada refused to recognize our conservation by-laws, we registered them with our Longhouse chiefs, and set up our own conservation authority with officers and by-laws that we fund ourselves. In this way we decided that, if Canada refuses to co-operate with us under its Indian Act powers, we will take our authority from the people and set up our own system.

The need for us to have these powers was emphasized by a developing situation in which guns, explosives, and gambling places were spreading into our areas of Akwesasne from the other side. Luckily, we already had a small Mohawk police force, a local judge, police cars, and a small jail and, on that basis, we have established an Akwesasne Judicial Society.

We pulled in people from the community who were interested in law and have established three different commissions to run our system of justice; the *Mowhawk Court Commission*, comprised of community members appointed by council, oversees the general conduct of the courts and judges; the *Legislative Commission* takes community and council recommendations and develops laws that are to be implemented by the police and courts, after being formally ratified by our community members under our own custom; and the *Police Commission* ensures that laws administered by the police and conservation authority are responsibly and efficiently enforced, according to a code of conduct.

A New Justice System of Akwesasne

Mohawks of Akwesasne realize that laws have to come from the people and the community.

Community people from both sides of Akwesasne and representing all three councils joined a task force that resulted in the formation of a "Justice Society" for Akwesasne. We are currently working on a justice code for all of Akwesasne.

The three justice chiefs and their three associates will be appointed jointly by the three governing bodies of Akwesasne — the Mohawk Nation Council of Traditional Chiefs, the St. Regis Tribal Council on the American side, and the Mohawk Council of Akwesasne. There is also a Grand Tribunal of Justice Chiefs to deal with appeals. A Mohawk Justice Conduct Society deals with any alleged misconduct on the part of the justice chiefs.

The Code of Offences administered by this structure has been established by the community, and has three categories of crime — capital, grievous, and minor — and punishments include banishment for serious crimes (in effect, the holding of an offender to be handed over to the outside authorities), community service, restitution, probation, and fines. Capital offences include unnecessary slaughter of game animals and fish, or unnecessary damage to plant life.

There is no place in our judicial process for lawyers. The emphasis is on mediation. For example, after hearing evidence from both sides, the justices ask all parties and their witnesses to state what they think would be a "just and equitable solution and end to the matter," and taking these into consideration, they pronounce their verdict. Anyone can bring a lawyer to the court to relate facts, but no questioning of witnesses by lawyers is permitted.

As our code states: "This Code is enacted with the intent of strengthening the Mohawk Nation at Akwesasne and affirming the determination of the Mohawk people to be one nation protected by one set of codes and procedures applicable to all regardless of geographical location. It is also affirming the determination of the Mohawk people to be governed by Mohawks rather than foreign governments."

This is one of the most important measures we have adopted. We will have it approved by referendum of the people, and we have gained a rather reluctant acceptance of the system by the Canadian federal authorities.

Canada's Face Set against Change

We have discovered that, under the elective system of government imposed on us by Canada, the chief and council may have the best intentions in the world, but their authority is fatally limited. In our effort to take charge of our own community we have passed many by-laws, and almost all of them have been rejected by the Canadian federal government. We can acknowledge that some of these rejections were the result of problems in drafting, but most can only be seen in terms of Canada's intention to deny the authority of our government, because the Department of Indian Affairs thinks it knows what is best for us, or because it is unwilling to allow us to test the strength of our law-making in the court. The Indian Act provides that any by-law made under section 81 may be disallowed by the minister within forty days after it is made, and usually such disallowance has been done at the end of the forty day period without consulting us. The long list of our disallowed by-laws would be laughable if it were not a serious matter for the health of our community. Here are some examples:

Our appointment of conservation officers as constables to enforce our conservation by-laws was disallowed on May 29, 1986. The Ontario Ministry of Natural Resources refused to train our officers as we requested, so we had them trained by U.S. Conservation authorities and the New York State Police. Yet, when these officers began their work in Akwesasne, the Ontario Provincial Police charged one of them with unauthorized possession of a restricted weapon — his service revolver, worn as part of his uniform. The RCMP had refused to register the weapon, because it did not consider the Akwesasne Police Force a law-enforcement agency, even though our officers hold police authority from both the Ontario and the Quebec provincial government. The charge against our officer was dismissed in provincial court, appealed, and dismissed again in a higher court.

Another variation of this type of harassment is the confusion of jurisdictions claimed by Canadian authorities. Early in 1988, two of our people were charged with fishing by means other than angling, because they were using a net in the St. Lawrence River, a place where our aboriginal right to fish has never been surrendered. Boat, motor, and nets were seized. The Ontario ministry says that, though it has powers to seize the equipment, it does not have the authority to release them, though it is willing to have a court order their release. Yet, this procedure comes under the federal Fisheries Act, and the federal department says it has delegated all its fisheries activities in Ontario to the provincial authorities! While they cannot make up their minds between them as to who has power to release our equipment, it remains in custody and our people suffer.

Our by-law forbidding the sale of fireworks was disallowed on February 29, 1988, a classic example of remote bureaucrats thinking they know what's best for a community whose problems they really know nothing about. This by-law was designed to give us power to confiscate enormous truckloads of some very lethal fireworks that began to creep into the Canadian portion of our territory from the other side. Though this law was rejected by Ottawa, we obtained community approval in the traditional way and enforced it anyway.

Our by-law respecting the regulation of small vessels was disallowed on July 15, 1988, because it "may not contain a sufficient description of the reserve to which the by-law is intended to apply," and because some of its provisions were similar to those of the Canada Shipping Act regulations and the Criminal Code of Canada.

We say: if the territory is not sufficiently described, let a court find that out — don't have lawyers and bureaucrats pre-empt a court decision. We say: it is perfectly sound for local and specific laws to regulate local situations, so why not allow them to do so?

Our trespassing by-law was disallowed in June 1988, because (among other things) it attempted to define trespassing. Yet, the only case ever reported under the trespassing section of the Indian Act resulted in an acquittal because "trespassing" was not properly defined.

Our dog control by-law was disallowed in April 1988, because it allowed for the destruction of a dog without prior notice to the animal's owner. Yet, this is consistent with our laws and reflects the wishes of our community. Who are these people in Ottawa to tell us how we should live?

Our wildlife conservation by-law was disallowed in May 1988 because, among other things, "the province of Ontario is concerned about the area of jurisdiction," and because it gives law-enforcement powers to our conservation officers.

Our by-law creating and empowering our police force in 1986 was disallowed because it was felt it was outside the authority of a band council. But what else could the Indian Act mean when it authorizes by-laws for "law and order"? And why have similar by-laws in other communities been enacted without being disallowed?

As can be seen, many of these by-laws dealt in one way or another with the problems of peace and order. In that category we have had eleven by-laws disallowed, having to do with nuisance, trespass, residency, explosives, weapons, and so on. We are convinced that, if these by-laws had been in force, we would not have experienced the problems we have had recently in connection with the smuggling of cigarettes, guns, liquor, and drugs.

Given this record, it is little wonder that we do not have much faith in the band-council system. It rests on a century-old document, the Indian Act, which has had very little modification, and it simply does not give us the powers to look after our community. It is a farce, and the time has come to change it. It is clear to us that we can break free of this imposed system of government.

A Massive Invasion of Akwesasne

It was because of this smuggling problem that our territory was subjected, on October 13, 1988, to a massive police raid in which 250 officers from the RCMP, the Ontario Provincial Police, the Cornwall City Police, and the New York State Police and Border Patrol invaded Akwesasne with 75 vehicles, a helicopter, two tow trucks, one front-end loader, and patrol boats. They sealed off Cornwall Island for four hours and searched twelve locations.

They were looking for cigarettes brought into the territory of Akwesasne on the Canadian side, later to be taken illegally into Canada proper, taking advantage of the ill-defined border between the two countries within our territory. These are Canadian cigarettes that are first exported tariff-free to border towns in the United States. They are then bought up in large quantities and smuggled back into Canada through Akwesasne.

This issue has unfortunately become confused in the minds of many people with our right to cross the borders with personal goods, a right that was confirmed in the Jay Treaty, and that we have been insisting on ever since. It is necessary to explain here that, though Canada has not ratified the Jay Treaty and denies the validity of these rights, nevertheless it has for some years informally recognized these border-crossing rights by establishing a separate lane at the border post on Cornwall Island for our people to pass through without being questioned. We have to pass this customs point if we want to travel from one side of our territory to another. Until now, the system had worked adequately, with the Indian lane governed on the basis of "trust."

From time to time, in the past, Canadian Customs authorities would insist on charging us duty when all we were doing was taking personal goods from one part of Akwesasne to another, as we believe we have the right to do. There was a celebrated confrontation on this issue in 1968, which became the subject of the National Film Board film *You Are on Indian Land*, which is still often shown in Canada in academic and other circles.

The point then — as it is now — was to establish our right to cross with personal goods. In practice, Canada has recognized that our people form one community, that we are really not divided by a border that was not Mohawk in its conception. But, unfortunately, these informal arrangements are fragile, and have permitted abuses by both Canadian and Mohawk people.

In 1988 we again challenged the meaning of these rights when we objected to a Canadian government ruling that goods destined for sale in community grocery stores within Akwesasne were commercial goods and not personal goods intended solely for the use of our people, and would not, therefore, be allowed to pass free of duty. So, in March 1988, I took a truckload of such goods to the border, deliberately courting arrest so as to provide occasion for a court challenge designed to get a definitive legal statement of our rights. (That case is proceeding at time of writing.)

This issue is of central importance to us, and it should not be confused with the smuggling problem. There are, of course, some Mohawk people who say that, since there is no border for us, we should be able to carry anything, anywhere, to sell to anybody.

Our people in Akwesasne have shown that they are against smuggling; they have co-operated with police, and our own Mohawk police have made a number of drug busts. Cigarettes are perhaps the least of our worries. Drugs, liquor, and automatic weapons, all of which are harmful to our people, have been brought into the territory in great quantities. Our people in our community have said that this is wrong under our laws, whether a border exists or not. Their view is that those native people who abuse our right to transport such property within our territory free of taxes and duties are opportunists. They are risking injury to the rights of all our people for their own immediate profit. Neither the community nor the Iroquois Confederacy supports smuggling.

We do, however, feel that it is Canadian laws that have permitted this smuggling to occur. We do not try to tell you what laws you should make — we agreed not to do so in our early treaties — but we can see that stricter control over exports, perhaps with a system of end-user permits and prohibition of sales to prior abusers, would solve much of this problem, but we do wish you to recognize our border rights for what they are, to protect the collective rights of all Mohawks.

Canadian law-enforcement agencies have been unsuccessful in dealing with what has become a large operation, with few seizures and few convictions to their credit, and almost none of the important figures charged.

The October 13, 1988, raid on Akwesasne was a particular affront to our people. The RCMP stated that seven individuals had been arrested, and substantial amounts of weapons, drugs, and cigarettes had been seized. In reality, the reported $200,000 worth of cigarettes seized was actually $50,000 ($150,000 in cash was seized); the weapons seized were three pistols, one rifle, and one shotgun, of which three were not in working order; and the "substantial quantities" of illegal drugs were only 30 grams of cocaine and a small quantity of marijuana taken from one residence. The RCMP did not touch people who have been smuggling drugs, liquor, and machine-guns through our community.

None of this justified the use of hundreds of police officers from five different forces, or the sealing off of an entire community for half a day.

Our people are very concerned about all of these things, and we believe the best way to deal with them would have been through co-operation between our own community and the police force and the authorities of outside jurisdictions.

Unfortunately, because of the massive abuse of police power represented by the October 13 raid, we cannot see ourselves trusting these outside agencies again. They have alienated the people of Akwesasne.

As a police action, the raid was a failure, but as an attack on our community it had a certain perverse success. The police came and went with very little to show for their effort, but in Akwesasne our leaders and our peacekeepers have had to deal with the aftermath of the raid. Much of the community anger has been directed at our Mohawk governments instead of at Canada, Ontario, and New York. We have learned a very hard lesson: unless we are in control of our own affairs and our leaders take their authority from the people in the community, the walls can come crashing in on us, no matter how hard we work or how good our intentions may be.

By this raid the Canadian authorities sent us a message: they do not trust us, nor do they want our co-operation. Our governing council and our police force were both kept ignorant of the planned raid, apparently because we were also suspects.

We find ourselves in the middle of an impossible situation: we have to defend our right to cross the border freely and have pledged this to our people. However, we cannot support or defend large-scale smuggling for sale to non-Indian people.

A Catalogue of Mounting Frustrations

"The raid by the RCMP has not done anything to make people respect the judicial system of Canada," I wrote to the deputy minister of Indian Affairs the month after the raid. "Quite the contrary: the heavy-handedness of that raid has made law enforcement more difficult at Akwesasne."

I outlined to him the difficulties caused to us by the indifference and obscurantism of his department:

> Our by-laws that needed support from your department have been rejected. Requests for adequate numbers of peace officers to protect our community members have also been neglected. Our Council...has pinpointed several problem areas that could be dealt with by a Mohawk-based judicial structure that protects not only the Mohawks of Akwesasne but the interest of Canada....A proposal by the Mohawk Council on the Border Patrol Program that was submitted by our Council two years ago also fell on deaf ears.
>
> You surely can imagine the frustration existing within our council and community due to the inaction at the various levels of government within Canada. Our Council and the people...have consistently reiterated their opposition to smuggling....If your government had paid some attention to the problem areas that we identified in the last few years, we certainly wouldn't be in the predicament that exists today...

> The Mohawk people of Akwesasne have resolved to overcome their problems with or without your assistance.…[But], without adequate resources for our law enforcement agencies, we are fighting a losing battle. Many of our leaders are ready to quit.

The leaders of our community, elected to our Mohawk Council, have quit their jobs and moved into our office to undertake responsibility for particular areas of Akwesasne affairs. This is almost full-time work, and no salaries are paid to them. Since we believe it an essential part of the development of self-government, we have been using some of our research funding for this purpose. If we are to succeed in what we hope to do, we need co-operation from the governments who control the resources we need.

To Restore Honour, Harmony, and Truth

We have before us a glorious purpose: that is, to replace these many frustrations and difficulties caused by the arrogance and indifference of the nations that surround us, with a consensual system of government that responds to our deepest needs, springs from the most profound wisdom of our past and our elders, and holds out for us the restoration of harmony, honour, and truth in our daily affairs.

In our traditional system, when a chief is ratified through what we call "a condolence ceremony," he takes office for as long as he is capable of hearing, seeing, has a good heart, and can produce a family in his whole adult life. That family he is capable of producing becomes his whole nation when he becomes a chief.

However, he is not necessarily there forever, or unconditionally. The Clan Mothers decide who will become chief, and if a chief they have chosen commits an offence of some kind against his nation, he is given three chances. The third time the Clan Mother will come with a man she has selected, and this man will take away the horns bestowed on the chief when he was installed in office. That is the greatest shame that a Mohawk leader can experience.

In this system, there is honour and justice. I grew up in this system. My grandparents raised me, and passed on to me the songs and speeches. Today I am a faithkeeper. I have to be present at the ceremonies, to pass the songs and speeches that have to be made, the prophecies, all the spiritual and ceremonial events that go with them. Today we do not have too many of the wise old ones left, so younger people have to carry on, building our base, the language, the culture: we realize that without those, even if we have the land, we are dying a slow death.

Now, working as I am in an elective system imposed by the white man, I find myself knee-deep in reports, lobbying, meetings, and paperwork. In white man's politics, I found that you have to learn to out-manoeuvre him. You not only have to be deceitful, you even have to try to keep a step ahead, to work out in advance what he is going to think of next. That's what everything is based on — deceit and manoeuvring.

So, it is peaceful when I go back to the longhouse; sitting there, listening, I say to myself: one time, it used to be this way. Those who were deceitful or lying, or were not ready to defend their nation, would not survive.

We are trying to reconnect with this ancient system of government that has watched over and guarded our people through all our troubles, right up to the present day. Of course, we do need to have our people educated — to become doctors, lawyers, teachers, and leaders. We do need resources and money for education, conservation, and administration. So, we must find the way to get the best out of both systems.

For us, however, our traditions are fundamental. Only last year (in November 1988), the U.S. Congress passed a declaration honouring the Iroquois Confederacy as a primary inspiration for the U.S. Constitution. Our system is based on consensus, arrived at by reasoning together. In the Iroquois Confederacy, the Mohawks and the Seneca sit on the same side of the House as the older brothers; the Oneida and Cayuga sit across from them as the younger brothers. The Onondagas sit between them, listening, and, when the older and younger brothers have agreed, the matter goes to the Onondagas, who can either support the agreement reached if they believe it to be good for the whole Iroquois Nation or send it back for further consideration. No agreement is lasting until it is unanimous.

Similarly, in our own longhouse, the six chiefs of the Turtle and Wolf clans deliberate and debate an issue and, when they are agreed, the matter goes to the three chiefs of the Bear Clan, who have been listening, and can either support the agreement or send it back for further discussion. It is easy to understand why the longhouse has always produced good speakers, men who have learned they have to reason, to talk things out together. I think of myself as a community leader, but my national leaders are the leaders of the Mohawk Nation. I am a citizen of Haudenosaunee; and if anyone says I am also a Canadian citizen, the most I can agree is that we have certain benefits in Canada, by treaty, the same benefits as we have in the United States.

If anyone thinks that Mohawks are anti-Canadian or American, then we kindly remind you that First Nations in North America, in ratio to other nationalities, sent more soldiers to the First and Second World Wars. Since we usually wound up on the front lines, many of our people didn't make it home. In Akwesasne, we have a Veterans' Legion where servicemen who enlisted in the Canadian or American Armed Forces are honoured (a historical footnote of interest is the fact that right after the United States of America declared war on Germany, the Haudenosaunee Confederacy went to Washington and also declared war as an independent nation and released their citizens to fight for either Canada or the United States armed services).

During the 1960s and 1970s, most Akwesasne men who turned eighteen signed up for the Vietnam War, not because they believed in the war, but because they believed they would bring honour to their Nation.

When I look at the Canadian and American systems, I see shades of the government that we have, but what is lacking is the reasoning, the honour, the truthfulness that is our tradition and our pride. I am proud to follow the ancient method of government, and am dedicated to restoring it to its full authority in our affairs.

If the Mohawk Council of Akwesasne as an elected community government is to bring about self-determination/self-government for the people of Akwesasne, then it can only do so by combining the modern elements of the elected councils of both sides of Akwesasne with the National Council of the Mohawk Nation.

ALGONQUINS
NORTH OF THE
OTTAWA

THE CONFRONTATION

In September 1989, after a year of fruitlessly trying to persuade federal and Quebec governments to listen to their complaints, the Algonquins of Barriere Lake, who live in La Verendrye Wildlife Reserve, Quebec, about 320 km (200 miles) north of Ottawa, blockaded many newly built logging roads, and brought logging operations to a halt in their traditional hunting territory.

A year before, in an effort to force federal officials to meet with them, the Barriere Lake people had pitched their tents on Parliament Hill in Ottawa, which they regard as unsurrendered Algonquin land. At that time many were arrested and charged with committing a nuisance in a public place.

Now, once again, the full force of the law was imposed in an effort to end their blockades of the loggers. Canadian Pacific, one of the largest corporations in the country, sought and obtained an injunction to prevent the blockades, and when the Algonquins defied the injunction, they were served with papers for contempt of court.

The Barriere Lake demands are unusual: their sole hope is that they can persuade governments to work with them towards a sustainable economy within their traditional lands. The hunting and trapping life on which they depend has been undermined by clear-cut logging and outside sports hunting. They have never been consulted about the activities allowed in their lands.

Mitchikanibikonginik Algonquins of Barriere Lake: Our Long Battle to Create a Sustainable Future

Chief Jean-Maurice Matchewan,
Barriere Lake Indian Government

Parliament Hill Is Algonquin Land

Parliament Hill is unsurrendered Algonquin land. And so is the entire watershed of the Ottawa River, which runs behind the Parliament buildings.

Since the time of first contact, Algonquin lands have been raped and ravaged by our European guests. It began with the fur trade; later, lumbering became the issue; then, it was settlement. Encroachment occurred first in the south and moved into the northern part of the territory. The consequences for our people have been grave. Through the decades we have been scourged by starvation and epidemics of smallpox and cholera, which at times wiped out almost our entire population.

Now, in the North, the pressures of encroachment have reached the point where they threaten the survival of our community. The heart of our territory lies at the source of the Ottawa River, at Barriere Lake. For a while we were insulated from impacts because of our location in the middle of a wildlife reserve, La Verendrye Park. But in recent times, clear-cut logging and sports hunting have intensified in our homeland, to the point where it is almost impossible to sustain our traditional lifestyle.

To bring attention to this situation, last year we made an encampment on Parliament Hill. We came to remind the federal government that this was our land, and to request their intervention to help us stop the activities that were threatening our survival.

We were urging the federal government to assist us in developing and implementing a conservation strategy for the La Verendrye area. This, we thought, could lead some day to a larger conservation strategy for the entire Ottawa River watershed.

Our proposal was consistent with the recommendations in the report of the World Commission on Environment and Development in 1987, the Brundtland Report. Since both the Quebec and federal governments had responded favourably to the report, we were expecting a positive reaction. We soon discovered that their commitments to environmental conservation were hollow.

On Parliament Hill, on September 28, 1988, our tents were seized and we were charged with trespassing.

We Have Always Been Here

We are known as Mitchikanibikonginik ("People of the Stone Weir"); this name refers to a site in our traditional territory, a natural stone ridge that once ran across a shallow narrow at Barriere Lake. We call this place Mitchikanibik.

Many fish used the shallows at this site for feeding and spawning. We harvested there since time immemorial and it became a central gathering place for our people. But this meant nothing to outsiders; in 1871, a dam was built there, raising the water level and forcing the fish to move elsewhere.

We are one of the communities in Canada that are called Algonquins by the general public. There are ten Algonquin communities in all. The collective ancestral territory of the Algonquin Nation includes all the lands and waters within the Ottawa River watershed, straddling the border between the provinces now known as Quebec and Ontario.

Historically, we regularly travelled throughout our territory, paddling down the Coulonge River that joins the Ottawa near Pembroke, or the Gatineau that emerges near Hull.

An archaeological study by the Quebec government dates our occupation of Algonquin territory back about 6,000 or 7,000 years, that is 4000 to 5000 B.C.; clearly, we have lived on our lands since long before any French or English peoples arrived in North America. And, within our collective memory, we have never lived anywhere else.

Many Algonquins were dislocated by settler encroachments many years before our community was directly affected and, eventually, two large reserves were set up for these dislocated people. The fact is, however, that none of the entire Algonquin territory has ever been surrendered or ceded to the Crown, and our pre-existing rights in these lands were specifically recognized by the Royal Proclamation of 1763.

Our memory of the agreement that was consummated at that time is recorded in what we call the Three-Figure Wampum Belt. Wampum belts were used by Indian nations in eastern North America to record agreements and laws, long before the coming of the white man. Wampum is a cylindrical bead, purple or white in colour, made from the hard shell of the clam. Woven together, the wampum form designs that symbolize actual events. It takes years to make a wampum belt and, once made, it is handed down from generation to generation, along with the memory of what it records.

In our view, our relationship with the governments of Canada and Quebec flow from the Three-Figure Wampum Belt Agreement made with their predecessors, the French-speaking and English-speaking nations. Our memory of this agreement is so strong that, when the final constitutional conference on aboriginal matters was held in Ottawa on March 27, 1987, we took the opportunity to remind Canada's First Ministers of its existence by laying the actual wampum belt before them.

"Our memory of this agreement is that any dealing with the land would involve Indians nations," we told Canada. "The French-speaking and English-speaking nations, as such, are symbolized by the figures on each side of the wampum belt. The central figure symbolizes the Indian nations.

"It was agreed, at the time, that the Indian nations would always be recognized by the French-speaking and English-speaking nations as leaders on our homelands, and that any negotiations regarding the use and sharing of the resources would necessarily involve the consent of the Indian nations." This historic agreement also provided that the matter of jurisdiction was to be based on mutual respect and equality.

"Upon concluding this sacred agreement, it was witnessed by a representative of the church. As such, this agreement was blessed by a representative from the Vatican who would see its fulfillment. This is why a cross appears on the wampum belt."

This remains the basis on which we enter any negotiations with either the Canadian or the Quebec government. Since we have never surrendered our title or jurisdiction, our position is that we continue to have the right of self-determination and self-government as indigenous peoples. And, unlike the French, we were never conquered. Our aboriginal and treaty rights are collective pre-existing rights given by the Creator. They cannot be taken away or altered by any government—imperial, federal, or provincial without our free and informed consent. It is these rights that make us distinct from other Quebeckers and Canadians.

As I told the constitutional conference: "Regardless of constitutional recognition, our traditional system of government continues. For centuries we have maintained the traditional feast which is our main institution of government. We have managed to maintain this feast even though federal and provincial policies are allowing for the systematic destruction of our lands, animals, and water."

Our society was organized through extended families that came together at certain times of the year for feasts and assemblies. The most important of these was the summer feast, after which public assemblies were held and decisions made on important matters for the coming year. During the other nine or ten months, people stayed in their family hunting territories.

We organized ourselves around the four seasons. The weather and climate determined what animals, plants, birds, and fish we would harvest throughout the year. This was our source of survival for many generations. Other feasts were held by families at the beginning of the other three seasons.

Our lands provided us with all we needed to survive. The waters were full of fish — walleye, pike, trout, and sturgeon. The forest provided us with plants such as strawberries, blueberries, and the various types we used for medicine. The trees provided wood and bark, which we used for fuel, shelter, transportation, and tools. Our traditional homes were made out of birch-bark sheets wrapped around frames of different shapes and sizes. We also built canoes out of birch bark for travel during the summer and sleds for travel in the winter, pulled by our dog teams. We hunted caribou, moose, deer, bear, geese, ducks, and partridge, and we also harvested beaver, marten, fisher, fox, wolf, lynx, and rabbit.

Newcomers Arrive
Upon the arrival of the Europeans during the sixteenth and seventeenth centuries, we had only rare contact with the French, either with traders looking for furs or the occasional explorer. We began to hear stories from our neighbours about the newcomers arriving in the big ships in the St. Lawrence River, and thus began a process of change that we are still experiencing today.

The French introduced us to firearms and other trade goods we never had before. From the 1620s to the 1680s the so-called Beaver Wars took place between the Algonquin and the Iroquois. It cost many furs for an Indian to get a gun in those days, which led to overhunting the beaver and then to invading other peoples' territory for furs. The Iroquois acquired firearms from the Dutch and then began to travel outside their own territory in search of beaver pelts. They took furs from the Algonquins and traded them to the Dutch.

It became a matter of survival to have a gun. The European demand for furs escalated the Algonquin-Iroquois feud. Those who had furs got guns or other trade goods; those who did not have furs to trade were attacked and driven away or annihilated. Many Algonquins were displaced or killed by Iroquois war parties that came into our territory through the Rideau and Ottawa rivers.

During these wars, the Algonquin territory around the Upper Ottawa, the Gatineau, and the St. Maurice rivers became an important secondary route for our Indian and French allies who wished to travel back and forth between the Saguenay and St. Lawrence to the main French posts in the west. Iroquois war parties penetrated these northern waters only occasionally during the Beaver Wars and, because of the difficulty of navigating the many channels, lakes, and rivers, they did not stay long. In fact, because of their unfamiliarity with the geography of our waters, our ancestors were able to ambush and kill them. Mostly, the Iroquois avoided our territory and travelled around us on their way north to where the Cree lived.

Trading Posts

The Algonquin territory around the Upper Ottawa remained distant from the main southern trading routes throughout the eighteenth century, but we would paddle during the summer to Oka, on the Lake of Two Mountains, where many southern Algonquins were living, to trade our furs and meet with

Algonquins from other communities. However, the Northwest Company did open some trading posts somewhat to the west of us and encouraged us to trade with the French instead of the English.

When the conquest of the French occurred, the Three-Figure Wampum Belt Treaty was affirmed in 1760 by the Articles of Capitulation, Article 40, and then reaffirmed by the Royal Proclamation of 1763. Only after that did English-speaking people begin to appear in our territory. Individual free-traders arrived and tried to get our trade away from the French.

Then, in 1774, the Quebec Act unilaterally extended the colony's boundary westward and northward to cover the Indian territory that had been specifically recognized in the Royal Proclamation.

This relocation of the boundary was done without drawing up a treaty to determine how best to share the land and resources. As a direct result of the boundary change, we began to be overrun by trespassers; by the end of the century, more French and English people than ever before were entering our hunting grounds and poaching the animals we needed for our survival.

These incursions brought European diseases — smallpox, tuberculosis, cholera—which raged throughout the Algonquin territories. Although we remained relatively isolated in the North, by the early nineteenth century the fur trade had become an important part of our economy and, in 1821, the Hudson's Bay Company opened a post at Trout Lake, not too far from our central place, Barriere Lake.

Lumbering and Settlement Encroachments

Lumbering began along the Lower Ottawa in the 1840s, and with the loggers came the settlers. Now began the destruction of the Algonquin hunting grounds in the Ottawa Valley and along the Gatineau. The Algonquins at Lake of Two Mountains were directly affected and began to complain to the settler governments that the Algonquin territory was being overrun by the trespassing colonists.

Actually, complaints about this had begun many years earlier, but the process of cutting forests into farmland really gathered steam as the century progressed. The Hudson's Bay Company opened a trading post at River Desert on the Gatineau in 1832, and some of the Algonquins from Lake of Two Mountains moved to that post in their efforts to get away from settler encroachment on their hunting grounds along the Lower Ottawa. But there was no escape. Lumberers, trappers, and settlers headed north, along the Gatineau, destroying the forest habitat and killing or driving away the animals.

Naturally, the church arrived with the businessmen. The Oblate missionaries came north in the 1840s and began to interfere in our internal affairs in their efforts to convert us to the Catholic religion. At Barriere Lake, the first church was built in 1841 and, as the Catholic Algonquins from Oka continued to arrive at River Desert, it became the aim of the priests to establish a mission where all Algonquin peoples would be more accessible to their conversion efforts. In 1845 and 1848 the priests at River Desert prepared two petitions bearing the signatures of some of the Catholic Algonquins, asking the colonial government of Lower Canada for a reserve.

There was going to be reserve whether the Algonquin people wanted it or not — the government and the priests saw to that in the next few years. In 1850, a law entitled An Act for the Better Protection of the Lands and Property of the Indians in Lower Canada was passed, without Indian consent, providing for a commissioner of Indian lands who was to take charge of aboriginal land issues. The next year An Act to Authorize the Setting Apart of Lands for the Use of Certain Indian Tribes in Lower Canada was also passed without the consent of Indian nations, setting aside land for eleven reserves in Lower Canada. Two of these reserves, River Desert (now called Maniwaki) and

Temiscaming (farther to the west), were located within the un-surrendered territory of the Algonquin nation.

The Oblate priests tried to persuade all Algonquins to move to these reserves, become Catholics, abandon hunting, and take up farming. However, in 1851, several of our people contracted smallpox and died while visiting the River Desert trading post, and after that our people stayed away from there for several years.

Although a few community members moved to River Desert after the reserve was created, collectively the Algonquins of Barriere Lake refused to do so. Our people continued to live in the Barriere Lake area, remaining quite distant from River Desert. There were still no roads, and it took a considerable time to paddle from Barriere Lake to River Desert. That our people stayed is confirmed by the fact that, when the Hudson's Bay Company established a post on Cabonga Lake in our hunting territory and provisions were sent from Mattawa by freight canoe during the summer, some of our people were employed to paddle the furs down to Mattawa and bring back provisions for the post.

Britain Transfers Responsibility to Canada

In 1867, when the newly created Dominion of Canada took over responsibility for "Indians and lands reserved for Indians," the Indian nations were never informed of the change by the British government. In 1876, the first federal Indian Act was passed, containing a consolidation of all pre-confederation legislation. Again, the consent of the Indian nations affected was not obtained.

In the second half of the century, lumbermen and poachers began to encroach more directly on our best hunting grounds. In 1871, dams were built by the Bennett-Gouin logging company on the southern part of Cabonga Lake and in the north at Barriere Lake. The company used the stored water to float logs down the Gatineau River to the Lower Ottawa River.

The killing of animals from our hunting grounds by the lumbermen and poachers brought our people to starvation during these decades, particularly during the 1890s when the logging companies began to cut the forests with horse-and-wagon teams, using roads that they built into Algonquin territory. Until this time, our people had remained relatively scattered throughout the territory in family hunting camps, but now began to move their homes closer together as a measure of protection against the Europeans who were coming in increasing numbers.

The railway reached Mattawa through Pembroke in 1881, consolidating the grip that the settlers were establishing within Algonquin territory.

In 1897, the Minister of the Interior, Mr. Clifford Sifton, was questioned in the House of Commons about the status of Algonquin lands and hunting rights. Canada expressed its concern to the government of Quebec about the application of provincial game laws to the Algonquins. Quebec chose to ignore the federal message, and continued to harass us while we were harvesting game and fur.

This has been a continuing problem ever since the colony of Quebec was created on top of Algonquin territory. Quebec government game wardens continue to harass our people to this day — in our view, quite illegally. As recently as April 1988, in a meeting with Premier Bourassa of Quebec, I had to protest against provincial charges brought against our people for harvesting fish and game. Charges were laid more than a year after the alleged incidents took place, and only after we had begun to protest publicly against certain Quebec government policies. One of these incidents involved one of our people, Arthur Ratte, who harvested a beaver for food for his family. So, it is still true, as it has been for many decades, that Quebec government game wardens are literally seizing the food from out of the mouths of Algonquin families.

The Railways Penetrate Algonquin Territory

In 1912, the Canadian Pacific Railway reached Senneterre, north of Barriere Lake. This opened up more land to settler occupation and to establishment of non-Indian villages along the railway line. By now, these transportation corridors reached the core of our territory, so overhunting by non-Indians intensified, and all this went totally unchecked by the governments of Quebec and Canada.

We had kept our distance from the French and English as much as possible, to live as our ancestors had lived, from the harvest of the land. We were not fluent in either of their languages. From the earliest times of contact until the 1960s, very few of our people spoke anything but Algonquin. This had not been a problem earlier when dealing with priests or Hudson's Bay Company agents because they were able to speak enough Algonquin to get by, even though they never fully understood the language (or our traditions).

In the early twentieth century, we were under immense pressure from trespassing hunters, and the impact this had on our diet led to an increase in sickness and death among our children. In 1919, our chief and council asked Ottawa for a doctor and hospital at Barriere Lake, but the request was ignored. We complained, also, about the poaching. Finally, after federal intervention, Quebec responded to our complaints in 1928 by establishing a 16,600 sq. km (6,300-square-mile) area for exclusive Indian hunting. This was known as the Grand Lac Victoria Hunting Reserve but, though non-Indians were excluded from hunting or trapping inside the reserve, there was no enforcement of any kind, so non-Indian poaching continued.

To make matters worse, the Quebec government, in 1928, authorized the construction of a series of water-storage dams on Cabonga Lake, which would raise the water level and flood our homes at Barriere Lake. We did not find out about these dams until a year later. Under this scheme, the old Gouin-Bennett dam, on the Gens de Terres River at the exit of Cabonga Lake, was replaced in 1929 by a dam built by the Gatineau Power Company, a subsidiary of Canadian International Paper, which held the majority timber interests in the lands that form our territory. The 1929 dam was built partly of concrete and partly of wood. In addition, numerous dykes were built to prevent waters from flowing to the Outaouais River basin. The reservoir extends for about 260 sq. km (100 square miles) and has a drainage area of about 2,750 sq. km (1,050 square miles), a capacity of 1.3 billion m³ (43 billion cubic feet), and cost $600,000 to build. According to Hydro-Quebec estimates, the water level in the Cabonga Reservoir is 6.6 m (22 feet) higher than the original (natural) level.

By the 1930s, our people had massive problems: our hunting territory was flooded and devastated by the huge Cabonga reservoir whose water levels can vary without warning; non-Indian poachers remained a problem; our people continued to starve because of the lack of fish and game. Not until 1939 did the federal government hire four game wardens to police the Indian Hunting Reserve and chase non-Indian trespassers out. But it was too little, too late.

A Road Driven Through the Centre of Algonquin Territory

In 1940, as though we were not here and as if our Indian Game Reserve was non-existent, the Quebec government built a road right through the centre of the hunting reserve, to connect Senneterre, to the north, with Mont Laurier, to the south. This suddenly made the area even more accessible to settlers and brought in droves of non-Indian poachers. The existence of the highway added to the pressure of commercial operators to have the whole region opened up to trade and commerce.

To this end, a 32-km (20-mile) -wide corridor, 16 km (10 miles) on each side of the road, was withdrawn from the hunting reserve and called the Mont-Laurier–Senneterre Highway Fish and Game Reserve. Algonquins were excluded from hunting, fishing, or trapping in this area. Of course, we refused to be bound by these regulations and continued to harvest this area out of necessity and in accordance with Algonquin customs. But, while we were officially excluded from the corridor, we learned that H. J. O'Connell was going to spend $30,000 to build a hotel, restaurant, and garage along the new highway at Wolf Lake, now known as Le Domaine, which is not too far from Barriere Lake. Until the lodge was purchased by the Quebec government in 1958, its private owners held exclusive hunting rights in the area.

To survive the invasion of non-Indians into our hunting grounds, we spent part of our time guiding the outsiders who came to fish and hunt. Some of our people who worked as guides built new homes for their families at a place about 40 km (25 miles) south of Barriere Lake, called Kitiganik, to be closer to where the tourists were staying. This was in the 1940s. Now known as Rapid Lake, this area is 8 km (5 miles) from the highway, near the former location of a lumber camp that was abandoned in the 1920s.

In the early 1950s, the Hudson's Bay Company and the Catholic church decided to move from Barriere Lake to Rapid Lake, to be closer to the road. Though the Canadian government had previously ignored our request for a hospital at Barriere Lake, they built a nursing station and small seasonal school at Rapid Lake, soon after the Hudson's Bay Company and the church moved there. The Algonquins of Barriere Lake were not involved in any of these decisions.

Twenty-four Hectares of Sand

The federal government had been discussing the creation of a reserve for us since 1919. Only in 1961, however, did the federal and provincial governments — urged by the church especially — decide between themselves to establish a reserve at Rapid Lake. Again, the Algonquin people did not consent. The reserve was set up by provincial order-in-council in 1961. The Quebec cabinet, in that order-in-council, referred to us as savages ("les sauvages") simply because we maintained our traditional way of life, harvesting from the land. The minister responsible for this racist insult was Jean-Jacques Bertrand, who was the Premier of Quebec before Messrs Bourassa and Lévesque took over in the 1970s.

This reserve at Rapid lake is only 24 hectares (54 acres) and totally inadequate for our needs. It is located on the ever-changing, ever-eroding shoreline of Cabonga reservoir. Though it was established without our consent, it has created an immense problem for us because the federal government now claims that its interest, and ours, in our territory, is limited to these few hectares. And, as far as the Quebec government is concerned, we have all the land we need or are entitled to.

This whole story is a classic example of the way in which Canadian society has acquired aboriginal lands, taking them over for other uses in violation of their own laws and completely without consultation or compensation. In other circumstances, Canadians call this sort of thing stealing.

For centuries, we have roamed our huge territory. We used the plants and animals for our livelihood and depended upon no outside agency to help us, trying our best to maintain our way of life, our language, and our culture. Increasingly, we became surrounded by people who proved to be alien to our way of life, hostile to our view of the world, and indifferent to our rights or our needs.

Through no choice of ours, we now find ourselves living on 24 hectares of sand, which is eroded year by year. The waters of the reservoir contribute to this erosion because the levels are changed according to the decisions of Hydro-Quebec, people living away from the land. The pattern of operation of the reservoir is determined by the needs of others, not ours. The very fine sand on which we live just cannot sustain such overcrowded conditions. Every spring and summer, the effects of wind, rain, and run-off cause terrific sandstorms and even the collapse of the foundations of houses.

We have a population of about 440, of whom only 40 live elsewhere. Of our 24 hectares, just 8 (20 acres) are suitable for housing and they are already being completely used. We have 77 families but only 65 houses, so many families are doubling up. Some houses, although small, have as many as 11 people living in them. One of our houses has 4 families living in it. A dozen or so of our houses are badly in need of repair. This situation is not regarded with any urgency by the Department of Indian Affairs, who are responsible for our housing. We used to get three or four new houses a year, when we had land. Now, because we have no more building lots, we have not had any new houses built for two years. Since our population is increasing rapidly, every year we are falling further behind. Our population is very young and it has been estimated that, within twelve years, we will number more than 900. Where are we all going to live? It is ironic that, in the middle of our vast territory, we are suffering from a shortage of land.

Our educational history also indicates how little attention was paid to our needs by people who assumed authority over us. The first school was established in 1955 in a large tent, and the language of instruction was English. Then, from 1962 until 1971, our children were sent to a residential school in Amos, where the language of instruction was French. But, when a school was finally built on the reserve in 1971, the language of instruction was English. It seemed that no one cared what sort of schooling we had: anything was good enough for us, so long as it suited the convenience of the bureaucrats making these decisions. One of the results of this system was that, for many years, few of our children made it through school. Indeed, in the twelve years after schooling began, only five students graduated from secondary school, and four of those made it after we ourselves became more involved in controlling education in the early 1980s. Now we do have some influence on education but we still have no control over the hiring of teachers. This is just one of many examples of how we no longer have the autonomy that most Canadian communities take for granted.

Though we have been so gravely affected by the wage economy of Canadian society, we have never been in a position really to benefit from it. In fact, traditionally, we have never really wanted to join it but now we have no choice. Today only sixteen of our people in the community have jobs for wages. But almost every family continues to rely extensively on hunting, fishing, and trapping for subsistence. Because of what is being done in our traditional hunting territory, it has become virtually impossible for our people to make even a subsistence living from these activities, so a large number of our people (in fact, more than thirty families and usually about forty single people) are on welfare, which has become an essential supplement to the traditional subsistence lifestyle. This is through no wish of ours; we have had no alternative.

Yet, in spite of our many problems on this tiny reserve, we still cling desperately to our way of life and prefer it to that of the city. Many of our people, having been out into the world, have decided to come back home and live the traditional style of life. While some Indian communities in Canada have more than 50 per cent of their people living elsewhere, we have fewer than 10 per cent, and more than half of these are students who are going to secondary school in Maniwaki, the nearest town.

The reason that people come back home was well described by one of our young people, Edward Wawatie, when, in 1987, the *Toronto Star* decided to compare a Canadian Indian community with an African community in South Africa. "We're a very privileged people," he told the reporter. "I'm not sure a lot of other people will understand that. But I've been in the city. You look up into the sky at night and you can't see anything. But here, in the bush, you can see everything. You have everything. It's just all there....

"Most people worry so much about living that they neglect their freedom. We don't ever forget that. That's what I have in the bush. It's where I choose to live, where I want to live." Yet, at the same time, Edward was so worried about the poor conditions in our community that he said he was not sure it made sense for a young person to think of having a family.

I once tried to express my views about this when I gave evidence before the House of Commons Standing Committee on Aboriginal Affairs: "In providing us with the land, the Creator gave us everything we needed to survive. It is our source of food, clothing and medicine. Our belief is that we cannot ask the Creator for anything more because he already gave us everything we need. This is why we respect the land.

"We Algonquins have our own system of government. It, too, is based on the land. In the feast we gather to thank the Creator for what he has provided and to discuss the affairs of our Nation. According to our beliefs, the feast and other important institutions of government were given to us by the Creator from the beginning of time.

"During the course of European settlement, many of our institutions were suppressed. In Barriere Lake, we are continuing the feast. However, an Indian government needs land."

An Environmental Crisis

By the 1980s we realized we were in a crisis because our traditional hunting territory had been simply taken over and handed to non-Indian people for their industry and recreation. The use they were making of it was appalling.

First of all, we were living in the middle of what was now called La Verendrye Wildlife Reserve — a place that we thought was supposed to be devoted to the preservation of wildlife. This reserve had grown out of that 32-km corridor that was originally carved out of our Grand Lac Victoria Indian Game Reserve when they built the road north, its name now changed from the Mont-Laurier–Senneterre Highway Reserve. We discovered, of course, when we set our researchers to work, that it never was the intention of the Quebec government to preserve wildlife in this so-called wildlife reserve. The 1940 provincial order-in-council, withdrawing this corridor from the hunting reserve, said that the purpose was "to derive the greatest possible advantage from the Highway and the numerous lakes and watercourses there situated, with a view to attracting tourists." There was no mention, of course, of Algonquin use; as a matter of fact, we were excluded from this area.

Ever since the 1960s, huge areas of this so-called reserve have been subjected to clear-cut forestry, which totally destroys the forest, drives the animals away, and has completely undermined our traditional way of life. We know definitely, for instance, that at least 45 per cent of the so-called wildlife reserve has already been subject to partial or clear-cut, and that logging companies normally have cut far beyond the maximum sustainable yield. The government's plans suggest that extensive logging will continue to be given priority far into the future, and reforestation plans now being put into place are ecologically unsound, involving chemical spraying and monoculture planting.

We are the only permanent population in the area; we have lived there for thousands of years; we understand this land like no one else, yet no one has ever bothered to ask us how it could best be developed.

When we began to look into the Quebec government's system for making these decisions, we found that the government divides its jurisdiction within this so-called wildlife reserve between two departments. The Ministry of Energy, Mines and Resources is responsible for the land (and, therefore, the habitat), while the Ministry of Recreation, Hunting and Fishing is in charge of the animals. In practice, the first ministry is interested only in taking the resources out of the territory and making a profit from them. The fact that this practice destroys animal populations is of no significance to them. If they'd asked us, we could have told them this did not make sense, but they didn't ask. Yet, in the 1980s, all white Canadians are supposed to have heard about the ecological relationships between all different forms of life. Somehow this seems to have escaped the notice of the Quebec government.

In fact, in the hundreds of orders-in-council concerning our land passed by the Quebec government between 1928 and 1980, Algonquin interests were taken into account only when we forced their hand. When it was decided to open up our lands to outside hunters, it was originally planned that Algonquins be hired as guides for them, to help monitor the impact of increased hunting. At first, outside hunters were required to have guides but, in 1980, this requirement was dropped. There is now little work for our people as guides.

In 1964, the government decided to allow an annual moose hunt in La Verendrye Wildlife Reserve (or Park, as it is often referred to): we were told it was to be "temporary," but this moose hunt has been renewed every year since, and the number of moose kills allowed has been increased. A sort of lottery system is set up and those hunters who win the draw are allowed to take not only moose, but also one wolf and one black bear. Some figures we gathered indicate that, in a typical year, 215 moose were taken out of our lands by this public hunt, while we take 125. We depend on moose meat for our survival. This fact was never taken into account when this system was created.

There is also evidence that the area is being overhunted. We have discovered figures that show, for example, that the success rate of hunting groups in La Verendrye Reserve dropped from 80 per cent in 1964 when the hunt was first allowed, to only 39 per cent in 1987 — that is, only 39 per cent of hunting parties obtain a moose. Yet, though fewer moose were being taken, the number of groups allowed into the park to hunt them had actually increased. This is a sign of poor management.

The 1980s: More of the Same

As we began to take up the question of the destruction of our land base with the federal and provincial governments through 1987 and 1988, we soon learned that modern Canadian governments care no more about our rights or our survival needs than did the governments of the nineteenth century. For example: in 1978 the Parti Quebecois government established a system known as ZECs (Zone d'exploitation controlee), whose purpose was supposed to be to protect animal populations in vulnerable areas, while providing increased and equitable access for hunting and fishing. This system arose from the government's desire to abolish the exclusive hunting and fishing rights of private clubs on public lands. After the Ministry of Hunting and Fishing has recommended an area as a controlled zone, citizens are supposed to volunteer to join organizations that take over management of wildlife — citizens' groups, in effect, given authority over development, harvesting, and conservation of wildlife. These organizations, financed through membership fees, have the power to charge rates for road access and daily harvesting activities, and their powers are in the process of being increased.

There are ZECs operating within our traditional territories; yet, the fact is that the ZEC regulations make no mention of Indian rights, make no provision for Indian hunting or trapping, and never include Indian communities in the management of the ZEC. We were, and are, treated as if we do not exist.

For the Quebec government, all priority is given to outside hunters, to tourist outfitters, and to private companies whose business is to exploit the natural resources of our lands. Presumably, because Quebec regards us as a federal responsibility, we are never included in any of the plans made by governments, at whatever level, for our region.

Our area is dotted with dozens of private campsites and private outfitters, some of whom have been given exclusive rights to operate such a business in a given area. This means, in the words of one Quebec document, that only outfitters' clients may hunt, trap, or fish in those lands over which the exclusive right is held. We reject these rights. In practice, we ignore them, but this leads to friction, which we would rather avoid.

The scope of this activity — and its seriousness for us is indicated by the fact that, in 1988 , more than 50,000 fishermen were active in La Verendrye Park, and they took 150,000 walleye and 40,000 northern pike. We do not wish to stop other people from using our lands entirely, but we do believe that, in deciding what use is to be made of our lands, our interests should be considered along with those of outsiders.

In 1987, the Quebec government introduced a proposal to privatize 40 per cent of La Verendrye Park by offering exclusive hunting, trapping , and fishing rights to private outfitters in what was called "underexploited areas." This proposal was shelved after strong public opposition to it. But the government has used a Crown corporation, SEPAQ (Societé des Etablissements de Plein Air du Québec), to accomplish something similar. This corporation now operates most of the hunting in La Verendrye Reserve. Its mandate is to break even economically, so it must look for ways to increase its revenue, which we believe is likely to result in increased quotas for moose hunting and the opening of the whole area to bear hunting, now confined to a smaller area.

It seems likely, from this approach, that wildlife-management principles will be traded off against profitability. Of course, all of these proposals exclude us. And, as an indication of how highly regarded we are by the Quebec government, when I wrote to Premier Bourassa protesting against this scheme on the grounds that it jeopardized our survival, I never received even an acknowledgement. Perhaps he did not appreciate it when I pointed out that we, too, are a "distinct society," just as Quebec claims to be.

As 1988 wore on, we decided we would have to move to more direct action to defend ourselves. In 1985, our community had been coerced into agreeing to be connected to the provincial electricity grid. But, as time passed and the provincial government's plans for our area became clearer to us, we began to suspect that the real reason for erecting a powerline was to tie us more firmly than ever into outside elements of provincial control. We decided to register our opposition to the project. Nothing we could say would sway Hydro-Quebec or the federal government, which was funding 75 per cent of the costs of this project on our behalf. Out of frustration, we decided to block the project by preventing the workers from working. Finally, Hydro-Quebec agreed to discontinue the line.

A Land-Management System Designed for Extinction

Even more serious, from our point of view, is the new forest-management system that the Quebec government has imposed on our lands, again totally without our involvement. Under this scheme, the government makes a CAAF (*contrat d'approvisionnement et d'aménagement forestier,* or timber supply and forest-management agreement) with private forestry companies. These agreements are made behind closed doors and give the companies forestry rights for twenty-five years, with five-year extensions thereafter. This new management approach is supposed to protect all functions and uses of the forest, not just logging, but there is no doubt that logging is the only interest of the companies and the Ministry of Mines and Resources. The companies are given a maximum allowable cut in the area for which they are responsible, and the legislation provides that, once this quota is established, the companies are to be compensated if any part of that allowable cut is subsequently withdrawn from them. This scheme is giving private companies a stranglehold over our traditional lands. But here again, even if other forest uses were taken into account, we are left out: sports hunting and other recreational uses are specifically mentioned; however, aboriginal use was never mentioned in any of the three years of planning for this change or in the legislation that has brought it into effect. Again, we are treated as if we do not exist.

This had become such a matter of survival for us that we called for the government to introduce an eight-month moratorium on the implementation of this new management scheme. Our proposal was that we should use those eight months to get

above: National Chief Georges Erasmus speaking on Parliament Hill.

right: The Innu flag blowing over the Innu future: Nitassinan children.

bottom: Fighter jets that fly over Nitassinan land.

top: Mohawk blockade at Cornwall Island.

bottom: Participants of the Golden Lake Algonquin protest in Algonquin Park.

right: Barriere Lake Algonquins set up information tolls on highway.

bottom: Chief Gary Potts defending his traditional home.

top: Lubicon supporter accosted by RCMP *during sovereignty exercise.*

bottom: Cheif Gwoimt's son drumming at Sam Green Creek before intrusion by logging company.

together with the federal and provincial governments, with municipalities and any other interests who are affected, to work out a long-term scheme for the development of our area that would be environmentally sustainable, and that would take the interests of everyone into account, including ours. We are not trying totally to exclude logging companies, sports hunters or fishermen, or any other interest in this environmental exercise. We are not entering a land claim either, at this point. We have, instead, based ourselves on the recommendations of the Brundtland Report on Global Environment and Development, presented to the United Nations in 1987.

We wrote to the Quebec minister for the environment, Clifford Lincoln, reminding him that Quebec had been one of the principle players in the task force that had endorsed the Brundtland Report in the Canadian context, and said the time had come to put principles into practice. Though Mr. Lincoln made a great reputation for himself with his radical-sounding speeches to international gatherings of environmentalists, he did not lift a finger to help us implement the principles he was so vociferous in endorsing in his speeches.

In July 1988, we blocked the road through La Verendrye Park, slowing down traffic for what we called an "information toll." We asked motorists to sign a petition supporting our conservation aims and, in a mere six hours, we received 1,400 signatures.

Still, no one in government would take us seriously; so, in September, we made an encampment on Victoria Island on the Ottawa River, almost opposite the Parliament buildings. Our intention was to get to see Prime Minister Mulroney, another politician who had been loud in his international protestations of virtue about the environment. Readers will remember how firm this commitment was. He told an interviewer of French-language radio just a week or two before we appeared in Ottawa: "Environmental protection is not only a consideration for government. We need a national vision. We need a collective commitment, as citizens, not only of Quebec but of Canada, to give ourselves, as citizens, the best environment that could exist....The kind of vision I am looking at [is] a collective commitment of the Canadian nation in favour of this great question of environmental protection."

Talk is cheap, as we found out. We never did get to see the prime minister.

So, we returned a week later; on September 28, 1988, we pitched our tents on Parliament Hill, unsurrendered Algonquin territory. We were immediately arrested, our tents seized, and we were charged with committing a nuisance on a public work.

This is the official government response to our attempt to do what every government in Canada has said they want people to do: to work towards an environmentally sustainable future, in which economic developments are designed to take into account the needs of our children and our grandchildren. We like this concept. It is a natural part of our traditional way of life and we have always organized our affairs in line with it.

The Brundtland Commission made special mention of the role of indigenous peoples in this struggle for a better global environment in the future. The commission recognized that indigenous peoples around the world "are the repositories of vast accumulations of traditional knowledge and experience that link humanity with its ancient origins."

Because of this, they continued, "tribal and indigenous peoples will need special attention as the forces of economic development disrupt their traditional lifestyles that can offer modern societies many lessons in the management of resources in a complex of forest, mountain and dry land ecosystems.

"Some are threatened with virtual extinction by insensitive development over which they have no control. Their traditional rights should be recognized, and they should be given a decisive voice in formulating policies about resource development in their areas."

Not only do we agree with this, we believe that our situation in our northern homeland illustrates perfectly what they say. We know from bitter experience that Canada's economic managers have made a tremendous mess in the way they have developed, are now developing, and propose to continue developing, our lands. And we also are confident that, if we had ever been consulted, we would have used our knowledge of how our land works to modify greatly the damages that have occurred. We are seeking that "decisive voice" in our own future that the Brundtland Commission spoke of.

The question is, can we persuade Canadians to listen to us?

At time of writing, I have to admit that we seem to be up against people who do not care what we say or what happens to us, or what happens to Canada in the future.

As a result of our civil-disobedience activities, the Minister of Indian Affairs, Bill McKnight, finally did agree to suspend work on the hydro line. We were able to meet only with his minister of state, Bernard Valcourt, to whom we recited the long litany of problems that now threaten our very survival:

- the clear-cut logging and the high future priority accorded to it;

- the many impacts of reservoir operations (water-level fluctuations; destruction of various traditional medicines, waterfowl and moose habitat, and fish spawning grounds; beaver mortality; shoreline erosion, altered travel patterns); and

- the pressure caused us by the continuing escalation of recreational hunting.

We asked for the federal government, which, historically, had condoned uses of our unsurrendered land that were contrary to our interest, at last to come to our aid to help us in engaging the Quebec government.

The politicians and bureaucrats involved merely shrugged and told the press that we were talking to the wrong people. We should be talking to the Quebec government. The Quebec government, of course, said we are a federal responsibility. Certainly, we have discovered, it is naive for any native group to expect the Canadian government to fulfil its obligations of trusteeship and protection that were so solemnly undertaken in the past.

A month after our Ottawa protest, we finally got to meet the Quebec minister responsible, Raymond Savoie. We reminded him that the Quebec government was offering to host a national conference on sustainable development in fall 1990, to review Canada's progress in implementing the measures suggested by the Brundtland Report, and that Canada was offering to host a global conference to review world progress in 1992.

"We are hopeful that significant progress could be made on our conservation strategy so that it could be put forward as a practical example at these important conferences," we told him.

But we were wasting our breath. Savoie is, of course, responsible not only for native affairs, but for mines and resources: in short, he is the very minister who is imposing on us, totally without consultation, the new schemes dreamed up by his department for the future management of Quebec's lands. With a defender like this, we have no need of enemies.

He told us that, perhaps by 1992, he would have time to think about land-claims negotiations with the Algonquins. We had to remind him that we were not even talking about land claims; we were trying to alleviate immediate pressures on our subsistence economy, and 1992 could be too late. By that time, Savoie will have behind him two big conferences about the environment, at which he will have trumpeted his government's commitment to conservation.

Even more significant than this misunderstanding of our purpose, however, was that he simply dismissed the idea of the eight-month moratorium on the new forest-management system.

"All we are asking," we told him in a letter responding to his refusal, "is that Quebec relieve the pressure under which we are operating....During this period we can, together, do a realistic assessment of whether forestry, sports hunting and other activities are being conducted within the limits of sustainable yield, taking into account our needs."

We have discovered that, to people in the Quebec and Canadian governments, sustainable yield is a concept that is only to be spoken about in speeches designed to impress foreigners.

For the next twelve months, Savoie totally ignored our repeated requests for some action on our demands. Finally, it became too much. In September 1989, our community took to the logging roads to prevent contractors from spraying our forests. This spraying with herbicides had already made some of our people violently ill, driven animals away, and affected fish populations.

Our action brought a promise from Savoie's department that further spraying would be delayed for a year.

But by this time our people had the bit between our teeth. We decided we could no longer afford to sit and watch while logging companies destroyed everything we had survived on for thousands of years.

We began to blockade new logging roads that were being built into forests right in the centre of our traditional lands. We stopped the loggers from working. Canadian Pacific Forest Products, owners of Canadian International Paper Company, the main lessee of timber rights in our lands, took out an injunction to prevent our blockade, at a hearing at which our lawyers were not even represented. We decided to defy the injunction, to risk and even to court arrest.

These tactics finally brought Raymond Savoie to make his first visit to our community, where, in a five-hour meeting, we obtained his commitment in principle to a selective moratorium on the logging of critically sensitive areas for wildlife. It was a struggle, but for the first time, we managed to move him a few inches towards meeting our suggested program.

We cannot be sure that he is not just agreeing to meet us as a means of stalling us. But by this time we are determined to press ahead with our effort to create a saner and more sustainable economy for our lands, from which everyone can benefit.

There is one final, ironic twist to our story. We have chosen to argue a conservation case, rather than a land-claims case, in defence of our future. Yet, the federal government has virtually forced us to make a claim for our share of the unsurrendered lands in the Ottawa Valley in the court case in which they are relentlessly pursuing nuisance-trespass charges against us.

The federal government has refused to withdraw these charges and forced us to argue that our aboriginal claim to Parliament Hill is a relevant defence. A provincial court judge has held that it is relevant, and we are therefore confronted by the need to enter a full defence on those lines.

This is what comes of trying to get Canadian governments, federal and provincial, to live up to their statement of environmental virtue.

Our history has taught us, unfortunately, that these governments cannot be depended upon to keep their word. And we find that is just as true today as it ever was in the past.

ALGONQUINS
SOUTH OF
THE OTTAWA

THE CONFRONTATION

On September 2, 1988, the Algonguins of Golden Lake First Nation set up a road block at the eastern entrance to Algonguin Park. There they handed out pamphlets and buttons emblazoned with the slogan "Algonguin Park — Algonquin Land." The thousands of motorists who frequented the park on this first day of a long weekend were also asked to sign a petition requesting the Government of Canada and the Ontario government to take immediate steps to deal fairly with the claims of the Algonquin people. The majority of the motorists were sympathetic to the cause and readily signed the petition.

The pamphlet stated:

> *The land you are travelling through belongs to the Algonquin people. We have been its guardians for thousands of years.*
> *When Europeans first came here, we welcomed them and became partners with them in trade. We have been the Crown's allies since 1760. We fought in most of Britain's wars, here and abroad.*

> *In 1763 the King promised us that our land would never be taken except in a formal treaty, and we relied on that promise.*
>
> *We have never made any treaty with Britain or Canada to sell any of our land. Beginning in the 1800s lumbermen began to cut the white pine forest; they moved up our valley, clear-cutting; and the settlers followed them.*
>
> *Our land was taken and our hunting grounds were destroyed by the loggers and settlers, leaving us poor and scattered. Out of the original 3.4 million hectares (8.5 million acres), we have less than 800 (2,000) left.*

The Algonquins took this action because they had yet to receive an answer to their latest petition, presented in February 1983.

The Chief said that "while we have been waiting for an answer to our petition, our trappers, hunters and fishermen have been taken to court for exercising their rights. The Government of Ontario has announced its intention to use our land as a 'Development tool' to attract investment, and to open new roads to promote logging and recreational use of our land."

The Algonquins of Golden Lake are fed up with the federal and provincial governments' cold shoulder, and Chief Greg Sarazin has announced that the Algonquins are prepared to do "whatever is necessary" to settle their claim, which dates back to 1772.

220 Years of Broken Promises

Chief Greg Sarazin,
Algonquins of Golden Lake First Nation

MANY CANADIANS TODAY mistakenly believe that the aboriginal peoples of this land were defeated in war and thus lost their lands to the conquering Europeans. Still others imagine that they "sold" all of their land for money or trade goods and most believe that the native people had all of the same opportunities to prosper as any of the newcomers in Canada.

Perhaps this narrative will serve to set the record straight and tell what really happened, particularly with regard to the Algonquin people.

The story of the Algonquins of the Ottawa Valley is a textbook example of how the solemn promises made to the aboriginal nations of this country throughout history were systematically violated as the Europeans consolidated their settlements and spread out across the land.

The Algonquin Nation was never a newcomer to its territory. Our occupation and use of an identifiable tract of land goes beyond the limits of what is now called history. The Algonquins have lived in the valley of the Ottawa River at least as long as the French have lived in France or the English have lived in England. Before there was a Canada, before Cartier sailed his small ship up the great river, Algonquins lived in, occupied, used, and defended their home in the Ottawa Valley.

The right of the Algonquins to their territory was recognized and confirmed by European laws and proclamations. When the French were defeated at Quebec they demanded that the lands of their Indian allies would not be disturbed, and the British agreed to this in the Articles of Capitulation. Four years later, through the Royal Proclamation of October 7, 1763, and the Treaty at Niagara that followed it, the First Nations were reassured that their lands would not be taken except by the Crown after a voluntary surrender, and then only under certain set procedures. Subsequent legislation confirmed the rights of the First Nations to their lands.

The Royal Proclamation of 1763 has never been repealed, and continues as law in Canada today. The Algonquin people have historical, moral, and legal rights to the land of the Ottawa Valley that we have not abandoned.

If any Canadians believe that the provisions of this proclamation were neglected inadvertently or through absent-mindedness, the detailed history of our people during these two hundred years will dispel that illusion. History shows that the Europeans in Canada knew precisely what they were doing. While repeatedly acknowledging the reality of Algonquin rights on paper, in speeches, and at meetings, they relentlessly moved onto the Algonquin lands in the Ottawa Valley, occupying and using those lands without any negotiation. Only then did the Europeans begin to declare shamelessly that they had never heard of any Algonquin rights.

Our people were painfully aware of what was happening. Some Canadians imagine that, after the initial contact, the aboriginal people simply sat, helplessly watching, only half knowing what was going on, as the juggernaut of European settlement rolled over us. The history of the Ottawa Valley Algonquins shows that, from the very first, our people knew very well the dangers posed by the newcomers.

Modern ethnohistorians agree that the Algonquins who lived astride the Ottawa dictated who could move up and down the river, thereby playing a vital role in the development of the fur trade, the economic basis for the European settlement of Canada. Our people were always reluctant to permit newcomers to move farther inland. Neither the French trading alliance with the Hurons nor the desire of European religious orders to penetrate to the Huron country could be implemented until the newcomers made terms with the Kitchesiprini Algonquins (the Big River People) who controlled passage around Allumette Island, near Pembroke.

Under our one-eyed chief, Tessouat, the Algonquins demanded tribute from all who passed. They provided a formidable obstacle to Champlain when he first mounted the river in 1713 and prevented his intended journey deeper into the interior in that year. Later, Tessouat proved to be a valuable ally for the French in both politics and war.

The Algonquins had long been traders with other native nations, trading furs, meat, and fish, and buying, for example, the corn and other agricultural products of their Iroquoian neighbours. European commerce affected this trade economy and the intensity of the work, but did not fundamentally alter the way of the Algonquins.

Algonquins from the lower Ottawa frequently went downstream to trade with the French. By the end of the seventeenth century, under French missionary influence, Algonquins, Nipissings, and Mohawks were established in three villages at Oka, north of Montreal, on the Lake of Two Mountains. During the fur-trade period Algonquins would arrive at Oka from their hunting grounds in late June to trade furs and pay off debts. They would occupy themselves in July and August with religious observance, political councils, socializing, and trade. By the end of August, the Algonquin and Nipissing villages would be almost deserted as the people returned to the hunting grounds, leaving behind only those too old or too sick to go into the woods.

Throughout recorded history, the Algonquin and Nipissing people have been closely linked culturally and politically. (For convenience, the term "Algonquins" is used to refer to both nations here.) By the mid-1700s, the Algonquins were part of the loose confederacy known as the Seven Nations of Canada, which also included three Iroquois villages, the Hurons of Lorette (near Quebec City), and the Abenakis of Becancour (on the south shore of the St. Lawrence, opposite Trois-Rivières). When the British and their allies attacked the French at Montreal, Sir William Johnson, the first British Superintendent of Indian Affairs, asked these nations to "stand aside." They did so, the French were defeated, and firm political relations were established between the First Nations and the British.

After the Conquest, however, western First Nations continued to attack British posts; Johnson needed to establish a larger political settlement with the native people of Upper and Lower Canada. Therefore, in 1763, King George III issued a royal proclamation reserving the land west of the Quebec colonial boundary for the Indians. The proclamation also set rules for the sale of Indian lands, in order to prevent the "great frauds and abuses" that had been taking place. Johnson sent printed copies of this proclamation to the First Nations.

The documents now in the National Archives of Canada are those copies of the Royal Proclamation that Johnson delivered to the Algonquins and Nipissings. Sixty years after the proclamation was issued, our leaders brought these copies forward to prove the justice of their many petitions, which simply demanded fulfilment of the terms of the proclamation.

Peace and trade were restored to northeastern North America by the Treaty of Niagara in 1764. Reassured by the Royal Proclamation and the treaties, our people went back to their hunting and trapping.

A History of Betrayed Promises

Now begins the unhappy story of the betrayal of all these promises.

Very soon Algonquin leaders protested that whiskey traders were moving into their hunting grounds. The traders could come as far west as Carillon, they wrote in one petition, but only with no liquor. They also said they would "clear their hunting grounds all the way to Lake Nipissing of any Traders that may reside thereupon, and so follow their hunting peaceably and quietly to the better interest of themselves and the Indian trade in general."

The government asked them to be patient, promising to deal with the problem so long as the Algonquins did not "meddle" with the traders; indeed, in 1776 an ordinance was passed, prohibiting the taking of liquor into Indian villages.

Twenty-five years later the Algonquins complained about Iroquois encroachments on their land and also about the movement of European settlers into the lower Ottawa Valley. They would agree to concede some lands along the Ottawa River, they said, but asked that these lands not extend more than 40 arpents (about 16 hectares/40 acres) in depth, and that no land be given out "in our rivers," since that process would take away "absolutely all the resources of life." They feared that those Algonquin whose lands were close to settlements in the valley would be "exposed to die of hunger."

In 1774 Lord Dorchester, the governor, again gave specific reassurances to the Algonquin people with respect to their rights: "All of that which belonged to the King of France belongs to your present Father, the King, but no one can give to another that which does not belong justly to him. That is why if you anciently held the rights to these lands, and if you have not been paid, the rights belong to you still."

The following year the deputy–superintendent general of Indian Affairs asked the Seven Nations Chiefs to describe "the nature of your claims to these lands, how you became originally possessed of them, and at what time." The Chiefs replied: "We ask you to observe that we have never been conquered by the French, that on the contrary we have always been the protectors of the white skins even against the Indian nations…you have asked us to prove how these lands belong to us: the best proof we can give is that God created us on these lands."

These representations continued. Year after year the Chiefs would meet with the authorities dealing with Indian affairs and ask for compensation. Despite the Royal Proclamation, land was being taken from US without payment of any kind. And gradually, in the face of this encroachment, our people's way of life became less and less viable. Even before 1800 one petition complained: "Our lands are infertile. We have almost no more hunting. The animals have become distant. We find very little for our families to live on."

In both the American Revolutionary War and the War of 1812, the Algonquins took an active part on the British side. Amable Chevalier, an Algonquin war chief, was instrumental in taking Michilimakinack in 1812, and Algonquin warriors took part in the Battle of Beaver Dams on the Niagara frontier.

Yet, by 1820, the Algonquin people again had to petition the governor general, Lord Dalhousie, about lost land, reminding him that the Royal Proclamation of 1763 had accorded them their hunting grounds exclusively, adding that the number of settlements continued to grow in their hunting grounds, causing the game "to become distant." Therefore, "the petitioners find themselves in a great need, which can only increase from day to day by this use of the lands on which they do their hunting."

Sir John Johnson, superintendent general of Indian Affairs, supported them, writing a glowing testimonial to the conduct of our people in wartime and thereafter, "such as to entitle them to every mark of favour and distinction." But the government now claimed that the King "cannot grant a specific tract of country, however remote, to any particular tribe or nation of Indians."

Johnson took up the cause of the Algonquins in a letter to the military secretary, again recalling the procedure laid down in the Royal Proclamation:

Notwithstanding which, extensive grants have been made of the territory claimed by the Algonquin and Nepissingue Indians without any compensation being made to them, although in all cases where lands claimed by other tribes are required by Governments, they have been purchased at stipulated price, or some other compensation made to the Indian in obedience to His Majesty's commands.

...Finding of late that the settlement of the country and the indiscriminate and injudicious destruction by the settlers of the beaver and other animals, from which the most valuable furs are taken, is likely soon to deprive them of the means by which they have hitherto supported their families, they very naturally solicited the interference of the government.

Your letter...was to them a source of much surprise and dissatisfaction, in that their request was not only refused but they were informed that the other tribes have an equal right with themselves to hunt upon those lands which for ages have been reserved for their use only.

Johnson explained that traditional hunting grounds were "originally defined among themselves [the Indian nations]," that the boundaries were perfectly understood, and that any encroachment by one tribe on the lands of another "is viewed by them in precisely the same light as is the invasion of one civilized state by another."

He warned that if something were not done soon to prevent settlers from hunting in Indian lands, "some lives will ere long be sacrificed." Yet, Johnson wrote, in spite of the many provocations they had suffered, even now the Indians were not asking that lands already granted should be restored to them, but merely for a written guarantee that they could hunt exclusively on "such parts of the tract claimed by them as are now unoccupied," and that they should be compensated for any further settlement on their lands.

It was on this occasion that the Chiefs gave to Sir John Johnson printed copies of the Royal Proclamation to buttress their claim, and it is these copies that have found their way into the National Archives of Canada.

European Settlers Move into Algonquin Lands

By 1827 the European settlement of the Ottawa Valley was well underway. Villages of retired soldiers were established at Perth and Richmond. Emigration societies were set up specifically to lure settlers from England to the new land, and finally, with the beginning of construction of the Rideau Canal, the settlement of Bytown (now Ottawa) was begun.

The Chiefs responded with great activity in 1827, pressing for the protections they had been guaranteed by the Crown more than sixty years before. They received many more promises, but no action. In February, the Chiefs asked the government to create a commission of inquiry into their claims, and to determine the compensation they were entitled to under the proclamation.

A month later the government warned the Chiefs that any violence against trespassers would be "subject to the utmost penalty of the law." Not only was the government unwilling to protect the Algonquin rights under the proclamation, it would also punish them if they tried to protect those rights themselves.

In July, the Chiefs again petitioned the governor general, noting their possession of the Ottawa Valley "from time immemorial," complaining of the unsustainable over-harvesting of fur by outsiders, asking for indemnification for the losses already sustained, but agreeing not to employ violent methods.

Then, in October, after most of the Indians had left for their hunting grounds, a council was held at the Lake of Two Mountains. Several older chiefs met with General Darling, superintendent general of Indian Affairs. The government, said Darling, "cannot by the laws of the land prevent white people from going through the woods or killing a bear or beaver, when they meet with it." He warned them again that tribes should not encroach on each other's grounds, and then told them that, though the people of the Lake of Two Mountains might have no land of their own, still they would not starve, "if you are disposed to follow the example of the white men."

Thus, the superintendent general offered the Indian people neither the protection against encroachments, nor the compensation, to which the Royal Proclamation entitled them, but instead urged them to assimilate, and warned again that any attempt to protect their hunting grounds would result in prosecution of the individuals responsible.

Officials of the Indian department wrote various letters to urge the government to take "immediate steps" to prevent further encroachment on Algonquin lands. "Their situation is becoming alarming by…rapid settlement," wrote General Darling in 1828. "The Indians have submitted to this species of plunder with a degree of forbearance quite foreign to their native character," Colonel Napier pointed out in 1829, and he went on to recommend that further trespass be forbidden by public notice.

Later that year, in fact, the Indians were advised that "any person who shall illegally settle or commit any cognizable trespass or depredation on their hunting grounds" would be prosecuted. There is no record of any prosecutions. Instead, settlement of the territory continued at an increasing pace.

The giant white pine forests of the Ottawa Valley were the habitat of moose, caribou, and beaver, as well as the Algonquin hunters, but the white pine was the prize tree of the lumberman, and as more accessible stands of forest in Southern Ontario were exhausted the valley became the source of the mast needed by the British Navy. The lumber industry was well established by the 1830s and demanded new waves of immigrants to clear the forests and then settle the cleared land, pushing the game, and the Indians who depended upon it, farther and farther north and inland.

By 1835, our Algonquin petitions began to focus on securing a homeland within the traditional hunting grounds. It shows how far the occupation of our lands had gone that, in his reply, the governor could promise no more than "to endeavour to prevent the Lumber Men and Squatters from molesting them on their hunting grounds to the west of the river Matawangue and between that river and Lake Nepissingue."

The Mattawa River and Lake Nipissing are, of course, in the western reaches of the original Algonquin territory (in 1764, remember, the Chiefs tried to stop liquor penetrating beyond Carillon). Now ostensible protection could only be "endeavoured" some 650 km (400 miles) to the west. This huge tract of land was taken, with no legal sanction, in a period of seventy years; a visible measure of the deprivation our people had suffered.

The Government Turns Full Circle

By the following year the government's position had come full circle. Six years before, Indians had been advised that trespassers on Algonquin hunting grounds would be prosecuted. Now, in February 1836, the government replied to Algonquin petitions with a pretence that it had never heard such claims before, and that full compensation had already been paid: "His Excellency has come to the conclusion that the claims of the present petitioners were fully settled and adjusted at the respective times when the lands were surrendered by those tribes to the Government, and the Lieut-Governor is the more strongly induced to consider this inference to be fair and legitimate, inasmuch as he is informed that no claim similar to the present can be found to have been preferred by any other Indian tribe, and that it is perfectly novel and without precedent."

It is difficult to understand how the government could have concluded that a claim so well documented by 1836 could be called "perfectly novel." But this reply was consistent with the government's cynical policy of the day.

The hunting grounds would not be protected. Indians were to be encouraged to abandon the hunt and become farmers.

Smaller reserves would be set aside for them and protected, as long as they were on land the government didn't want. We see here the genesis of the policies later adopted in the Robinson and numbered treaties covering Northern Ontario, western Canada, and the North.

Two months later, the Chiefs sent another petition, reminding the government of their faithfulness in time of war, the clear promises made to them in the Royal Proclamation, and the pattern of "grievances and deprivations which we…have long endured patiently and submissively without complaint."

This time they asked for the hunting grounds on the north side of the Ottawa to be accorded to them, acknowledging: "We do not presume or venture to entertain the belief that the lands already dismembered from our hunting grounds and converted and erected into Townships for settlement by the government…will be restored to us." In this petition they mentioned the Royal Proclamation no fewer than nine times, often quoting from it directly.

In 1837 a committee of the Executive Council of Lower Canada reviewed the claims, acknowledging that there was no reason to doubt that the Algonquin hunting ground "may have" covered the whole territory they now described, and that the Algonquins' right to use it was little disputed and well defined. The committee noted the Royal Proclamation had been acknowledged as the basis for possession of lands for some of the tribes of Lower Canada, and stated that the Algonquins "may have some ground to complain" if deprived of protection for their claims.

The committee concluded, however, only that: "the claims of these…tribes in respect of their former territorial possessions are at the present day to be resolved into an equitable right to be compensated for the loss of lands…and that the measure of such compensation should be to place and maintain them in a condition of at least equal advantage with that which they would have enjoyed in their former state." The committee recommended that "a sufficient tract of land should be set apart for them in the rear of the present range of Townships on the Ottawa river," and that the Algonquins should be located there.

The committee's thrust was towards adoption of farming as a way of life for the Algonquin people. Rather than protect the remaining hunting grounds, the committee suggested that the government should pay compensation in the form of assistance to adopt a more settled way of life.

This story of the persistent derogation of the rights of the First Nations is interspersed with occasional bursts of what might be described as honesty by various officials of the Indian department. For example, nine years after Indians were promised that trespassers in their land would be prosecuted, someone noticed that the instruction had never been repealed. A Captain Ducharme was told that, as all the islands in the Ottawa River and all lands on both sides of the river that had not been made townships by the government still formed part of the Algonquin hunting grounds, "you will be pleased to warn and order all persons who might have taken possession of any of the said or other lands situated on the Ottawa river without any authority to show you, to leave them as soon as possible."

Colonel Hughes of the Indian department acknowledged in a letter to the government that the tribes claimed indemnity for the dismembered lands and asked "to be reinstated and secured" in the remaining lands south of the Ottawa. "They desire the expulsion of all intruders and Squatters," he said, "and complain grievously of the frauds and impositions to which they have been subjected in relation to their hunting grounds." He added that the tribes also asked for leave to occupy "the island of Allumets" (Tessouat's strategic old toll point).

But this short-lived burst of conscience was to no avail. Though some Algonquins apparently were authorized to settle on Allumette Island, the Executive Council finally decided that equity would be best served by setting aside a tract of land north of the Ottawa and behind the established townships.

The Government Loses the Evidence!

As the years went by, various authorities delivered one blow after another to the Algonquins' ancient and valid claims. In 1839, for example, Mr. Justice Macaulay, in a report on Indian Affairs for the government of Upper Canada (now Ontario), dealt with the fact that the Mississaugas had surrendered and been paid for an extensive part of the Ottawa Valley. Although the Algonquins had objected, he concluded: "The Mississaugas' right as occupants had been implicitly recognized by the government, and there is not sufficient evidence to support the counter-claim of the Algonquins. If it exists it must repose in the early history of the tribes frequenting the great Canadian rivers."

Any reader who has followed the story through the countless petitions and responses recorded since 1763 will find this an extraordinary claim. The evidence certainly did exist, and it reposed in the files of the Indian department.

But Macaulay was reporting to the government of Upper Canada, and because the summer trading place of the Algonquins was at Lake of Two Mountains in Lower Canada (Quebec), the papers concerning them were kept in the Lower Canada branch of the department.

It was simple for Macaulay to dismiss the official correspondence that supported the claims of the Algonquins by saying that they "assume rather than prove the right of those Indians to territory within the limits of Upper Canada," since he believed that the Algonquins were "Lower Canada Indians," without rights on the west side of the Ottawa Valley. He had read enough to know, however, "that all this requires attention," and he urged the government to "compound with proper parties for the cession of all this territory and…for all the unconceded lands embraced by the Great Lakes and the Ottawa as far as Lake Nippissing [*sic*]…extinguishing the Indian title for a fair equivalent."

The Executive Council did not take the action recommended by Macaulay. Instead, it fastened on his conclusion that the

Indians had no rights south of the Ottawa River to countermand the actions Captain Ducharme and Colonel Hughes of the Indian department had taken to deal with squatters in Indian lands on the river. Thus, the one step ever taken by the Indian department to secure any form of compensation from squatters on Algonquin land was overruled. The government ignored Macaulay's recommendation for a treaty and completely ignored the terms of the Royal Proclamation, which, as the Algonquins had so many times insisted, had never been repealed and was still in force.

In 1840 Colonel Hughes met with the Algonquins to tell them that the government had not yet answered their petitions. Chief Ka-on-di-no-ketch replied with a sad and remarkable summary of the entire eighty-year experience:

> Our hunting grounds, which are vast and extensive and once abounded in the richest furs and swarmed with deer of every description, are now entirely ruined. We tell you too true, we now starve half the year through, our children, who were formerly accustomed to be comfortably clothed, are now naked.
>
> Brother, we are partly the cause of these our present misfortunes. We were too good and generous. We permitted strangers to come and settle in our grounds and cultivate the land, and traders to destroy our valuable timber, who have done us much injury, as by clearing our rich forest, they have annihilated our beaver and our peltries, and driven away our deer. Had our hunting grounds belonged to the whites, they would not have allowed this, but we had good hearts and took pity on our white brethren.

The Chief cited the Royal Proclamation: "Our Father, Sir William Johnson, gave our ancestors a writing on parchment, we still hold. This document tells us that we shall never be disturbed on the hunting grounds reserved for us...that we could not make away with these to strangers, but that whenever we should wish to part with them our Great Father...would pay us for them." He objected again to the fact that the government had paid the Mississaugas for the surrender of Algonquin lands, and ended: "We have no choice to make. We must one and all become tillers of the ground, otherwise we must starve."

The Algonquin effort to move on to Allumette Island also had a melancholy result. Algonquins were told in 1837 that the governor would have the land surveyed for them, but when they later sent a deputation to Toronto, they were told that the land on which they were to settle had been sold to a tribe of Mississaugas who had sold it in turn, though they were well aware that it formed a part of the Algonquin hunting grounds.

Fiddling the Boundaries of Algonquin Territory

The occupation of the Ottawa Valley by lumbermen and settlers was matched by a movement to exploit the timber and mineral resources north of Lake Huron and Lake Superior. Mining locations of 260 sq. km (100 square miles) each were granted to friends and members of the government. Petitions by Ojibway chiefs were ignored, just as Algonquin petitions had been.

It was not until 1849, when the Ojibways living near Sault Ste. Marie took over a mining location and evicted the miners, that the government decided a treaty was necessary.

Here again, as so often, the extent of the territories surrendered was very vaguely described, and this has had a negative impact on the Algonquins, northern neighbours to the Ojibways.

The eastern boundary of the land surrendered by the Ojibways in the Robinson-Huron Treaty of 1850 was not clearly defined; it includes "the eastern and northern shores" of Lake Huron, and "inland to the height of land" separating the Hudson's Bay Company lands from Canada. A royal commission that preceded the 1850 treaty, however, gives a clearer definition of the Ojibway area, and notes that a tract of land lying between the "last three bands" of Ojibways and the Ottawa River "is supposed to belong to the Indians of Two Mountains, Canada East."

The obfuscation of this boundary extends right to the present day. Maps produced by the Department of Indian Affairs in the 1960s show the Ontario side of the Ottawa Valley as being covered by no valid surrender, but in 1971 the department produced a map that extends the territory covered by the 1850 treaty to the banks of the Ottawa.

By the 1840s the Algonquins were drifting away from the settlement at Lake of Two Mountains and establishing settlements closer to their traditional hunting grounds. There were several reasons for this. There was a bitter battle between the Mohawks and the priests at the seminary at Oka about control over the land, there were many diseases in the village, and more trading posts had opened up closer to the trapping areas.

Getting the Algonquins Out of the Way

By the 1840s the Algonquins of Ontario had become a marginalized people, at least in the eyes of the white man. Our people lived in scattered settlements, where according to official policy they had no rights except those granted by the government.

The Algonquins who left Lake of Two Mountains restarted settlements on their own initiative at River Desert, on the Gatineau, 150 km (90 miles) directly north of Ottawa, and at Golden Lake, on the Bonnechere River, 140 km (85 miles) west of Ottawa. The story of how these settlements were turned into reserves, intended as gathering places for the scattered Algonquins, illustrates another persistent theme of Canadian government Indian policy: the determination to gather the native people who had been forced off their hunting grounds into consolidated settlements, called "points of concentration," where they could be subjected to the "civilizing" influence of priests and teachers and turned into Christians and farmers. This policy was tried (and failed) in deliberate experiments in the 1830s at Coldwater in the Muskoka region, and Manitoulin Island; it was the chief impetus behind the reserve policy extended into the Canadian west by the numbered treaties in the 1870s.

In 1851 the heads of three or four hundred Algonquin families petitioned the House of Commons, complaining that the government had never done anything "to help to come to pass...the awaited advantages of the civilized state"; that they had been stripped of the land that was their inheritance with "nothing given to them in exchange." They had, they said, "been brought to believe, as a result, that the principles of religion and humanity that civilized men profess are not well rooted in their hearts. Having thus remained a hunting people while you have destroyed all the means of hunting," they said, many remained discouraged, without hope, and without resource. The resultant poverty "has as its companions miseries of all kind, and diseases which quickly harvest their wives and children."

A year or two before, other Algonquins had applied for 40,000 hectares (100,000 acres) of reserved land at the head of Lake Temiscaming and 24,000 hectares (60,000 acres) at River Desert. But in this petition these family heads said they did not want the Temiscaming land, because of "the ingratitude of the climate and soil of that place, its distance, the absence of roads and neighbours, of any example in the practice of farming, and of any means of procuring any tools, seeds and animals." They asked for a township nearer the Ottawa River, and financial assistance to help establish a modern farming community.

The money, they pointed out, could come from the savings the government had made by diminishing the annual presents, or from the "public funds to which your petitioners have as much right as their fellow citizens of European origin."

It took six years before two tracts of land were set aside for the Algonquins: 15,360 hectares (38,400 acres) — not 40,000 hectares — at Temiscaming, and 18,300 hectares (45,750 acres) — not 24,000 hectares — at River Desert, which the Algonquins named Maniwaki ("Mary's Land").

Not everybody wanted to go to these two places. In September 1857, five families living near Golden Lake petitioned the governor general, stating that since their hunting grounds had been opened up for settlement and sale by the government, they had "no resource left but to try to raise sufficient from the soil to support (themselves)."

They asked for 80 hectares (200 acres) per family, much the same kind of grant white settlers were receiving from the government. The local Crown Lands agent wrote in support of the petition: "These men appear to be unusually intelligent and respectable; I have been informed that they are moral and industrious and well-deserving."

In spite of this the Commissioner of Crown Lands wrote to the Indian Affairs department in November 1857 that there was no provision for the disposal of public lands for such an application: "This department cannot submit the application to the favourable consideration of the government," and they would have to see if there were Indian funds for such a purchase. Besides, wrote the commissioner, the Algonquins at Golden Lake were reported to be "half-bred, half-civilized Indians."

For six years the Algonquins continued to apply to the local Crown Lands agent for response, all the while worried that the government might sell the land on which they were living to someone else. Finally, in 1864, the Indian department used Indian funds to pay $156.10 for the 624 hectares (1,560 acres) that became the Golden Lake Reserve.

Over the next few years several more families joined those already there, until in 1880 there were eighty-three Indians, seven log houses, sixteen wigwams, and thirteen barns and stables. The Algonquins asked for more land, but the Indian department decided, "there is evidently plenty of land for all."

The written record of the following decade shows a government determined to restrict the rights of Algonquins who persisted in living outside the three designated reserves. As these reserves were being established Algonquins living in two other places not far from Golden Lake tried to obtain reserved Indian land grants. The usual response was that they should go either to Golden Lake or to Maniwaki. In 1866, one-quarter of

Lawrence Township, within the boundaries of Algonquin Park, was reserved from sale, but the Indians living there, who had requested this, were not told until two years later. Then they were advised: "The land has been reserved for the use of the Algonquin Indians during the pleasure of the Crown, not granted....Also, the Indians are not to have the right to the merchantable timber on the land nor are they to interrupt those parties who hold timber licenses from cutting and carrying off the timber."

Twenty years later, the people there tried unsuccessfully to exchange this location for another, since hunting was poor and fur scarce. Ontario was now in charge of Crown Lands, but did not respond to the request. Later still, in the 1890s, further efforts were made to secure formal protection for the land set aside, but the Commissioner of Crown Lands did not agree:

> The formation of a settlement of Indians upon the borders of a territory of this kind would, in my opinion, be attended with great danger to the preservation of game in [Algonquin] Park. You know the predatory habits of these people, how they roam about, and how difficult it is to keep watch of their movements in the forest, or to get them to recognize that a law which applies to white people with respect at any rate to the killing of game, should be made to apply to the Indian, who depends for his livelihood in great measure upon what he can kill in the forest.
>
> It would therefore be also impossible to keep these Indians, thus situated, from hunting and trapping within the Park, and the attempt to do so would no doubt be attended with great expense and continual friction and bad blood between Indians and the ranger, which might lead to unfortunate results.

The commissioner then learned that there was an Algonquin settlement nearby, in Nightingale Township. Although these people had been living there for a generation, he hastened to warn them that "they have no rights there, and they must not expect that these lands will...be allowed to them." Similarly land was ultimately denied to the Lawrence Township Indians, who were advised that "they should confine themselves to the reserve which has been set aside for them at Golden Lake."

Algonquin Park, set up at the instigation of the lumber barons as a means of keeping timber land from being settled, was now used to deny land to Indians living in the vicinity. In vain did Chief Peter Sharbot say that he had no designs on land within the park. Bewildered by the bureaucratic runaround, he wrote: "We are getting such poor satisfaction by running and writing and nothing ahead yet we do not wish to be humbugged...we wish you to try and get the land."

Chief Sharbot tried to get a land grant in a third township, Sabine, but again Indian Affairs headquarters refused: "If these people belong to the Golden Lake band, they should be instructed to return to the reserve at Golden Lake."

Of course, they were not from Golden Lake. But the bureaucrats had never been to Golden Lake, although it was one of the closest reserves to Ottawa.

Indian Affairs later wrote to the Ontario government that the lands in question were unoccupied except by the Indians, and "unfit for settlement." However, the provincial government steadfastly refused to part with them, since the timber had not yet been harvested. "This department's...experience is that Indian settlements render the localities in which they are situated less attractive for settlement than other localities in which there is no Indian population," observed the province. One might remark that this had not, of course, stopped them from settling the Algonquin lands in the first place!

By the end of the nineteenth century, the federal government had issued its final word about the Algonquins living in Lawrence, Nightingale, and Sabine townships: "These Indians are merely stragglers from other bands and are allied to those for whom the Maniwaki reserve was set apart, as well as those for whom the Golden Lake reserve was established in 1870."

Thus had our proud people — hunters, traders, great travellers, masters of a huge wilderness — been reduced by bureaucratic and political duplicity to "mere stragglers" in our own land.

The Algonquins at Golden Lake had received a formally recognized Indian reserve. Those who lived 80 km (50 miles) west of them, equally Algonquin, ended up with nothing.

When the Government of Canada began to decide who was an "Indian," according to the strange definitions written into the Indian Act, the people living on the reserve at Golden Lake were recognized as "status Indians." The Algonquins of all other parts of the Ontario side of the Ottawa Valley were not even granted that recognition.

Algonquins Defend Their Hunting Rights

In 1897 the local Indian agent wrote that one of the Golden Lake Indians had asked for "a permit to kill a deer now and then for meat to support his family. I feel sorry for the poor man," the agent continued. "I know him to be a good and kind man...the people threaten that if they ever know him to kill a deer they will have him before a magistrate and fined."

The department replied that the Indians did have the right to kill deer for food. The local agent must have informed the people of Golden Lake about this, since in April 1898 he wrote back to headquarters: "The majority of the Indians at Golden Lake reserve are summoned to appear before the game warden...for killing deer out of season. Now they expect me to save them as if not I suppose they will make a complaint to the department." But the secretary of the department replied that "even if the department felt justified in defending Indians...it has no funds at its disposal for such purpose."

Most of the Algonquins were convicted, but instead of imposing fines (in view of their poverty they could not pay fines and would have ended up in jail) the magistrate gave suspended sentences and a warning that the men would be jailed if they were caught hunting again.

This court action did not stop the Algonquins from hunting and fishing. It did, however, make us much more careful. Algonquins continued to use the land as they had for so many thousands of years, and what we called making a living, the newcomers now called "poaching."

Our elders tell stories of hunting in Algonquin Park; of the man who used stilts to confuse the rangers who might try to track him, of the man who wore his snowshoes backwards, and of the family whose children were wrapped in "poached" furs under their snowsuits, which the rangers failed to search. At the portage store at Canoe Lake the Ontario Ministry of Natural Resources displays a birch-bark canoe blackened to avoid detection, seized from "an Indian poacher." There were few court cases for nearly a century, not because the Algonquins ceased hunting and fishing but because we did so with much more discretion.

In 1954 a new regime of fur management in Algonquin Park arrived. The government realized that proper harvesting of fur-bearing animals would strengthen the populations and ensure their survival — something the Indians always knew. The entire eastern half of the park was opened to the trappers from Golden Lake (and only to them) and, ever since, each trapline has been in full use and occupation.

When the Algonquins of Golden Lake began to reassert their land rights, in the late 1970s, the Ontario Ministry of Natural Resources responded with a new series of charges under the Provincial Parks Act and the Game and Fish Act.

In many cases the charges were perused through several adjournments of the court and then dropped on the date set for trial, after we had gone through all the trouble and expense of preparing for the hearing. The Algonquins have stated that these charges are harassment, that we consider the practice an abuse of the court process by the Crown, and that we seriously consider taking court action to prevent any recurrence.

At Golden Lake the Algonquin people have instituted our own community hunting, fishing, trapping, and gathering rules, which are to be respected and enforced over the entire traditional territory, rules that are consistent with traditional Algonquin values of conservation, sharing, and safety.

Reasserting Our Rights

In 1974, Chief Dan Tennisco asked the Rights and Treaty Research Programme of the Union of Ontario Indians to examine the taking of the railway right-of-way through the Golden Lake reserve. Before the Research Programme could give any opinion, though, it had to find out how the land had come to be a reserve in the first place.

The inquiry led to the discovery of the 1857 petition asking for reserve, and then to the realization that there had never been any treaty or surrender by the Algonquins. From that point the entire sorry tale of petition upon petition, promise and delay, emerged.

In 1978, at a meeting in Golden Lake, representatives of the Canadian and Ontario governments were given copies of all the research that had been accumulated to that time. Ontario was asked to refrain from issuing any further land patents.

Also in 1978 the Algonquins of Golden Lake hosted a meeting of the chiefs of all the "status Indian" Algonquin communities in Ontario and Quebec. Golden Lake's research was nearly finished; the research work of the others had barely begun.

An agreement was made that Golden Lake would claim the Algonquin territory on the west side of the Ottawa River, while the other communities would concentrate on the east side, that if any negotiations were to take place one designated representative from each side of the river would be invited to attend meetings on the other side, and that all research materials would be shared.

In 1983 the Algonquins of Golden Lake delivered a petition, as dictated by protocol, to the governor general, Edward Schreyer. The document was signed by almost all the adult population of the Algonquin Golden Lake First Nation.

Writing the petition was easy; most of what needed to be said had been stated many times over in the petitions of the previous two centuries. Most of the 1983 petition was taken directly from earlier ones, especially the forceful and clear communications of the 1820s and 1830s.

After reiterating the long history that has been outlined in this article, the petition details at least twenty-three previous petitions "for protection and simple justice" that had been made by Algonquins between 1791 and 1863. Then it continues:

> Innumerable squatters and lumberers, authorized by your governments, have taken possession of and established themselves on the most fertile parts of our lands, destroyed our magnificent forests, abused our ancestors, and forced them into pitifully small tracts of land in abject poverty...
>
> The Crown's governments have participated in these attacks on our just rights, gaining profit from the sale of our lands and resources. We have seen our people stripped of their nationality in violation of all laws. We have seen them jailed or fined for seeking game or fish for food. These attacks on our rights continue in our woods and lakes and your courts to this day...
>
> In violation of your laws and ours, your governments took purchases of our lands from Indians who never lived on them and claimed no title to them.

The petition acknowledges that in seeking justice today the Algonquins do not want to create injustice for others by dispossessing others without compensation, "as we have been dispossessed ourselves."

> We therefore pray:
>
> That all lands in the province of Ontario which form part of the watershed of the Ottawa River below the

Mattawa River that are now in the possession of the Crown be immediately confirmed and recognized as belonging to our Nation;

That the governments of Canada and of the province of Ontario make no use or disposition of these lands or any parts of them or any resources appertaining to them, without the consent of our Nation;

That discussions begin with your governments under your personal auspices and direction to settle the questions of compensation for their past use and occupation of our lands and resources, and of compensation for the taking of those lands which have been patented.

Our Rights Contested in Court

Meanwhile, as this was developing, the Algonquin claim was beginning to be tested in the courts. In a case involving Algonquin Boyd Tennesco, Provincial Court Judge Russel Merredew stated that the Algonquins had aboriginal rights to the areas that have never been surrendered. Merredew found the 1923 treaties purporting to be a surrender of the Ottawa Valley by the Mississaugas and Chippewas to be a cynical act by the governments. And he found that the Algonquins, in accepting, relying upon, and complying with the Royal Proclamation of 1763, had elevated that document to the status of a treaty, which would override the provincial Fish and Game Act.

The Supreme Court of Ontario, dealing with the narrow issue of whether the proclamation was a treaty, disagreed. It held that the Proclamation was a unilateral act of the Crown, and that nothing the Algonquins did would change the nature of the document into a treaty.

The decision is ironic. If any other Crown official had communicated the reservation of the land in the Royal Proclamation to the Algonquins, the Algonquins' acceptance would have created a treaty, according to this decision. But since the Proclamation was the King's word only, and did not require Algonquin acceptance, it provides no legal protection at all.

Yet, the findings of fact of the Provincial Court still stand: the Algonquins have unsurrendered aboriginal rights in the area.

By 1987 the provincial and federal governments had been in possession of our land-claim documents for four years. Although the federal claims policy indicates that there should be a formal response within twelve months of submission, we had not yet received any response from the Government of Canada. The Province of Ontario did say, however, that its land policy would continue as before: disposition of Crown land would proceed without any requirement for notice to, or consent from, the Algonquins.

In September 1987, as Chief of the Algonquin Golden Lake First Nation, I met with Ian Scott who was both the provincial minister responsible for Native Affairs and the attorney general of Ontario. Scott promised at that meeting that he would provide the Algonquins with the official reply on behalf of the province of Ontario "by mid-1988." That time has come and gone and we have yet received no reply.

Dispositions of Crown lands and the alienation of Crown land to third-party interests, however, began to increase at an alarming rate within the claim territory. The provincial government formally announced its "Crown Lands as a Development Tool" policy, and designated the Whitney area, Algonquin heartland, as a "Primary Development Area." Under this development policy the provincial government intends to make land available to developers at subsidized rates for a variety of uses.

At the same time Ontario announced its intention to build a Pakkotina Forest access road, to open up an area of about 12,000 hectares (30,000 acres) of Crown land near Golden Lake to more intensive forestry and recreational use, a clear attempt by the Ontario government to extinguish aboriginal title to the area in question as per the federal land-claims policy.

Road allowances around lakes in the area (which are still considered Crown land) have been "stopped up" and sold with no consideration given to the Algonquin claim, and "new" provincial parks have been created in Algonquin territory.

We feel that the federal and provincial governments have been neither diligent nor sincere in their dealings with Algonquin rights, and this perception has led us to consider taking various actions in an attempt to provoke a response after more than two centuries of inertia.

We thought that perhaps one reason the government did not respond to our latest petition, that of 1983, was that they lacked any vision of how a claim, so well documented, so well justified, and of such a magnitude, could be settled fairly. We therefore decided that we should help the government to overcome this apparent short-sightedness.

A Proposed Resolution of Our Claims

In August 1988, on behalf of the Algonquins of Golden Lake, I delivered a settlement proposal to the governor general, again as protocol dictated, and to the responsible Canadian and Ontario ministers. The proposal is a serious attempt to resolve this issue, and represents major concessions on the part of the Algonquin people. Compensation in direct dollar value for loss of land and loss of land use would reach astronomical amounts. We have, therefore, based our proposal not on direct compensation but on the requirements for the establishment of an independent, self-sufficient Algonquin economy, and the rights and powers necessary to protect that economy and land from ever being threatened again.

The proposal states, in several parts:

- that the Algonquins would take over administration and control of Algonquin Park, which would remain a public park while also remaining Algonquin land. The proposal calls for a joint Ontario-Algonquin management board to oversee a transition period, which would ensure no reduction in the quality of service and administration in the park;

- that other unpatented land in traditional Algonquin territory would either be acknowledged as Algonquin land or be transferred to the Crown with compensation. "Crown land" within that territory includes what is now called Algonquin Park, Canadian Forces Base Petawawa, and the lands of the National Capital Commission in Ottawa (including Parliament Hill);

- that the government of Canada would continue its program and services in education and health care;

- that there would be sufficient financial compensation to ensure the establishment of a non-dependent Algonquin economy;

- that Algonquin social and political rights would be recognized.

In making this proposal the Algonquin people emphasize that non-Algonquin land owners in the area should not be concerned about the loss of their property. The land portion of the proposal applies to Crown land only and not to private land, and the Algonquins have made every effort to ensure that private individuals' land rights are protected.

On September 2, 1988, the Algonquin people of Golden Lake took to the road to draw attention to their plight, to educate the public and to gain support for their struggle. About 70 percent of the adult residents of Golden Lake as well as Algonquin and non-Algonquin supporters from the Whitney, Lake St. Peter, and Sharbot Lake areas gathered at the eastern gate of Algonquin Park. Here a road block was set up and buttons and pamphlets explaining the Algonquin situation were handed out. The thousands of motorists stopped were also asked to sign a petition asking the government to take immediate steps to deal fairly with the claims of the Algonquin people.

There is no question that the demonstration was effective. Most of the motorists readily signed the petition and several newspaper and TV crews were present to cover the event. Cooperation with the police and the park staff was very good, and the involvement and support of so many of our people was heartwarming to see — evidence, surely, of our renewed interest in our heritage and of our commitment to the future of our children.

On October 5, the Ministry of Natural Resources announced that the Pakkotina Forest Access Road Development had been "postponed" because of lack of financial resources — although the funds had in fact already been allocated to the project.

On October 17, the heads of the respective land-claims departments of the federal and provincial governments came to Golden Lake to discuss the claim. After presenting a brief historical background, we stated our positions on the variety of federal and provincial initiatives affecting our claim. The Pakkotina Forest Access Road, which remains as a stated objective of the Ministry of Natural Resources, would not be built. Crown Lands as a Development Tool would not proceed in Algonquin territory without Algonquin consent. Algonquin hunting, fishing, trapping, and gathering would continue over the entire Algonquin territory according to our own established hunting, fishing, and gathering rules, and the road-allowance sales as well as any other land-use initiatives must proceed only with Algonquin consent.

The province agreed to work with us at that time to establish an "interim agreement" that would resolve some of those "issues of common concern" while we were seeking settlement of the Algonquin land claim.

Once again we asked these government officials when we could reasonably expect an official response from their respective governments regarding the acceptance of our claim for negotiation. We were assured that both the federal and provincial cabinets would review the land claim, together with the required supporting documentation, by the end of December 1988 and that we could expect to receive a cabinet response by the end of January 1989. We were also advised, however, that this probably would not happen without more detailed information demonstrating continued aboriginal use (hunting, fishing, trapping, and gathering) over the entire territory in question. We began immediately to work towards this end, but in the meantime they hesitated to submit our claim to cabinet until after the Bear Island appeal decision was announced.

On February 27, 1989, the Ontario Court of Appeal issued its decision in the case of the Attorney General of Ontario *v.* the Bear Island Foundation et al. This decision had serious implications for many aboriginal people in Canada. Among other things, it said that, if there is clear proof that the sovereign had the plain and unambiguous intent to take the land in question, then the aboriginal rights in that land are extinguished. Our legal opinion as to the effect of the *Bear Island* case on the Algonquin land claim is that the two cases are sufficiently different so as to make that decision, although serious, not significantly damaging to the Algonquin claim. Provincial government people unofficially confirmed our position and also commented that the *Bear Island* decision might even help the Algonquin claim. Federal justice lawyers were split on the issue, with one side being of the opinion that the *Bear Island* ruling completely negated the Algonquin claim and the other side believing that the ruling did not significantly damage our claim. On April 25, 1989, our land-claim committee — myself, Kirby Whiteduck, Dan Cooco, and legal counsel Paul Williams — met with Richard Van Loon, the assistant deputy minister of Northern Affairs (where the Comprehensive Claims Branch had been transferred to in the last cabinet shuffle, away from the Department of Indian Affairs). Also present at that meeting was Ian Potter, the director of Comprehensive Claims, and John Leslie, the chief of Treaty and Historical Research Centre of the Comprehensive Claims Branch.

At this meeting we presented our aboriginal land-use data that proved current and continued aboriginal land use on and over our entire territory. Here we were presented with a document entitled *Indices of Current Use: An Approach to Data Collection and Reporting.* This document, which we had never seen before,

outlined further and much more detailed information requirements concerning aboriginal land-use activity, for example,
under "Gathering": "list roots, berries, medicinal herbs, etc.
collected....What is the intensity....What is the frequency....How
many members of the claimant group are involved? and gathering locations should be indicated."

To our dismay we were also advised that the Comprehensive
Claims Branch was now not prepared to submit our claim to
cabinet because "in our opinion the Algonquin land claim
would be rejected by cabinet, if submitted in its present form."
As an alternative, since our claim was neither a true comprehensive nor a true specific land claim, yet with elements of both and,
in our opinion anyway, undeniably a valid claim, we were advised
that the Comprehensive Claims Branch would submit for
cabinet's consideration a "Modified Comprehensive Land Claim"
categorization before submitting the Golden Lake land claim.
This, we were assured, would give our claim the best chance of
being accepted for negotiation by cabinet. This, of course, raises
the question, "Is the federal government attempting to water
down the land claim process to make the Golden Lake claim that
much more affordable?"

The effect of having this cabinet document going forward
ahead of our land claim would mean, considering that cabinet
recesses for the summer, that our claim would not be put
forward for consideration until the fall and that we would then
not be able to expect a response much before the end of 1989,
a full seven years from the date of our last petition and six years
from the date that the federal government's own policy dictates
that we should have a formal response.

On May 9, 1989, the committee met with Mark Krasnick,
executive director of the Ontario Native Affairs Directorate; Lise
Hansen, director of Claims Unit; and Mark Stevenson, the
lawyer for the province. At this meeting we were advised that they
were hesitant to submit our claim to the cabinet at the present
time as "it probably would not be accepted for negotiation in its

present form. It was also admitted that the provincial government more than likely would not agree to negotiate our claim until after the federal government accepted it for negotiation.

Work on the "Interim Agreement" was discussed as well, and we were advised that the provincial government, to wit, the Ministry of Natural Resources, would have a lot of difficulty with our positions. However, the province did agree to enter into a discussion process with us, parallel to, yet separate from, the land claim process, that would attempt to provide a practical pro-active approach to addressing some of the immediate needs of the Algonquins of Golden Lake.

So we continue to struggle with government bureaucracies that have stymied the desire of our people to defend their land, almost ever since white men came among us. We have always been reasonable, yet after two hundred years, our patience is wearing thin.

TEME-AUGAMA
ANISHNABAI

THE CONFRONTATION

On June 1, 1988, members of the Teme-Augama Anishnabai Nation in Northern Ontario set up a blockade on a road that the Ontario government was in the process of building to provide logging companies access to the last corner of ancient white pine forest left in n'Daki-Menan, their aboriginal homeland for 6,000 years.

"If our land dies, we die," said Chief Gary Potts, that day. "This land is our Crown. This land, along with the seasons affecting it, is our touchstone to past life and the gateway to future life, both human and non-human."

The blockade prevented further work on the road, and was kept in place until ordered removed by the Ontario Court of Appeal on December 8. That judgment also forbade all further work on the road by the province, except for surveying with a transit and chain.

The road blockade was established only after 112 years of fruitless efforts by the Teme-Augama Anishnabai to negotiate with the Ontario government the defence of their traditional homeland and human rights.

Last-Ditch Defence of a Priceless Homeland

Chief Gary Potts,
of the Teme-Augama Anishnabai

For 112 years, we, the people of Teme-Augama Anishnabai, while trying to survive, to get along with others, and to avoid confrontation, have had to watch the exploitation and destruction of our traditional lands by outsiders.

The lands on which our people have always lived cover nearly 10,000 km (4,000 square miles) surrounding and north of Lake Temagami, roughly 160 km (100 miles) northwest of the city of North Bay. When, in 1850, the colonial government signed the Robinson-Huron Treaty, accepting surrender of aboriginal lands north of Lake Huron, our people were omitted from the treaty. A quarter of a century later our Chief Tonene began to ask to be taken into treaty to gain protection from encroaching lumbermen and settlers, and the authorities then admitted that we had never surrendered our lands, and agreed that a treaty was in order.

In fact, in 1884, the federal government surveyed a 260 sq. km (100-square-mile) reserve for us at the southern outlet of Lake Temagami, but the Ontario government, by this time in control of Crown lands, refused to transfer the area, apparently on the grounds that there was too much valuable timber within the proposed reserve.

Thus, we can see at work a persistent theme of Canadian history, the effort to ensure that the aboriginal people be confined not only to small tracts of land, but to worthless and valueless land on which it has since been impossible for most of us to create a viable livelihood and way of life.

The People of the Deep Water, as we have always called ourselves, we were for thousands of years a self-governing Nation who regulated land possession and civil affairs by a communal system of law. Each family, in those days, maintained its own tract of 500 to 800 sq. km (200 to 300 square miles), and Wendaban and Misabi (the names we gave to the two camps of our 1988 road blockade) are the names of two such traditional family hunting grounds.

We have always been deeply attached to the magnificent forests in which we have carried on our traditional life. Before the coming of the white man we made use of more than three hundred plants — sugar maples, for instance, and basswood fibres for making twine snares and fishing nets — and our trails, called nastawgan, some of them as old as 3,000 years, still criss-cross the area. They are a testimony to our system of year-round travel by foot, canoe, snowshoe, and toboggan: few people anywhere have ever lived more intimately with their environment than we have.

I can illustrate this by describing the tradition of wisana, under which an animal would come close to a wigwam shortly after the birth of a child, apparently with the intention of seeing the baby. This could happen any time in the first year of life, and traditionally the child would treasure the name of the animal all its life. Even if the family was in need of food, this animal would never be molested or disturbed. The coming of this animal was expected and looked for by the mother, and often the child would carry the wisana's name until some episode in life would earn the child another name, a sort of nickname. Everybody in those days would know everybody else's wisana.

Of course, we have inherited communal and collective traditions that explain our continuing emphasis on community values. When a child was born, the parents would always hold a feast and invite all relatives, and when the child was about a year old the mother would choose some old man or woman, selected on account of his or her good qualities, to give the child a name. At a feast held at this time, the name-giver would lift the child and announce the chosen name; then, as food was passed around from right to left, the child was also handed from one person to another, each guest kissing the child in turn. Thus, in the most fundamental way, the birth and welfare of that child became a matter of collective and communal interest.

Like many other nations, our people were also divided into totems or clans (traditionally, loon, kingfisher, rattlesnake, caribou, porcupine, and beaver) whose members would in normal circumstances marry only outside their clan.

In Teme-Augama our rules of proprietorship, trespass, and conservation and ideas of inheritance and marriage were traditionally similar to those of other members of the Algonkian family of Nations. The emphasis on conservation was fundamental to all our practices: each family's hunting district was divided into quarters, hunted on a rotational basis. Each year a tract would be left unused as a sort of bank not to be hunted over unless shortages in the other parts of the family's territory made it necessary. This system, which, of course, is still practised throughout the country by aboriginal hunters, allowed time for diminishing resources to replenish themselves.

Our system of chieftainship traditionally provided for a head chief, a second chief, and a third person known as the man who collects for the chief (one of his main duties was to divide and distribute the meat). The duty of the chiefs was to regulate contact with neighbouring Nations and the government. These leaders were always supposed to be planning for the interests of the people, were to take care of widows and orphans, and would occasionally preach on the rules of the camp or other topics on which they thought the people needed instruction or encouragement.

In this preaching or lecturing the second chief would normally do the talking, telling people what it was the chief had to say. This reflects the practice among people with an oral tradition that those in authority should not waste words, should not speak idly or without due weight. Immense influential authority was invested in the chief, and he chose to exercise it in a measured way. But, in time of war, the chief would decide the fighting policy, where to camp, where to move, when to retreat, when to advance, and so on. Election of these three officials was decided by the men of the tribe. This form of government was extremely stable: records gathered towards the beginning of this century indicate that, throughout the nineteenth century, chiefs lasted in office for an average of sixteen years.

Naturally, we watched with dismay when logging was first allowed in our lands from 1920 onwards, but a turning-point was reached in the 1960s, with the construction of all-season roads and the introduction of clear-cutting. Suddenly, the virgin stands of our marvellous forests became accessible to the loggers, and ever since then clear-cutting has devastated our territory.

Our patience in the face of constant rejection by the Ontario government was finally pushed too far in 1972, when they proposed to build an $80-million resort in our sacred area, Chee-Baiging, "the place where the spirit goes after the body dies."

In response, early in 1973 we decided at last to act decisively and aggressively to defend our land against these depredations that had been going on for many years.

We filed land cautions in 110 townships within our traditional territory, and thus asserted aboriginal ownership over it. The effect was to freeze the development of all Crown lands. But logging, which is the most damaging of all land uses, has continued.

Ever since filing that caution we have been fighting our way through the courts: it took us until 1989 to reach the Ontario Court of Appeal, and the matter will now go on to the Supreme Court of Canada.

This prolonged battle has been fought against the background of continuing destruction caused by the Ontario government's decision to open up the area to too many logging companies, who have long since pushed their operations beyond a sustainable level. In the 1980s, only 26.5 per cent of logged forest in the Temagami district has been replanted — a replanted forest is never as rich as a natural one — and it is admitted that there is incredible wastage, said to be as high as 32 per cent, through poor forestry and logging practices.

Clear-cutting Our Land to Death

The flashpoint that brought about our road blockades in 1988 was the decision of the Ontario government to extend logging into the so-called Wakimika triangle, which lies at the very heart of n'Daki-Menan. In the centre of this area is what we call the Conjuring Rock, among our most sacred sites, one of the places to which we have always retired, alone or in groups, to make contact with the spirits. Two other nearby rocks, which we call Shomis and Kokomis, are among our offering sites, where passing travellers may leave offerings of tobacco to the spirits. There are ancient pictographs nearby, a traditional village site, a winter fishery, and many nastawgan trails.

The forest that the government proposed to allow the loggers to destroy is one of the last significant old-growth pine ecosystems in North America, and the last major accessible wilderness in eastern Canada; because of the environmental aspect of the argument, the environmental movement became involved, hoping, like ourselves, to preserve the purity of our lands. In fact, the forest in question represents the last 5 per cent of virgin forest in our area and, even if loggers were allowed to cut it, it would not supply them with more than five years of work. Of course, at the end of those five years, not only would employment cease, but an irreplaceable, precious forest would have been destroyed forever.

When the government took that decision to proceed with two logging roads — known as the Red Squirrel Extension and the Pinetorch road, 48 km (30 miles) in all — our people, on May 22, 1988, adopted by consensus the position that we would not allow the roads to be built. On June 1, we closed the road, and a month later we had a visit from representatives of the Ontario government, asking us to allow road surveyors in. We held an assembly to consider this, but, on July 10, our people decided to refuse the request.

Before I outline the detailed story of how we have been denied our rights over the last 112 years, it would be appropriate, I think, to describe our attitude towards the management of the lands we claim.

During the months of the blockade we worked with an Ontario government representative to develop a concept of forest stewardship. On November 6, we proposed a stewardship council, to cover the Wakimika, the council to include two Anishnabai, two Ontario government–appointed representatives, and a mutually agreed-upon chairperson.

Our View of Stewardship

The council would draw up a Forest Stewardship Plan, governed by two major principles that we call Sustained Life and Sustained Development. Our attitudes are contained in the definitions we proposed:

Forest stewardship means: the forest belongs to the life that lives within it and that the future generations of this life are dependent upon the continuity of the forest. Human beings must respect forest life and integrate human uses of the forest in a manner compatible with the continuity of forest life. Forever.

Sustained life means: protecting and maintaining the life of the earth, air, and water that gives life to the forest, which protects and replenishes the earth, air, and water, as well as creating an interdependent home for all biological lifeforms within it. Designated trees and/or forest areas must be allowed to die, fall to the earth, decay, and return to earth, thus giving life to earth, which can then support the growth of a new forest for future generations, forever.

Sustained development means: (1) a political system that secures effective citizen participation in decision-making; (2) an economic system that is able to generate surpluses and technical knowledge on a self-reliant and sustainable basis; (3) a social system that provides for solutions for the tensions arising from disharmonious development; (4) an education system that respects the obligation to preserve the ecological base for development; (5) a technological system that can search continuously for new solutions; and (6) an administrative system that is flexible and has the capacity for self-correction.

Ontario Prefers Logging

Far from meeting us in a combined effort to deal with this problem of sustaining life and development, the Ontario government has coldly rejected these proposals. On November 29, 1988, the government declared its intention to proceed with the logging roads, and to seek legal injunctions preventing us from maintaining our blockades, or from imposing a third blockade on a proposed Goulard Road Extension into the same area. The government claimed that we were trying "to shut down the North." Far from it: we are trying to save the North for the future.

Why should the forest industry have the right to destroy our forests? Why should forestry companies be allowed to clear out our forests, and then move on elsewhere, leaving a wasteland behind them? What about the rights of Ontario's citizens to use a forest? Where will the animals and other life forms go when the forests are gone?

The environmental impact of the removal of a forest is long-term; the economic gain is not. We made it clear to the government that the wish of our people for the future is to have our traditional area governed by an area residents' land-use council that cannot be overruled by short-sighted politicians who do not appreciate fully the principles of sustained life and development. The traditional boundaries would also reflect thousands of years of native continuity, thus joining new institutions with ancient traditions.

For all this, we received a chilling refusal from the ministers of the Ontario government, coupled with a request for an injunction against us.

This injunction was heard by the same three justices — Zuber, Cory, and Finlayson — who were to sit on the Ontario Court of Appeal to hear our case a month later. In our opinion, by sending the matter of our blockades to them before they had a chance to hear the appeal, the Ontario government was playing public-relations and political games with us, and with the honourable court.

Nevertheless, we won our major point. On December 8, 1988, 191 days after we established our Wendaban blockade camp, the appeal court decided to adjourn the injunction application until after the hearing of the appeal proper, which was to begin on January 9. The court did order us to cease the blockade, but also ordered that the Ontario government could do no work other than surveys with a transit and chain.

We honoured the appeal court's directive and removed the road blockade.

History of Our Claim
On September 9, 1850, the government of the province of Canada and the chiefs and councils of the tribes inhabiting the northern and eastern shores of Lake Huron and an area a considerable distance inland negotiated the Robinson-Huron Treaty. Minerals had been discovered in the area and the Crown wished to purchase the Indian lands to obtain for itself a free and clear title to the lands. By the terms of the treaty, the Indians received a certain cash payment as compensation for surrendering their lands, and were promised a perpetual annuity and that certain lands within their hunting grounds would be excluded from the surrendered tract and maintained as reservations.

In all of the hundreds of documents gathered in preparation for the court case surrounding the Teme-Augama Anishnabai claim, nowhere was it expressly stated that the Robinson-Huron Treaty boundary extended far enough north to cover n'Daki-Menan. Moreover, no evidence that these particular lands were even contemplated by those who drafted that treaty appears in it. We have always maintained that regardless of the boundaries of the treaty, our people were not a party to the treaty, and therefore we still own our ancestral lands. Although the federal government has historically agreed with us that the Indian title to the land was not extinguished, they seem to have assumed that the lands were none the less included within the treaty boundary. Ontario has always expressly stated that it believed the lands to be within the treaty's bounds, and that they were ceded by the treaty. The boundary issue was raised on a number of occasions during the trial and, at the eleventh hour, a Department of Indian Affairs file was presented to the Teme-Augama Anishnabai legal counsel, Bruce Clark, by Canada's legal representative, William Hobson.

This file contained a detailed report respecting annuitants under the Robinson-Superior and Robinson-Huron treaties. It was prepared in 1899 by a Mr. McRae, Inspector of Indian Agencies and Reserves, and had a map attached showing the Teme-Augama Anishnabai lands to be outside the boundaries of the treaty. That this map was not known to department agents who were investigating our claim may have been the result of compartmentalization within the department. It could have been overlooked because the report in question addressed membership under the treaty, and not land or boundaries.

In 1867, the British government passed the British North America Act. Under the terms of confederation, the new federal government was given responsibility for "Indians and lands reserved for Indians." The homeland of the Teme-Augama Anishnabai fell well within the boundaries of the new province of Ontario.

In 1877, Chief Tonene first brought the Teme-Augama Anishnabai claim forward. For several years Tonene travelled to Lake Nipissing to intercept Charles Skene, the Indian agent stationed at Parry Sound, as he arrived there yearly to pay the Nipissing Band their Robinson-Huron Treaty annuity.

Historical records of Skene's letters to his superior at the Department of Indian Affairs, L. Vankoughnet, describe his meetings with Tonene. In 1880 Skene writes: "It has been 3 years since 3 Indians came upon me representing themselves as belonging to a Band living north of Lake Nipissing. Of course as they are not mentioned in any Treaty no reserve has been set aside for them...they wish to know whether a reserve is to be laid out for them and on what conditions they are supposed to cede their lands."

And in February 1881: "The Chief expressed his hope that before any settlement was made I would be sent to meet the Band in Council — I told him I could say nothing about that — but I had no doubt that before any Treaty was made someone would be empowered by the Government to meet the Band and arrange matters."

Skene wrote several letters to Ottawa relaying Tonene's requests to be taken into treaty. Skene suggested that a party be sent to meet the band in council offering a certain sum ($1,500–$2,000) as compensation, that a reserve be marked out, the band having the privilege of selecting the site; and that the band be paid annuity on the same terms as the bands in the Robinson-Huron Treaty. In his letter of May 28, 1881, to Vankoughnet he adds: "I think the Band would be pleased with this — the Chief when I asked him about this would say nothing without the Band. All the same I think some such arrangements would satisfy the Band and be fair to all parties."

Canada Admits Our Claim — in 1881

Also in 1881, Vankoughnet brought the Teme-Augama Anishnabai claim to the attention of Sir John A. Macdonald, Superintendent General of Indian Affairs:

Relative to a claim made by the Chief of the Temogamingue Band of Indians to compensation for the hunting
grounds belonging to that Band...it does not appear to
have ever been surrendered by the Indians in question
or by any other Tribe. The Lands within this tract are
held by the Ontario Government....The tract is reported
to be well-timbered and the Chief of the Band who claim
it is somewhat alarmed at what he considers encroachments of lumbermen....The undersigned respectfully
submits that in the settlement which may be made with
the Ontario Government, the right of this Band of
Indians to fair compensation for the territory...may be
insisted upon.

In June 1881, Skene was instructed to write to Tonene to ask
on what terms the band would surrender. Tonene replied that,
for the surrender of their lands, his band wanted money and a
reservation "wherefrom to be able to provide for the children
and that forever."

In June 1883, Skene was informed by the Indian branch that
the "Temogamingue Band of Indians" were to be paid annuities
under the Robinson-Huron Treaty, and further, a surveyor
would be sent to investigate the band's wishes regarding a
reserve. On September 5, 1884, Thomas Walton, Indian superintendent, wrote to the   superintendent general reporting:
"Chief Tonene and his Council desired me to express to you
their earnest wish that a Reserve be surveyed for them 26 sq. km
(10 miles square) at the Southern outlet of Lake Temogamingue where the Temogamingue River begins its course to the
Sturgeon River. They desire that the River shall run through the
centre of the Reserve."

Thomas Walton forwarded to Tonene a map sketched by
G. B. Abrey, public land surveyor, and suggested that he accept
the proposed reserve since the Indian department had already
sent Abrey's map to the Ontario government, asking that the
land be set apart as a reserve.

The records show that when Abrey came to Lake Temagami to meet with Chief Tonene in 1884 regarding the site of the Teme-Augama Anishnabai reserve, the chief was out on his hunting grounds and the information was given to Abrey by Second Chief Mattias. Hence, Tonene accepted the reserve as mapped by Abrey, it being much like the sketch Tonene himself had prepared.

In 1901, the provincial government established the Temagami Forest Reserve including Teme-Augama Anishnabai lands and without providing for their claim to a reserve.

A report from the Privy Council, approved by the governor general, was issued to Ontario in 1890 "to make a further effort to obtain from the Ontario Government a definite statement of the position it is disposed to take with reference to this claim."

Article 6 of an Act for the Settlement of Certain Questions Between the Governments of Canada and Ontario Respecting Indian Lands, S.C. 1891, reads: "That any future treaties with the Indians in respect to territory in Ontario to which they have not hitherto surrendered their claim aforesaid, shall be deemed to require the concurrence of the Government of Ontario."

In 1894, pursuant to the above-mentioned act, a board of arbitrators was established to settle matters contemplated in that act. The "Statement of Case of the Dominion On Behalf of the Temogamingue Band of Ojibbewa Indians" reads in part:

> The said Temogamingue Band...was not represented at, nor did they take any part in, the negotiations which culminated in the said [Robinson-Huron] Treaties....By the British North America Act, 1867, the lands in the Province of Ontario became vested in that Province, subject to any existing interest, other than that of the province in the same...the said Temogamingue Band have always occupied and do still occupy the said tract of land...they allege that they have never surrendered their title thereto, or that their said title has never become extinguished...they have claimed and do still claim that

their rights and interests in the said tract, were not and are not in any way affected by the said Robinson Treaties....The Dominion on behalf of the said Indians says that the lands which were and are inhabited and occupied by the Temogamingue Band of Ojibbewa Indians, are subject in the hands of Ontario to the interest of the said Indians, and that the said Province ought to allow a reserve to be set apart, or approve of the reserve so surveyed by the Dominion as aforesaid, and the Dominion claims that the Arbitrators under the facts and circumstances above set out, should direct the Province of Ontario to grant to the said Indians a reserve, or to acquiesce and approve of the said reserve so surveyed as aforesaid, and upon such terms as to surrender of the Indian title in the remaining portions of the said tract as the Board would seem just and fair.

On the representation of Mr. Amelius Irving, counsel for Ontario, it was held that the Teme-Augama Anishnabai case was not a proper subject under the statute for submission to the Board of Arbitrators. Ontario successfully argued that the case was, rather, a matter for treaty.

Ontario Digs in Its Heels

In 1901, Aubrey White, Assistant Commissioner of Crown Lands (Ontario), reported to the commissioner regarding the Reserve proposed for the Teme-Augama Anishnabai: "The reserve would cover an area of 260 sq. km (100 square miles), taking in a great portion of Lake Temagami and many million of Pine timber...this Department was aware of the great quantities of Pine...and that the area asked for was entirely out of keeping with the numbers of the Indian population, and it being further considered that we were not legally bound to give a reserve, no action was taken."

Chiefs François White Bear and Alex Paul wrote to George Cockburn, Indian agent, on February 23, 1907, again requesting a reserve. Attached with the letter was a petition signed by members of the Teme-Augama Anishnabai.

Again in 1910, Ontario refused the Department of Indian Affairs's request for a reserve for the Temagami people, saying: "In view of the fact that the Treaty does not call for any reserve in this locality, and because of the importance of preserving the timber, the Department [of Lands, Forests and Mines] cannot promise a favourable reply to your request."

To this the Department of Indian Affairs replied "that the land provisions of the Treaty have not been carried out" and "the title of the Temagami Indians to the surrendered tract has not been fully extinguished."

In a letter to the Indian department in Ottawa, dated May 21, 1910, Chief François White Bear again requested a reserve. He also complained that his people were "being annoyed" and that they had "to get permission from the Chief Fire Ranger to cut even firewood" and could not "cut timber for building purposes."

Replying to the Department of Indian Affairs's inquiry regarding Ontario's intentions to set apart a game and fish reserve and as a consequence, any disposition made with regard to the Temagami Indians, Aubrey White, Deputy Minister of Lands and Forests, wrote: "I have to say that shooting and fishing have been prohibited in the Temagami Reserve. We have treated the Indians there in an very generous way since we set apart that reserve....If you would be kind enough to state under what authority they claim the right to fish and shoot there" (June 28, 1911).

In September 1912, Chief Alexander Paul addressed this complaint to Ottawa: "We have been forbidden by Chief Ranger C. C. Minden to build small shacks for our own use on Bear Island. Now we deem it only our right to have the privilege to live like people....Also we ask for our Reserve at Austin Bay. These we deem fair and justly coming to us."

Chief François White Bear wrote to George Cockburn, Indian agent at Sturgeon Falls, on May 27, 1913, saying: "We were indeed surprised to learn that your proposed visit to us has been postponed indefinitely.... [We] quite expected to have our hopes realized, but we are now greatly disappointed...we were promised a reservation some 30 years ago, so surely we have been lenient in our demands."

On September 3, 1917, Chief Alexander Paul again requested a reserve: "We think that we deserve something in our reserve. We have been here before any government was born in Canada. So we earnestly ask your Honour to grant us what we ask, it is, a reserve for the Temagami Band."

Ontario Demands Rent for Our Own Land!

In June 1929 notices were sent to Alex Mattias, William Peshabo, John Catt, and Pete Misabi by the Department of Lands and Forests, requesting rental payments for lands they occupied on Bear Island. This action by Ontario was heavily protested, and in reply to the Department of Indian Affairs's request for some arrangement "whereby these Indians could have special permission to remain without charge upon the land until such time as a reserve might be obtained for them," Ontario said: "These Indians have the same privileges to occupy these lots and do business, as other people, but they should not hold up the development by refusing to pay rental for the lands they occupy...and it is very doubtful if they would be satisfied to occupy other lands on Lake Temagami....If you can assure this Department that the Indians would remove to some particular locality as referred to, the matter might receive further consideration."

And, in 1930, in a letter to Indian Affairs, Ottawa, Ontario's position was: "As time goes on there seems to be less and less reason why lands should be set aside for that Timagami Indians in Austin Bay...there is not much likelihood of these Indians going to Austin Bay to live permanently."

Chief William Peshabo again protested against paying rent to the Ontario government for land occupancy. He added: "In the first place we have not got the money to pay with. The

Provincial Government sold licenses to hunt and trap to anyone who cared to apply and now there is no fur to get in this country. As you know we have no other means of making money all winter and we are not allowed to net fish or to shoot moose or deer so we are not in a position to pay out anything. The Government promised to give us a reserve some years ago and we are still hoping that this promise will be fulfilled."

The federal government again detailed the Teme-Augama Anishnabai claim to Ontario in 1933, stating, "The Department [of Indian Affairs] considers that the Province has a moral as well as a legal obligation to provide these [Temagami] Indians with a reserve."

In 1935, another petition, headed by Chief William Peshabo, was addressed to Ottawa requesting a reserve at Austin Bay.

In a letter dated May 10, 1939, to Mr. Walter Little, MP, Chief Alex Mattias wrote: "We held a meeting here last night to act on this suggestion by the Dominion Government about moving from Bear Island to Austin Bay and it is the unanimous decision of our band to vacate Bear Island as soon as a suitable site is set aside for us."

On October 20, 1939, Ontario stated that it could not "consent to disposing of any portion of the Township of Vogt." Ontario's view was that it was "too valuable from a timber point of view" and that the Temagami Indians "should be allotted a portion of Bear Island." The deputy minister of Lands and Forests, W.C. Cain, said that, in his opinion, "irrespective of where they might otherwise be located...the Indians will not 'stay put' should they be given an area elsewhere on the Lake."

An interdepartment memo from Indian Affairs says: "It would appear that the provincial attitude is that we must take land that they are willing to give us on Bear Island or nothing."

An order-in-council issued by Ontario, on June 15, 1943, vested the "Bear Island Subdivision" in the Crown (Canada) for the use and occupancy of the Temagami band. The property was conditionally sold to the Dominion for $3,000. The province retained certain rights on Bear Island for itself, one of which was the reversionary interest whereby "the lands shall be revested without charge by the Crown...in the right of the Province of Ontario...should the said Temagami Band of Indians become extinct or abandon the lands."

In November 1945, the deputy minister of Indian Affairs wrote to the Ontario premier's office, requesting "a small additional Reserve at Austin Bay to accommodate the families there." He adds: "They have always claimed that they are entitled to a Reserve to be selected by them and some of them have resided at Austin Bay...since about 1880. The Province has not recognized their claim to that land."

The North American Indian Brotherhood Grand Council intervened on behalf of the Teme-Augama Anishnabai. President Andrew Paull wrote to the Department of Indian Affairs, on September 4, 1948, saying: "I have been instructed by Chief John Twain and his people to take whatever steps may be open so that the reserve which was surveyed for them in 1884 be finally and officially recognized as being for their explicit use and benefit...from the record it is quite evident that the two Governments have failed to carry out a sacred obligation in compliance with the edicts of the Imperial Government and the Proclamation of King George III."

Our Leaders Reiterate Our Claim

At a meeting of the band-in-council, presided by Chief John Twain, on January 22, 1947 it was resolved: "That the Temagami Band of Indians originally of Austin Bay, now residing on Bear Island, do hereby declare that Austin Bay was never surrendered by the said Band, nor neither was a Party to any Treaty making convention, we also declare that our forefathers were not a Party to the Robinson-Huron Treaty of 1850 and we further state that our Band never gave consent to a surrender or ceded any tract of land or lands of what we occupied from time immemorial."

In connection with charges laid against Ben McKenzie, which were dropped subsequent to the matter being taken up with the Fish and Wildlife division in Toronto by J. R. Garland, MP, H.R. Conn, fur supervisor, wrote to Chief John Twain: "You must realize that living in Temagami instead of on your reserve on Bear Island, you are constantly under observation by non-Indians who are jealous of the extra privileges you enjoy and delight in complaining to the Game Warden…the Game Warden has no alternative but to investigate and if evidence is found he must lay a complaint or lose his job. It would be only fair to warn you that as long as you live in Temagami you can expect recurrences of the recent incident."

Chief John Twain replied to Mr. Conn in a letter dated April 5, 1954: "As regards to Bear Island…it's not a reserve by any means. You cannot show me the registration number or agreement signed by the Temagami Band that Bear Island has been accepted as an Indian Reserve. We have every right to live wherever we decide to live because Temagami Band is in the same position as before any treaty was made; we never surrendered our reserve — our hunting grounds — or any of our original rights to the Crown. We never signed the treaty with no government. I am not afraid to say this because I know I am right and you are wrong about Bear Island…all these troubles we got now will be put before the Supreme Court of Canada to definitely settle the whole matter for once and for all."

In the late 1960s, under the leadership of Chief William Twain, the Teme-Augama Anishnabai living at Bear Island undertook to develop the land for economic reasons. However, as the island was not an Indian reserve as such was defined in the Indian Act, but rather property of the Crown held for the use of the band according to restrictions imposed by the provincial executive order-in-council of June 1943, Indian Affairs appealed to the province "to remove the restrictions so that the lands can be made an Indian Reserve, with the Band having control over the use of the land."

By an order-in-council of the province dated November 17, 1970, the reservations and conditions contained in the 1943 order-in-council were released and the "administration, control, disposal and the exercise of the beneficial use" of Bear Island transferred to Canada provided that "Bear Island shall be held...as a reserve for the Temagami Band of Indians." A further order-in-council issued by the governor general of Canada set apart Bear Island Indian Reserve Number 1.

This brings us to August 1973, when band council instructed our lawyer to file a "caution" against all unregistered "Crown" lands within the bounds of the Teme-Augama Anishnabai ancestral lands, n'Daki-Menan, asserting that the area was Indian land within the meaning of the Royal Proclamation of 1763. The province of Ontario unsuccessfully tried to have the caution removed, and in April 1978 the case was before His Honour Judge Fernand Gratton of the Ontario District Court, North Bay.

The attorney general for Ontario sued the Teme-Augama Anishnabai in the Supreme Court of Ontario in May 1978. Ontario sought a number of declarations, one of which was that the Teme-Augama Anishnabai had no interest in, or aboriginal title to, the lands in question.

In 1979 the Teme-Augama Anishnabai resolved to return cheques that the status Indian members received yearly from the Department of Indian Affairs under the Robinson-Huron Treaty system. A declaration was issued "because of references made by the provincial government that these are Treaty monies, and payment for our lands." It reads in part: "The Federal Government recognized that we are a separate tribe of Indians and were given Indian monies because we became registered Indians under the Indian Act in 1883. We did not sign any Treaty in 1883 so any monies received then and since cannot be Treaty monies, it can only be Indian monies."

While the legal action was going through various procedural tasks leading to trial, preliminary negotiation meetings of Canada, Ontario, and the Teme-Augama Anishnabai were held.

The negotiation process, which began in July 1980, terminated on October 13, 1982.

On June 21, 1982, the case went to trial in the Supreme Court of Ontario. The trial was adjourned March 15, 1984, after 119 days of proceedings. Justice Donald Steele delivered his decision on December 11, 1984, wherein he found that the Teme-Augama Anishnabai had no interest in, nor aboriginal rights to the lands they claimed. Immediately following Justice Steele's delivery the Teme-Augama Anishnabai met in Council, and it was decided to appeal the judgment.

The question at issue in our appeal was our aboriginal rights in our ancient homeland. Mr. Justice Steele had returned a most unfavourable verdict, finding basically that we were untrustworthy, that we were not as civilized as Europeans, and that any rights we have or had were frozen by the Royal Proclamation of 1763, and remain so.

Justice Steele Steps Back into the Past

For example, he held that our view of our history as presented to the court was "pieced together" by "a small, dedicated and well- meaning group of white people" on our behalf, and he threw doubt on the credibility of the oral evidence we ourselves had given the court. (This is the sort of language that was used by Parliament and the courts back in the 1920s, when Indian rights were being totally denied and denigrated by Canadian institutions.)

In interpreting the meaning of the Royal Proclamation, he leaned heavily on a report laid before the Legislative Assembly of Canada in 1845 by a commission of inquiry. This report referred to the government policy of offering compensation to induce Indians "to move quietly to more distant hunting grounds, or to confine themselves within the more limited reserves." The authors of that report, said Mr. Justice Steele, "considered that the Indians did not have any proprietary right in the lands, that the Indian occupation could not be considered as a true and legal habitation, and that the Europeans were lawfully entitled to take possession of the land and to settle it with colonies." He added that this 1845 view was consistent with his own interpretation of the meaning of the Royal Proclamation.

"In 1763 George III did not grant ownership of vast tracts of lands to Indian bands, subject to a limited right of repossession by repurchase, surrender or conquest, when a war had just been fought to acquire those lands. At that time Europeans did not consider Indians to be equal to themselves, and it is inconceivable that the King would have made such vast grants to undefined bands, thus restricting his European subjects from occupying these lands in the future, except at great expense."

His list of nine aboriginal rights that he admitted to exist at the time of the signing of the Royal Proclamation certainly is more restricted than in any other recent judgment. Indeed, in the context of changing perceptions about aboriginal rights in the last twenty years, his list is derisory: the right to hunt animals for food and personal use, the individual family right to trap fur-bearers; to fish; to use berries, herbs, roots, and so on; to use stones for tools (but not for mining); to use clay for pottery, pipes, and ornaments; to use trees for housing (but not for lumbering), and for fires, canoes, sleighs, and snowshoes.

It is little wonder that we had to appeal such a judgment, in view of its far-reaching importance, not only to us, but to all aboriginal Nations.

Re: Appeal Court of Ontario

On February 27, 1989, the Appeal Court of Ontario, in an unanimous decision (3 to 0), rejected the appeal of the Teme-Augama Anishnabai from Justice Donald Steele's decision at trial on December 11, 1984.

More specifically, the appeal court set out three reasons as to why the aboriginal title of the Teme-Augama Anishnabai was gone: (1) Taigawene signed the treaty on behalf of the Teme-Augama Anishnabai in 1850 at Sault Ste. Marie; (2) the acceptance of treaty money in 1883 constituted an adhesion by the Teme-Augama Anishnabai to the treaty; and (3) the Sovereign intended to take the lands of the Teme-Augama Anishnabai.

On the first point found against us, they ignored the fact that there is no evidence that Taigawene represented anybody at the treaty negotiations leading up to the treaty signing on September 9, 1850.

On the second point, the judges found that acceptance of treaty money by some of our people in 1883 constituted an adhesion to the 1850 Treaty. This decision by bureaucrats in Ottawa was made under the belief that our people lived on Lake Huron. The Royal Proclamation of 1763 and the Dorchester Regulations of 1794 made it clear that the Crown could not take Indian lands by deception of any type, as the honour of the Crown was paramount.

On the final point, the judges found that the Sovereign intended to take our lands. While we put forward documented evidence that there was no intent to make a treaty with us, the province argued that the Sovereign intended to take all lands in Canada West. The judges ignored the wording on the face of the Robinson-Huron Treaty of September 9, 1850, which made it clear that the lands being transferred from the Indian tribes and bands to the Crown are only those that they are inhabiting and claiming, as well as all unceded lands within the limits of Canada West "to which they have any just claim," and "Kitcheposkipigun by Papasainse." These words make it clear that the people know their lands and that when someone is representing someone else, it says so on the treaty — for example, "Kitcheposkipigun by Papasainse."

Our oral testimony stating that we signed no treaty and were not invited to any treaty-making process was ignored by the judges.

The judgment also states in part "that there is no contemporary evidence of Nebanegwane or any members of the Temagami Band attempting to disassociate themselves from Taigawene's actions at Garden River."

For our side, I say there was no need to dissociate because there was never any association to begin with. The province of Ontario fabricated this interpretation of history at the trial; nowhere can there be found any evidence linking the Teme-Augama Anishnabai with Taigawene historically, or as a spokesperson for us at the treaty negotiations.

With regard to the adhesion in 1883, there is, in fact, no evidence that any treaty negotiation took place; the Indian agent at Parry Sound was instructed by a senior bureaucrat in Ottawa to pay the Temagami Indians because he thought they were resident on Lake Huron.

In 1984 Chief Dokis who signed the Robinson-Huron Treaty of 1850, told a representative of the Ontario government that Nebanegwane and his people were not invited to the treaty-making and that they did not find out about it until it was over. In 1899 a federal government commissioner, in a report submitted after visiting Bear Island and other reserves along Lake Huron, concluded that the Temagami Indians and their lands were not part of the Robinson-Huron Treaty.

The judges followed Justice Steele's reasoning for his decision and complimented him by saying he had bent over backwards to be fair to us. They also threw out the Royal Proclamation of 1763, saying that it had been repealed by the Quebec Act of 1774. This line of reasoning enabled them to say that a public meeting with the Indians to purchase their lands was not required as set out in the 1763 Royal Proclamation, that all the Sovereign had to do was want the lands, and, thus, no treaty with the people was necessary.

The treatment of our oral history by the Appeal Court of Ontario is very disturbing. They take bits and pieces of statements by Europeans to legitimize their position that we were not organized until a Hudson's Bay Company post was set up on Lake Temagami in 1857. Again, they use the statement of Frank Speck, in 1913, in which he assumes we migrated from the Great Lakes, and says the Temagami themselves say they came from

Sault Ste. Marie. There is no evidence anywhere, oral or written, of a migration from anywhere. Three people from the Great Lakes areas married into our group in the nineteenth century. Our genealogical charts go back to the eighteenth century and they show that we did not come from someplace else that was already despoiled by white people.

The appeal judges reasoned that we were not organized enough in 1850 to be considered a band, so Taigawene represented us, although there is no evidence anywhere that he did so. They then go on to say that four days after the treaty was signed, Nebanegwane received $25 and is listed on the same voucher 11 as Taigawene, Maisguawzo, and Dokis, who also received $25 each. There were 2,400 Indians paid that day; no treaty negotiations took place. The original vouchers were lost, the ones available to the court were made up by Indian agent Ironside in June 1851. It was shown to the court that other people received money also on September 13, 1850, and thereafter, who were not a party to the Robinson-Huron Treaty of September 9, 1850, and in fact some of these people negotiated and signed Treaty 9 at Matagami, near Gogama, Ontario, in 1906.

The appeal court's finding that an adhesion had taken place by virtue of money's being accepted has never been upheld by any court to our knowledge. Historically the process followed in Canada is that set out in the Royal Proclamation of 1763, whether it be in reference to a new treaty or to an existing one.

The Teme-Augama Anishnabai must face the awesome power of the British Crown, which has now passed its powers to the federal government of Canada, of which the judges are an administrative arm. The oath of allegiance to protect the Crown has, I feel, led to acts of patriotism from Ontario judges that contravene the true history of Canada and its evolution to a nation-state.

But the honour of the Crown in 1763 disappeared into the darkness of racism in the mid-1800s. Many Europeans in local government grew up believing, as had their parents, that they were superior to the indigenous citizens of Canada. The country's political parties see us as an impediment to progress, as they have defined it. All of these human-rights abuses, including the theft of land and natural-resources are sanctioned by the same people who denounce the fascist regime in South Africa and label the P.L.O. as terrorists for their struggles for justice. When will these double standards be brought to the attention of the world? When will Canadians see the violation of First Nations' rights undertaken by their government and bureaucracies in their name?

We are not giving up our struggle for justice; we are now focusing on public education. We have a twelve-minute documentary called *Frozen Caution*, which is available from a Toronto distributor. Our application to the Supreme Court of Canada, asking them to hear our appeal, has been granted. We hope the appeal can be heard soon, as the Ontario government continues to build all-season roads into our wilderness areas, which will be clear-cut by the logging companies. We are financially broke and in debt, thus preventing us from seeking injunctions to stop the clear-cutting and all-season bush roads; any funds we now raise will be targeted for the appeal procedures. Lawyers have highlighted the serious problems we will have in convincing the Supreme Court of Canada that four judges from Ontario are wrong in their findings against us. The particular problem is that Justice Steele, the trial judge, carefully constructed his decision in such a way as to protect his interpretation of the facts. This is important because the Supreme Court of Canada does not ordinarily read the trial transcript and could therefore base its deliberations on Justice Steele's interpretations. Despite this negative viewpoint, that we have almost no chance of success, some of our people still hold on to hope that the Supreme Court of Canada will agree that we have not surrendered our ancient homeland to anyone. Should we be successful or not in the Supreme Court of Canada, we intend to maintain our honour and integrity as our forefathers have done in dealing with the

Crown since 1763. We began our struggle for justice in 1877, and after 112 years, have no intention of giving up. Who can lie for 112 years? We can't; we have not and never will. This land is our land, as well as that our descendants 6,000 years from now; there is no other motherland for us on earth. Our principle of sharing with all people will continue, a commitment based on the principles of Sustained Life, Sustained Development, and Stewardship.

> *Our story is a story of human beings.*
> *Our story is a story of struggle.*
> *Our story is a story of injustice.*
> *Our story is a story of peace-time genocide.*
> *Our history is a part of Canada's history.*
> *Our future is a part of Canada's future.*

THE LUBICON
OF NORTHERN
ALBERTA

THE CONFRONTATION

On October 15, 1988, the Cree people of Lubicon Lake in northern Alberta, after more than a decade of fruitless negotiation about their land claims, established a blockade on roads leading into their traditional lands. Three days earlier they had declared, in the name of the Lubicon Lake Indian Nation, "jurisdiction, ownership, management, control and administration" of their traditional lands, and promulgated a law forbidding exploration, drilling, mining, extraction of gas and oil, and logging, and restricting access to the territory.

Six days before that the Lubicon had formally withdrawn from all legal proceedings, having decided no longer to recognize the jurisdiction of Canadian courts to pronounce on "our aboriginal rights or any other matters within our unceded traditional area."

After five days of blockade the RCMP arrived with a force of fifty officers, smashing the barricades and arresting twenty-seven people. Two days later Chief Bernard Ominayak and Alberta premier Don Getty agreed on establishment of a 250-sq. km (95 square mile) reserve, conditional upon agreement with the federal government.

On January 24, 1989, after three months of negotiation with the federal government, the Lubicon, frustrated again by federal double-dealing, refused a "final federal take-it-or-leave-it offer"; at time of writing, their struggle for a secure land base continues.

Wrestling with the Canadian System: A Decade of Lubicon Frustration

Boyce Richardson

*B*Y OCTOBER 1988, when the people of Lubicon Lake formally denied Canadian jurisdiction over their traditional lands and withdrew from all Canadian court proceedings, they had already spent nearly fourteen years trying to defend themselves by pursuing their cause through the Canadian justice system.

To say they had got absolutely nowhere in this struggle would be an understatement. In fact, during those fourteen years they were stripped of their traditional economy, reduced to penury, and plunged into a social and economic crisis caused by the ruthless seizure of their lands by the Province of Alberta and countless oil companies, with the knowledge and consent of Canada.

They had pursued all avenues of redress that are supposedly available through Canadian legal and political institutions, and had arrived at a bitter awareness that they had no hope of defending their legitimate aboriginal rights by this route.

Foiled at home, they had taken their case to the United Nations Committee on Human Rights, which had instructed

Canada to do no further irreparable damage to the traditional Lubicon lands and way of life, pending determination of their aboriginal rights. But Canada ignored that decision, and Alberta continued to exploit their lands.

Their story is a case-book example of the frustrations native people in Canada have always encountered in dealing with the federal and provincial governments. Right up to time of writing, the Lubicon people have had to confront, on a daily and weekly basis, spread out over many years, an antagonist — the white power structure — that will not give an inch of ground without a fight, one ready to use every delaying tactic in the book, and every legal and political manoeuvre that can be dreamed up. The story of the Lubicon struggle calls into question, to say the least, the integrity and honesty of the people and institutions, supposedly operating in the name of the Canadian people, that they have had to grapple with.

Though the Lubicon, under Chief Bernard Ominayak, have always maintained that Canadian government and courts have no jurisdiction over their lands, from 1973 on they entered into court proceedings in an effort, as they said, to compel the Canadian government to obey its own laws.

By 1988 it was evident that this was a hopeless effort: they now realized it would take millions of dollars and years and years of time (neither of which they could afford) to squeeze any kind of decision about their aboriginal rights out of the Canadian court system.

So, in October 1988, they turned their backs on the whole process.

They did not believe that, as the press suggested, they were taking the law into their own hands; as far as they were concerned, they were simply acting on what they knew to be true; namely, that they have never relinquished their status as a separate nation. And they decided that the time had come to exercise their jurisdiction over lands that they had never given up.

The claim of the Alberta government to jurisdiction over the Lubicon land relies upon the Alberta Natural Resources Transfer Agreement of 1930, which transferred vast tracts of unpatented Crown land (unpatented land is land that has never been assigned to anyone) from federal-government to provincial-government jurisdiction. In other words, Alberta says it obtained jurisdiction from the federal government.

The federal government, in turn, claims to have obtained rights to these lands through negotiation of Treaty 8 in 1899. However, the federal negotiators at that time did not enter the traditional Lubicon area, and they didn't negotiate any treaty with the Lubicon people. This is why they now claim that their jurisdiction over their traditional lands continues. The two levels of Canadian government do not agree with this.

The way such disputes were resolved in the past was through negotiation of a treaty between the aboriginal group and the federal government. This process has never been an ideal one from the native point of view, but it does at least establish some minimal requirements for the taking of aboriginal land that the federal government is supposedly obliged to follow.

The Lubicon Lake people have been willing to negotiate a settlement of their aboriginal rights not because they particularly want to, but because, as in many other parts of Canada, they really don't have much choice. As Chief Ominayak has said, however, though they are willing to negotiate, "we are not prepared to allow Canadian governments and oil companies to wipe us off the face of the earth," in violation of even the minimal requirements laid down by Canadian law for dealing with aboriginal lands.

Since the signing of Treaty 8 in 1899 and the land transfers of 1930, both levels of government have proceeded as if the federal government had negotiated treaty with the Lubicon, had properly obtained the rights to Lubicon lands, and had therefore been able to transfer these rights to Alberta.

The Lubicon say they never signed treaty. They never took scrip (given in payment to non-status people for their rights in land). They never sold their land. They never lost it in battle. They never ceded it to anybody.

In fact, it was not until 1939 that officials of the Indian Affairs department ever visited their area. Then, these officials recognized the Lubicon as a separate band, and promised them a reserve of their own. The Lubicon selected land at the western end of Lubicon Lake. This was approved in 1940. The land was held by Alberta for several years against the day it would be declared a reserve, but was never surveyed.

A People Who Would Not Disappear

The fact is that, during all of this century, the federal government has treated the Lubicon as if they were a people who would magically disappear, thus, the government hoped, forestalling the embarrassment of having to deal with them. When they did not disappear, the government moved heaven and earth to make them do so. For example, for years games were played by federal officials with band membership lists. Some Lubicon people were added to the membership lists of other bands early in the century, and then, in 1942, an Ottawa civil servant arbitrarily decided that many of them were not really Indians. The full story of this transaction is shocking: the civil servant's actions were denounced by two judicial commissions of inquiry, yet, beavering away in the Ottawa office, the man responsible for the injustices was able to ensure that these two reports were buried, and no action was taken to restore people to band membership.

All this would be of no importance, perhaps, except that, in the 1980s, forty years after these people were unjustly removed from the band lists, the government has been trying to restrict the size of the Lubicon reserve by arguing that many of their people are not entitled to be considered members of the Lubicon band.

The government has fiddled about with the size of the land to be retained, too. When it was brought to the attention of the federal government in 1952 that the reserve promised in 1940 had never been surveyed, a new generation of officials declared it would be inconvenient to administer a reserve in such an isolated, inaccessible place as Lubicon Lake. At that time pressure was brought by both governments to get the Lubicon to accept a reserve in a more convenient place. A departmental letter of the time reveals the motive: "There were so many inquiries from oil companies to explore the area that it was becoming embarrassing to state that it could not be entered." Other people now wanted the mineral rights, which both governments admitted were included in the land originally agreed upon in 1940. But no mineral rights would be included with any land except that originally agreed upon. So, there is one good reason for not accepting an alternative site.

The governments certainly knew what they were trying to do. "In approaching the subject with Indians," wrote the regional director to a local Indian agent, "I think it would be well to keep in mind that the mineral rights may be very much more valuable than anything else, and if the Indians were deprived of these rights, they could make it very unpleasant for Branch officials." This is the language of, one might say, cautious theft.

When the Lubicon rejected this generous offer, Alberta demanded, in 1953, from the federal government an answer about the reserve's location within thirty days or the land would be struck from the record.

Having failed to con the Lubicon out of the land they wanted, in the next few years federal officials put their major effort into trying to eliminate them as a separate band. The officials now began to question the validity of their separate existence, which they had accepted in 1939, and continued to transfer members to other band lists, at the same time encouraging Lubicon people to enfranchise (that is, to abandon Indian status).

A letter of the time from the regional Indian Affairs supervisor was very explicit about the strategy:

> The Whitefish band have no objection to [the Lubicon Lake people] being transferred...to their band, and I am suggesting to [the local Indian agent] to contact those members [of the Lubicon Lake band] who are at present residing at Whitefish and Grouard and ascertain if they wish to file application for transfer. If they all wish to transfer it would reduce the Lubicon Lake band membership to approximately 30 and if the remainder cannot be persuaded to transfer, their land requirement would be much less that the present membership would be entitled to.

The archives of Canadian history are full of such information, in relation to the way Indians have been treated, but only now are such facts being researched, as has been done by the Lubicon in preparation of their case. This is giving us a whole new perspective on the history of our nation.

These various strategies failed, and in 1973 the existence of the Lubicon as a separate band was reaffirmed by order-in-council. But these long-term efforts to make the Lubicon disappear were not without their effect: some band members have never been added to the treaty list; others were removed and never reinstated. Some enfranchised. Some are on the lists of other bands, even though they were born, raised, and consider themselves members of Lubicon Lake band, and are not considered by the other bands to be their members.

Yet, all of these manoeuvrings didn't really bother the Lubicon much until a few years ago. Their area was relatively isolated and inaccessible by road. They were left pretty much alone, and had little contact with provincial officials, federal officials, or outsiders generally.

The Invasion from Outside Begins

That began to change when in 1971 the province started to build an all-weather road into their traditional lands as part of a plan by the Lougheed government to open up northern Alberta for resource exploitation. The Lubicon joined together with people from five other northern Alberta communities — Chipewyan Lake, Sandy Lake, Trout Lake, Peerless Lake, and Loon Lake — to press a joint land claim over a huge area of north-central Alberta, of some 65,000 square kilometres 65,750 sq. km (25,000 square miles), roughly bounded by the Athabasca River in the east, the Peace River in the west, Buffalo Head Hills and Wood Buffalo National Park in the north, and roughly on a parallel with, and slightly north of, Lesser Slave Lake in the south.

None of these communities had taken part in Treaty 8, or received reserve lands, and their traditional lands included several large tar-sand deposits, as well as large reserves of oil and gas.

The government had a land-claims commissioner at the time, Dr. Lloyd Barber, who went north and took evidence from people showing that there were in existence identifiable groups and bands of Indians who exercised dominant control over their traditional lands, and that representatives of these bands and groups did not take part in the treaty-making process.

These isolated communities decided to file a caveat with the Northern Alberta Land Registration District, putting outsiders on notice that they retained aboriginal title. The effect of such a caveat, if accepted, would have been to place a caution against development of such lands, and to preserve the state of title while any court action was being argued.

The caveat was entered on October 27, 1975, and it could be said that, from that date, the Lubicon entered what might be called the modern era of renewed bad faith, manipulation, and judicial and political double-talk, which eventually brought them to take the extreme measure of blockading entry to their lands.

At first the federal government gave the impression that, as trustee for the native interest, it would help them in the legal proceedings. The registrar decided to ask the Supreme Court of

Alberta whether he was obliged to accept the caveat, because, he claimed, aboriginal rights had not been proved. The Lubicon then applied to the federal government for funding for the case, and were amazed to discover that the federal government intended to enter the case, but not in their defence. Ottawa came in on the side of the Alberta government, arguing that the caveat should not be allowed. Evidently, with a protector like this, the natives were in deep trouble.

Decision on this issue was postponed for more than a year until the Supreme Court of Canada decided on a similar case in the Northwest Territories. That case went against the Indians. But the court intimated that the Indian caveat there would have succeeded had there been a provision in NWT law, as there was in Alberta law, for the filing of caveats against unpatented Crown land.

The specific mention of Alberta in the NWT judgment made it clear that caveats could be entered in that province against unpatented Crown land. As most of the Lubicon land was of this type, according to their legal advice the only issue that would have to be decided was whether aboriginal title was the kind of issue that could be registered in the form of a caveat.

If there were those among the Lubicon who retained any faith in the Canadian system of law, so cherished as one of the enduring values of Canadian society, they now received a rude awakening. A year and a half after they had filed, a hearing on the acceptability of caveat was scheduled for March 28, 1977. The court had postponed hearing the case at the request of the Alberta government, which said it wanted to tidy up a few loose ends in the law. Three days before the hearing, they tidied it up, but good!

They not only eliminated from the law the provision that caveats could be entered against unpatented Crown land, but made the change retrospective to a date before the filing of the Lubicon claim. Tidy indeed! Having discovered a law that could have worked to their advantage, the natives now found it whipped away from under their very noses by a government that never ceased to tell them that they should work within the framework of the law.

Grave Damage from the New Roads

So, the caveat came to nothing. The all-weather road into the Lubicon lands was completed in 1978, and their years of relative peace and contentment were over.

In 1980, the Alberta government and the oil companies launched a major invasion of Lubicon lands. Dozens of oil companies began moving in, building roads, cutting seismic lines, drilling wells, putting in pipelines, and so on. They scared away (or killed) much of the game the Lubicon had always depended on for food and furs.

Between 1979 and 1982 more than 400 oil wells were drilled within a 24-km (15-mile) radius of the Lubicon community of Little Buffalo Lake. Traditional hunting and trapping trails were taken over and turned into private oil-company roads, posted with "no trespassing" signs and protected by guards and gates. Traplines were systematically bulldozed on orders from the province and oil companies. Game was deliberately chased out of the area by firing rifles into the air, a sport entered into with such enthusiasm that some workers described it as being "almost like a competition."

Between 1979 and 1983 the number of moose taken by Lubicon Lake people for food dropped from an average of more than 200 to under 20 per year. Annual income from trapping during the same period dropped from more that $5,000 per trapper to less than $400. Local hide and handicraft buyers were told not to buy from Lubicon Lake. Dependence on welfare soared from under 10 per cent in 1981 to more than 95 per cent in 1983.

Destruction of the Lubicon traditional economy and way of life was not simply the unfortunate result of contact between a traditional aboriginal society and a modern industrial state. It was the calculated result of a deliberate provincial government legal strategy.

This is how the Lubicon leaders felt it worked: the lower courts have held that those who would assert unextinguished aboriginal rights must be able to show that they continue to pursue a traditional way of life. In the view of the Lubicon, the Alberta government deliberately destroyed their economy and way of life so that their lawyers could go to court and argue that, since they no longer depended on their traditional economy, they no longer had aboriginal rights.

Another Generous Gift — Hamlet Status and Land Tenure

Government efforts to undermine the Lubicon legal position now switched to an attempted administrative and legal takeover of their communities. In 1981, the Alberta government declared the Cree community of Little Buffalo to be a provincial hamlet, divided it up into little four-fifths-hectare (two-acre) plots, and tried to get people either to lease these plots or to accept them as "gifts" from the province. People were promised services and security if they supported the hamlet and land-tenure program. Those who opposed it faced difficult consequences, including no phone service, no power, and no new housing. Some people who decided to build houses outside the so-called hamlet boundaries were told to obtain provincial leases or face having their houses bulldozed.

Chief Ominayak and the Lubicon leaders realized that to accept the provincial hamlet and land-tenure programs would jeopardize their land rights, so they asked the province to delay the program until its effect on land rights could be determined. The province refused, claiming that they had already checked this out, "and there is no relationship between land claims and land tenure."

When the leaders continued to question this finding, according to Lubicon statements of that time, the province then resorted to outright deception in an effort to get people to sign up. One old woman who could neither read nor write was told that she was signing, not for one of the plots, but for free firewood. They told another, desperately in need of adequate housing, to make her mark so she could receive a free Alberta housing trailer. They told a third that she was required to sign a census form.

At this time the provincial government publicly described the Cree of Lubicon Lake as "merely squatters on provincial Crown land," and sent them property-tax notices.

These notices stated that a 15 per cent penalty would be imposed if the taxes were not paid by a certain date, and unpaid taxes could be recovered under the provisions of two provincial acts. They did not spell out in the notices that the proposed method of recovery involved seizure and sale of assets.

Most people were financially unable to pay provincial taxes, but the pressures went even further: the property-tax assessment notice included a separate charge to support building of a new school in the community of Little Buffalo Lake. The council had opposed construction of this school because they believed it would be used by the government as proof that they were not an Indian community, but rather a provincial hamlet. They realized that once they accepted that, this "hamlet" would not be eligible to be included in the reserve lands they were fighting for.

So, in effect, with this tax demand Little Buffalo was being asked to finance a school that its people didn't want in order to bolster the province's claim to jurisdiction, which they opposed. And if they refused to finance this new school, the government was claiming the right to seize and sell up their very limited assets.

Alberta Decides They Don't Really Exist

At one point the federal government did ask Alberta for a six-month delay in the land-tenure program, but in reply the provincial minister questioned the very existence of the band, and stated that the community could not be part of a land claim because it was now a provincial hamlet and was no longer classified as unoccupied Crown land — thus confirming all the people's worst fears about what could happen if they were to sign up for the hamlet program.

In 1980, the Lubicon filed an action in the Federal Court of Canada asking for recognition of their right to the exclusive use and enjoyment of their traditional lands, including mineral rights, naming both levels of government and a number of oil companies as defendants. A promise by the federal minister of Indian Affairs to provide seven communities with $1 million to allow this action to be pursued was quickly withdrawn. The court held it had no jurisdiction over the provincial government and oil companies, but allowed the action to stand against the federal government and Petro-Canada, the oil company owned by the federal government.

Meantime the Office of Native Claims and the federal Justice department agreed that the Lubicon should indeed have land, with mineral rights, located where it had originally been selected, and said that, in addition, they were prepared to discuss special hunting and trapping rights, membership problems, and the possibility of special programs. Believing that there was now sufficient common ground to justify negotiations, the federal government decided to involve the province, and a federal-provincial meeting was held in January 1982.

To use the idiom of Hollywood, this introduced to the Lubicon the good cop–bad cop syndrome, with the federal government appearing for the moment as a good cop. The province, however, played the role of bad cop to the hilt: they rejected out of hand most of the points under discussion. They refused to consider land entitlement until they were first satisfied as to its merits. They refused to agree on a timetable for determining those merits. They refused to consider the land originally selected, or to include the traditional community of Little Buffalo Lake. They refused to include mineral rights. They refused to consider compensation. They even refused to meet with representatives of the band.

So, in February 1982, the Lubicon initiated a second legal action, this time in the Alberta Court of Queen's Bench, asking for a declaration that they retained aboriginal rights over their traditional lands; that these rights included mineral rights, that they were under federal jurisdiction; and that the gas and oil permits granted by the province were null, void, and unconstitutional, or at least subject to Indian rights.

In addition they asked the court for an immediate injunction preventing the oil companies from undertaking further development in the area. This application for an injunction dragged on for years: as it dragged on, the damage that the Lubicon feared was done.

Heads We Win, Tails You Lose

First, the province argued that the Crown was immune from injunction. Even the oil companies made the same case, arguing that they were merely agents of the provincial government. The court found in the Cree's favour on that one, so the provincial and oil-company lawyers entered a raft of procedural objections. They argued that the injunction application should not be heard, even if all it claimed were true, because the damage wasn't really irreparable. The trees would grow back. But, even if the damage was irreparable, they said, the case should not be heard because such irreparable damages claimed could still be compensated with money. Further, even if the damage was irreparable and could not be compensated with money, the case should not be heard because an injunction would have such a detrimental effect on the provincial economy. And, finally, they said the injunction should not be heard because, even if everything said about the destruction of the Lubicon economy and way of life was true, they might still lose the main action (calling for recognition of aboriginal rights) and if they did, they would never be able to repay the provincial government and the oil companies for the revenue lost through the application of an injunction.

No one could say that the province did not oppose the injunction with enthusiasm, root-and-branch.

I do not want to weary readers with too much detail, but there may be no other conflict in Canada that so precisely illustrates the disadvantages that aboriginal peoples confront when they try to achieve justice through the established legal system. Everything appears to be stacked against them, and it is only by examination of the details that one can grasp the full enormity of their problem.

The arguments of the province and oil companies were basically procedural arguments, which are normally decided from the Bench. As the Lubicon have explained in submissions to the United Nations, the judge in this case was a former oil-company lawyer. The three months during which he pondered his decision coincided with the winter development season of the oil companies, when they move into new areas and construct roads that will enable them to proceed with development throughout the year. So, while this former oil-company lawyer considered the matter, the companies were accomplishing the very things that the Cree were seeking to prevent through their application for an injunction. This is justice?

They beat back these procedural arguments, and were granted a hearing of their application for an emergency or interlocutory injunction. That hearing was held in September and October 1983, immediately before the oil companies' next winter season. Sworn affidavits were submitted from community elders, an anthropologist, a wildlife biologist, an ecologist, and others about traditional ways of life and the adverse effect development activity was having on them. Government and oil companies submitted no evidence at all on traditional life, basically asserting that it was now the twentieth century and any traditional way of life that may have existed had long since disappeared, and that any decline in the catch was the result of natural causes, such as moose ticks and the hare cycle. The government, of course, also argued that the Lubicon had no aboriginal rights and that a hunting right could not override a development right.

The former oil-company lawyer, now provincial judge, agreed with the oil companies and declined to grant the injunction, since he concluded — despite uncontested evidence to the contrary — that no traditional way of life had been shown.

The story gets worse. The Lubicon then appealed this judgment to the Alberta Court of Appeal, where Chief Justice McGillivray put himself at the head of a three-judge panel to consider the case. Before becoming a judge he had been the lawyer for the family of Alberta premier Peter Lougheed, and indeed had given Mr. Lougheed his first job in his Calgary law firm. A senior member of that law firm was now the senior oil-company lawyer on the case. Before the law, where all are supposed to be equal, one cannot escape the feeling that some may be more equal than others.

Chief Justice McGillivray died before hearing the case, but the court, predictably, decided against granting an injunction because, according to the learned judges, the natives would be able to restore the wilderness with money paid in damages if they were ever able to prove that they retained continuing aboriginal title in the area. This is justice?

The Lubicon then appealed for an emergency injunction to the Supreme Court of Canada, but that court declined to hear the case, without bothering to say why. Again a three-judge panel was involved. In practice these three judges operate on the basis of consensus, and unless they all agree, cases are not accepted for hearing. One can hardly avoid observing that here again, the cards seemed less than equally stacked. One of the three judges was another former oil-company lawyer, who has since retired from the court and been appointed to the board of a large western Canadian petrochemical conglomerate based in Alberta, with significant interests in the traditional Lubicon area.

The Supreme Court's refusal to hear the case seemed notable, especially when, two weeks after the Lubicon were refused leave to appeal, the British Columbia Court of Appeal granted an emergency injunction sought by another band in a case that was virtually identical. The B.C. Court of Appeal concluded that native rights would be adversely affected if development were allowed to continue on Meares Island, on the west coast, rejected argument that the developers would suffer economically, and said that a solution must be found through "a reasonable exchange" with the Indians in the area. The Lubicon lawyers then went back to the Supreme Court of Canada to point out the discrepancies between the B.C. and Alberta appeal court judgments, and asked for reconsideration of the decision not to hear their appeal. That same justice who has since retired into the embrace of the resource industry said the Supreme Court has a rule against rehearing applications for leave to appeal, and dismissed the renewed application without even hearing argument.

Goodbye to the Courts

This virtually slammed the door shut on the Lubicons' hope for justice through the legal system. Since it had become obvious they could in all likelihood never get justice through this route, they began increasingly to press their case outside the usual political and legal channels, and internationally. They had previously asked the World Council of Churches to investigate, and that body had come to the conclusion that the actions of Alberta and the oil companies "could have genocidal consequences."

The World Council's Commission to Combat Racism, after visiting the Lubicon, decided that the hamlet and land-tenure programs of the Alberta government would "effectively wipe out any remaining ability they [the Lubicon people] might have to withstand the provincial and oil company effort to undermine and subvert traditional and aboriginal rights."

The Council wrote to Prime Minister Trudeau:

> The situation of the band and band members is...desperate, crucial and urgent. They know no other way to live. They have no money, many have never been out of their traditional area. Many speak only Cree. Many neither read nor write. None have completed Grade 11. Those who try to pursue a different lifestyle will both deny their heritage and break their traditional bond with the land, an essential legal requirement of their aboriginal claim.
>
> They are literally in a struggle for their very existence as a people with the rich and politically powerful Alberta provincial government, and with dozens of multinational oil companies, each of which possesses more resources than many nation states. They cannot be expected to achieve a just and fair settlement of their legitimate rights and claims without help. They cannot be expected to survive as a people unless they receive immediate financial, political and legal help.

In July 1985 the Lubicon filed a formal complaint to the U.N. Committee on Human Rights, alleging that Canada was in breach of international undertakings on human rights because of their denial of the right to self-determination.

The international interest in the Lubicon's plight stimulated both levels of government into heavy-handed and cumbersome defence of their actions. Alberta set their ombudsman to investigate the Lubicon claims that the provincial government had acted improperly; but he specifically excluded from his investigation anything related to the land claim, which lies at the base of everything that had been done. Also he said he could not investigate the actions of the oil companies, which were destroying the Lubicon way of life. What the oil companies were doing was the basis of the charge made by the World Council of Churches that there could be "genocidal consequences." But, in spite of not investigating these things, the ombudsman found there was no factual basis for the World Council's charges. Some investigation!

Canada — The Lubicon Are Not "a People"

Canada, of course, denied the allegations made to the U.N. committee. They said the Lubicon did not constitute "a people" and were not entitled to assert the right of self-determination. They described them as a "thinly scattered minority group living within the midst of a more numerous population grouping, and occupying territory co-extensive with that grouping." Furthermore, Canada argued that the Lubicon had not exhausted all domestic remedies, because the substantive issue of their aboriginal rights had never been heard by the Canadian courts.

In response the Lubicon argued again that, because of the Canadian government's failure to intervene on their behalf, the people had effectively been deprived of their means of subsistence, their economy had been decimated, their culture was in disintegration, and "any final judgment recognizing aboriginal rights or...treaty rights can never restore the way of life, livelihood and means of subsistence of the band.

"The government of Canada has completely ignored this fundamental issue of the immediately threatened and imminent extinction of the band's means of subsistence and way of life."

In response to Canada's denial of any act of genocide, the Lubicon reminded the committee that genocide, as officially defined by the U.N. convention, includes acts that "deliberately inflict on the group conditions of life calculated to bring about its physical destruction in whole or in part." They put forward the view that Alberta and the oil companies had acted with a clear intent to destroy the people's means of subsistence and the cultural base that binds them together as a group. Canada had refused to act "with full knowledge that these actions were bringing about the rapid and thorough destruction" of this economic and cultural base, and it was at least arguable that this negligence could be considered a basis for holding Canada responsible "for the genocidal (or at minimum, ethnocidal, that is, cultural genocide) actions of one of its provinces."

The Lubicon did not gain the committee's backing for their full argument, but the committee did decide that their claim that they couldn't achieve effective political or legal redress within Canada was admissible, something that Canada had sought to prevent.

Gradually, by assiduous and indeed indefatigable effort, the Lubicon managed to make a broad range of contacts across North America and Europe, with other aboriginal groups, churches, universities, environment and human-rights organizations, and others. This brought about growing public awareness and concern about the fate of this small group of aboriginal people struggling against such terrible odds in northern Alberta; and this concern put pressure on the government to do something.

A Brief Breath of Hope

With the election of the new Canadian government in 1984 came what seemed to be a hopeful development. The Lubicon gave the new Indian Affairs minister, David Crombie, a list of the vital points at issue and of the elements of a solution, as they saw it: the minister then appointed E. Davie Fulton, a former federal Justice minister, former judge of the B.C. Supreme Court, and a distinguished Canadian jurist, to conduct an investigation and try to suggest possible solutions, a task he undertook with the agreement of all parties.

Mr. Fulton took evidence from both levels of government and from the Cree, checked that evidence, did his own independent research into the issues, and delivered his conclusions to the government in the form of a discussion paper. A further round of negotiations was to be based on his paper.

He investigated the major problems that the natives brought to his attention — land entitlement, subsurface rights, wildlife and environmental management, compensation for past and future losses, membership, and so on — outlined the positions of all parties, and recommended possible ways to a solution. He realized there was a fundamental disagreement between the Cree insistence that their claim rests on their aboriginal right, and Alberta and Canada's refusal to consider that as a basis for negotiations. But he was flexible on the question of band membership, and from the Lubicon point of view, this was important.

Here is why: for many years the Lubicon had argued that in the matter of land they should be treated no differently from the Indians who signed Treaty 8. These Indians had determined their own membership, and thus were able to include persons of aboriginal ancestry with family ties and ties to their traditional areas. Reserve lands were then determined by population at the time of first survey.

Chief Ominayak had always claimed that his people should have the right to do the same, to determine their own membership. Fulton reported that the band claimed a membership of at least 347, with more than 400 eligible when recent changes to the Indian Act were taken into account. Canada claimed the band had only 183 registered members, but admitted the figure could rise to between 350 and 400 when Bill C-31 returned many non-status people to band membership.

Given these figures, under the treaty formula of 51 hectares (128 acres) per person, the band argued, they were entitled to at least 240 sq. km (95 square miles) of their traditional territory as a reserve.

Alberta's position was that they were prepared to transfer the 67 sq. km (25.4 square miles) at the western end of Lubicon Lake agreed to as a reserve in 1940 — an area that was calculated on the basis on a band membership of only 127. The federal government agreed that the land area should be based on current population figures determined after the passing of Bill C-31. Mr. Fulton himself favoured a figure of about 400. According to this, the reserve would be more than 210 sq. km (80 square miles). At least with such figures they were beginning to play in the same ballpark.

Unfortunately, Alberta adopted a hard position: if the amount of land claimed was based on any population figure above 127, they reserved the right to challenge the whole basis of the calculation, including the 1940 figure. Because of their hostility on this issue, the Lubicon refused to share with Alberta the genealogical research that they had carried out in 1984 with the federal government.

Fulton agreed with Alberta that Canada was entirely responsible for the fact that the reserve was not established in 1940. He suggested, therefore, that any land above the original figure of 66 square kilometres (25.4 square miles) should be compensated for by the federal government. (In the end the Lubicon's position in relation to membership was vindicated: four years later, after a period of intense confrontation, Alberta and Canada agreed that the reserve, when established, should be 250 sq. km/95 square miles).

Though they had many reservations about Fulton's conclusions, the Lubicon were pleased that in many areas he confirmed their claims: specifically, he held that subsurface rights should be transferred with all reserve lands; that wildlife- and environmental-management programs in the whole of the Lubicon territory should be accepted in principle; that the Lubicon were reasonably entitled to first consideration for employment in new oil and gas development in their territory; that compensation should be paid for resource revenues not received in the reserve lands promised but not given in 1940; that compensation was due for facilities not provided in the areas of housing and community infrastructure, because of the delay in establishing the reserve, and also for "the substantial and damaging decline" in their income from traditional activities, caused by resource development.

The Governments Get Rid of Mr. Fulton

Lubicon spokesmen said they were ready to continue the negotiations on the basis of this discussion paper, and they expected that these negotiations would be conducted by Mr. Fulton himself. But, once again, they encountered a major frustration. The Alberta government simply refused to discuss Mr. Fulton's paper with him. In fact, four days after he delivered his paper they called a press conference to announce that they had settled the Lubicon land rights, with an offer to transfer less than a third of the reserve land proposed by Mr. Fulton. They claimed this had been accepted by the federal minister, though the minister himself said he had rejected it.

Ten days after that the senior civil servant in Indian Affairs, Bruce Rawson, dropped another bombshell: he told the Cree he was already discussing with the Alberta government dropping Mr. Fulton from all further discussions. It was now time to "move beyond" Mr. Fulton, he said. He did not see Mr. Fulton as playing a useful future role, and was not much interested in the band's recommendation as to what Mr. Fulton should do next.

While this was happening, strangely enough the minster, Mr. Crombie, continued to express confidence in Mr. Fulton and instructed him to proceed to the next stage.

Much of the early work done by the Lubicon in putting forward their grievances had been paid for with a bank loan underwritten by the Cree of James Bay, Quebec, but, at about this time, Crombie arranged for the Lubicon to receive $1.5 million, against part of the legal costs and other expenses (although excluding the cost of the court proceedings) that they had accumulated during their decade of fruitless struggle for justice.

But Crombie's authority as a minister appeared to be disintegrating.

Six weeks or so after Mr. Fulton delivered his discussion paper, it became clear, as a Lubicon statement of the time said, that Crombie was no longer relevant to decision-making in his own department. Fulton was out, and so, by April 1986, was Crombie, presumably because he had undertaken a number of initiatives, such as the Fulton inquiry, that might conceivably have led to some just settlements of aboriginal issues in various parts of the country.

A new federal negotiator, Roger Tassé, was soon appointed, with the assurance that negotiations would proceed on the basis of the Fulton discussion paper. But, in July 1986, when the Lubicon had their first formal meeting with Tassé, they found that the rules of the game had been arbitrarily changed again. After making a little speech about his personal commitment to justice and equality, Mr. Tassé announced he was prepared to talk only to those Lubicon people who were recognized as "Indians" by the federal government before the passing of Bill C-31. Any others who thought they had claims could go to court, he said.

The meeting lasted less than an hour: the Lubicon told him they were not prepared to sacrifice the rights of any of their people, members of their own families, as a prerequisite for even talking with him. He then announced that these putative negotiations had supposedly broken down, and for the rest of the year flooded the country with what the Lubicon in their press statements called "a tissue of falsehoods": for example, that the Lubicon were trying to obtain more land than they were entitled to by adding "non-Indians" to their membership lists; that the federal government was trying to settle, but the Lubicon were refusing to negotiate; that disappearance of the game from their traditional territory was not the result of development activity, but of Lubicon overhunting. In the game of good cop–bad cop, the feds had now taken over the role of bad cop.

Early in 1986, the Lubicon began their campaign for a boycott of the Olympic Games, and more particularly of the art exhibition, "The Spirit Sings," mounted by the Glenbow Museum of Calgary and financed by the very oil companies that were destroying Lubicon life. They made successful trips to

Europe, receiving the support of many organizations and museums. Their intervention there was so successful, indeed, that many of Canada's embassies began to put out propaganda designed to counter the story of their long struggle (by now widely understood in Europe), and the growing support for their boycott. The campaign may not have halted the games or the exhibition, but it certainly raised the consciousness of many people, and confronted many Canadian and other museums with a crisis of conscience that was long overdue.

The Canadian government certainly was displeased, and at one point even refused to resume negotiations unless these international publicity efforts were halted.

A year later, Mr. Tassé was replaced; he never met with the Lubicon again, and never even acknowledged receipt of a letter they sent him reiterating their willingness to proceed with negotiations using the Fulton discussion paper as a basis.

Tuberculosis, Alcoholism, Suicide — New Companions

The year 1987 produced terrible proof of the impact that resource development was having on the Lubicon people. Oil companies were taking something like $1 million a day out of their lands, but their people were becoming destitute and disoriented. They began to experience the first suicides they had ever known. Family breakdown and alcoholism and other addictions began to affect many people, and in the last half of the year there was an outbreak of tuberculosis, a disease directly linked to poor housing, lack of sanitation, unclean water, overcrowding — in short, poverty. By the end of the year 37 people were under treatment and almost 100 more had been exposed to a disease that had supposedly disappeared from Canada in the 1950s.

In October 1987, Brian Malone, a Calgary lawyer, was appointed to replace Tassé as federal negotiator, and he brought with him yet another change of tactics. He now said Tassé's approach had been wrong because he had failed to involve the Alberta government as a full party. They should be there,

Malone said, because Alberta "holds title to the land." The Lubicon disagreed: like other aboriginal people in Canada, they believe their business is with the federal government only, because Canada is responsible for the undertakings given by the Crown in the Royal Proclamation of 1763 and in the treaties.

Certainly the Lubicon never had any doubt that their settlement had to be with the federal government, and they refused to concede to the new negotiator the right of Alberta to be at their meetings. They had become convinced that the provincial government wanted only to block negotiations for an equitable settlement, while the federal government wished to use provincial involvement as a means of avoiding its own responsibility. This became a big sticking issue in 1987 and 1988.

Late in 1987 came yet another body blow: the very minister who was supposedly responsible for protecting Indians announced (in his capacity as minister responsible for the Western Economic Diversification Program) that a huge pulp mill was to be built in Peace River, near Lubicon territory. The mill would have a capacity of 910 tonnes (1,000 tons) a day, and would feed the paper mills of Daishowa Canada Ltd., a Japan-based pulp-and-paper company. The trees to be used were on Lubicon traditional lands, but the federal government view was that the Lubicon had no right to these trees.

The Lubicon feared that logging on the scale needed to feed such a mill would be yet another nail in the coffin of their traditional rights and of the way of life that was now in process of crumbling.

They felt the minister was in evident conflict of interest, promoting the destruction of the very people he was supposed to protect. But that didn't worry him, and at the beginning of 1988 timber-cutting rights were granted to 30,000 sq. km (11,400 square miles), mostly in Lubicon lands, to the Daishowa company. To add insult to injury, the Japanese company was granted $65 million in subsidy by the province, and $9.5 million by the federal government, the same government that said it could not afford to pay reasonable compensation for the losses the Lubicon had suffered through federal negligence over many decades, particularly since 1940.

The feds were now settling down into their bad-cop role with a vengeance. In December 1987, they took the law into their own hands and announced that they were actively negotiating a settlement of Lubicon land rights with the province, but without any involvement of the Lubicon people. Malone said he had no choice since the Cree had refused to talk to the province. He claimed to have the right to do this by virtue of Treaty 8 (even though that treaty clearly stipulates that reserve lands are to be set aside by the federal government only after "consulting with the Indians concerned").

It was in response to this squeeze play that Chief Ominayak began to make it clear that he was being forced into a situation in which his people would have no choice but to assert jurisdiction over their traditional lands. On January 21, 1988, the Indian Affairs minister, Bill McKnight, gave him eight days to agree to provincial involvement, or, he said, he would call a federal inquiry to determine the Lubicon land entitlement without their involvement. On February 1, he said the deadline was past; but now he said that he might take the province to court to settle the claims.

The Provincial Premier Comes to Life

This brought Alberta premier Don Getty to life, and Chief Ominayak met with him to discuss what was obviously a worsening situation. Getty proposed that a binding tribunal be created to resolve any questions that could not be agreed with the federal government. Ominayak agreed to Getty's suggestions, but McKnight would not. So again they met: Getty now suggested an advisory, not a binding, tribunal. Again Ominayak agreed. Again McKnight refused.

By this time it seemed that the province was beginning to slip into the role of the good cop in this little chamber-of-horrors drama. But the bad cop was now unstoppable. In May, McKnight asked the provincial Court of Queen's Bench to declare that the Lubicon are covered by the 1899 Treaty 8, and that, therefore, they are "entitled" to a reserve under the provisions of that treaty. He also asked the court to agree that the size of this reserve should be decided by a membership formula never before employed in Canada, to determine aboriginal land rights. He said he was forced to go to court because of Ominayak's refusal to negotiate with the province. Yet, the situation now was that Ominayak and Getty had agreed to a framework for negotiations, but McKnight was bulldozing ahead to get the matter back into the courts.

The upcoming election must have had something to do with it: if the matter was before the courts, it might, with any luck, not become an embarrassment for the government during the election. But, naturally, putting the case back into court didn't work either: the courtroom itself became just another arena in which the issue was argued, and in August, McKnight wrote to Ominayak expressing concern about his assertion of jurisdiction and "about the time it may now take a court to decide." As an alternative he now proposed suspension of the government's legal action, and establishment of "a forum for addressing the band's grievances," including appointment of a mutually acceptable independent mediator.

This had truly become theatre of the absurd.

And things simply became more and more absurd as the year dragged on. The silliest item on the program was the dance of the accepted-and-rejected mediators. The federal government first suggested as mediator a Supreme Court justice known for his fairness and independence, a hopeful sign. But when the Lubicon accepted this suggested candidate, this man was suddenly declared unacceptable to the federal government, supposedly because of "some negative vibrations from higher up." Several more names were then suggested by the federal government, accepted by Chief Ominayak, but then withdrawn. On the native side they began to get the distinct feeling that the feds were interested more in creating the illusion that they were serious about negotiating than in actually negotiating.

Next they hired a Calgary public-relations man to be their new spokesman on Lubicon affairs, and he kept repeating that the two sides just couldn't agree on a mediator. But the federal government rejected all of the candidates the Lubicon put forward, while the Lubicon accepted four of the proposed federal candidates, only to have three of them later withdrawn by the government (the fourth was, in the end, unavailable). This sort of thing went on into October, with the feds stalling and adding names to the proposed list.

Assertion of Jurisdiction and Sovereignty

On September 21, Chief Ominayak announced that the Lubicon were ready to assert their own jurisdiction, which would involve check points and blockades on four routes leading into their traditional territory, if the government did not agree to a settlement by October 15.

As that day approached they received the support of many Canadians who could no longer believe the federal government's protestations of good intentions. For example, the Edmonton Inter-church Committee on the North urged its members to lobby the federal government for a negotiated settlement, and failing that to hold a two-day prayer vigil in the days before the blockades were established.

The spectacle of this huge federal government screwing the natives' noses into the dust was too much even for the editorial writers of the nation, and such words as "abomination," "shameful," and "cynical" were used in many editorials to describe what was going on.

Almost everyone who looked into the situation came to the same conclusion. For example, just before the assertion of jurisdiction, James G. Smith, curator of ethnology at the

Museum of the American Indian in New York, gave an excellent description of what had happened.

He noted that in fall 1988 the Lubicon had been able to take only about 10 moose, compared with 200 they used to take in the days of their isolation, only a decade before. He said:

> Moose hunting for these people was like whale hunting for the Inuit, or buffalo hunting for the Plains Indians. Take it away and you drastically change the nature of the society.
>
> The disaster came with the highway, and the oil roads, white hunters and so on. The whole subsistence base was knocked out, not just involving foods, but in the cultural sense as well. The moose is the basis of the status system among the men. Killing a moose was the event that changed a boy into a man. A good hunter had a prized place in society. This was what men did. Take this away and you destroy the prestige system, the status system.
>
> Now the men go hunting day after day and come back with nothing. The older women who know how to handle moose and dry the meat have nothing to process.

Two days before the Lubicon deadline, Premier Getty again sprang into life, and last-minute emergency meetings began, to try to avert drastic action. But the provincial offer remained unacceptable to the Lubicon. (Indeed, they didn't even recognize that the province could "offer" them their own land.)

On October 12, they declared themselves a nation at a general assembly and passed a law "respecting the use of our traditional territory."

By this law they set out the rules governing any exploitation of the resources of their territory, established their right to set up entry, exit, and check points, and formed a tribunal to consider violations of the new law, this tribunal taking account of traditional laws, customs, and practices. They declared that no federal or provincial laws shall apply to their lands "unless otherwise determined" by their council. Simultaneously, they drew up permit forms for access to their territory.

On October 15, they carried out their stated intention and established road blocks. The action was witnessed by some 70 media representatives from all over Europe and North America.

For some days there was confusion among the 100 resource companies working in the territory, but eventually they decided to shut down their operations, thus lending tacit support to the native claim of jurisdiction over their land.

But not only the oil companies were thrown into confusion. Two days after the Lubicon took this action, Premier Getty was saying he was ready to offer a reserve of 236 sq. km (90 square miles), not far short of what the Lubicon figured they were entitled to, but he had never made that offer at earlier meetings. Later still, he said the talks broke down because the natives asked for $100 million in compensation, and he rehearsed what has become a persistent theme (one that has been repeated throughout Canadian history): that the Lubicon were in the grip of advisers who did not want any kind of settlement.

The support the Lubicon received was amazing; people came to help from many countries, and in other parts of Canada other aboriginal peoples held their own symbolic blockades in solidarity. Premier Getty said he would not talk so long as the blockade was maintained, but promised the RCMP would enforce the law with "sensitivity and flexibility." For a few days they did keep their distance, a kilometre down the highway. But when the media left, the sensitivity and flexibility of the police suddenly evaporated, and five days after the blockade began RCMP officers armed with chain saws, rifles, and a court injunction, and accompanied by dogs, moved in just after dawn, smashing the barricades. They arrested twenty-seven people, who were taken to jail in Peace River.

Minutes after all this happened Getty was on the phone to Chief Ominayak, suggesting they should get together to settle this thing.

Two days later they got together and, after seven hours locked up in a small hotel room, managed to come to an agreement. After many years of struggle and neglect, the Lubicon were to have a reserve of 250 sq. km (95 square miles). Of that they would have mineral rights over 208 sq. km (79 square miles), with the province keeping oil and mineral rights on the other 42 sq. km (16 square miles). They would sell the surface rights on the second parcel of land to the federal government, which would also compensate many leaseholders on the 208 sq. km, at a total cost estimated at anything between $7 million and $20 million.

This agreement did not give the Cree everything they wanted, but it was certainly better than anything they had been offered before. They were all extremely happy, of course: their people felt they were on the way to confirming their ownership of their traditional lands, as they had been trying to do for so long, with the possibility of making an arrangement with the governments that would provide for a decent future.

Until this day Alberta had never moved beyond agreeing that they should have a reserve of 67 sq. km (25.4 square miles), as provided for in 1940. Chief Ominayak said at the time that Premier Getty deserved a lot of credit for having the courage to take the bull by the horns and deal with him.

The only snag was that it was all conditional on the agreement of Ottawa. Most people in Canada probably thought this was a mere formality: after all, Ottawa had now lost two of the major arguments by which they had always justified their refusal to make a deal; namely, that the province and the band were unwilling to settle. Now they were both willing, and the ball was in the federal court.

The Feds Erect Their Own Blockade

The feds did not take long before they began to call into question Premier Getty's deal with Chief Ominayak. A spokesman for the minister said they believed Alberta had the responsibility to hand over the land, free and clear of encumbrances, and the federal government would not undertake to compensate third parties for any interest they might hold in the lands.

The two governments began to argue back and forth about this for the next two months. On the one hand, the Indian Affairs spokesman told the public that the land issue was settled — he claimed they agreed to the size of the proposed reserve "within 15 minutes" — but, on the other hand, they kept arguing about the financial details. Lubicon-federal negotiations started on October 31, but by the end of January the federal government had found so many things to be difficult about that, once again, Chief Ominayak felt obliged to reject their unjust take-it-or-leave-it offer.

The federal government insisted, for example, that the Lubicon should "preserve the right" of lessees and licensees to gain access to their reserve "for future exploration and development of mines and minerals." That wasn't really the idea when they entered their long struggle: the land was supposed to be theirs, to administer as they thought fit, but already the government was trying to dictate how they should use their own land in future.

In addition, they were unable to reach agreement on who should be included as members of the band: the Lubicon insisted, as they had always done, that they should be free to decide that themselves, as other aboriginal groups had done in 1899 when they signed Treaty 8. But, again, the federal government wanted to exclude some people on the grounds that they were not status Indians.

The Lubicon asked for compensation of $113 million for benefits they had not been able to collect since 1940, when they were first promised a reserve: they figured such compensation would amount to $167 million, if calculated back to 1899, when other bands signed Treaty 8.

Ottawa offered $45 million in total — about $35 million for reserve construction, and $10 million for economic development — and made it clear that they also regarded this as adequate compensation for past losses. In fact, since they continued to insist that the Lubicon had no aboriginal rights in their traditional lands, they actually denied any obligation to pay any compensation at all, despite the fact that provisions for compensation are included in both the federal government's comprehensive and its specific land-claims policies.

The Lubicon considered the $45 million offered inadequate to cover their great needs if they are to catch up with other Canadian communities and overcome decades of neglect. Like other communities, they need a health centre, vocational-training centre, senior citizens' home, day-care centre, arena, garbage incinerator, satellite dish and transmitter, storage sheds, natural-gas installation, community hall, band office, firehouse, road grader and other equipment — all facilities needed if their community is to function in such a way that their people can pull themselves out of the desperate poverty into which they have been plunged by the heartless recent invasion of their lands. They believed these things could not all be provided with the funding that the federal government was willing to make available.

This was more especially true since it was written into the government's offer that all monies to be provided would be subject to parliamentary approval during the applicable fiscal year — in other words, if the government happened to be (or claimed to be) short of money one year, then the Lubicon could well get nothing. These sums, in short, were not guaranteed. In fact, every detailed offer on the table was phrased in an extremely conditional way.

The Lubicon wanted as part of the package some $14 million for agricultural development, which would enable them to clear 12,800 hectares (32,000 acres) of land, irrigate some of it, build a dairy herd, create a wild-rice industry and a Saskatoon berry farm. But Ottawa would not agree beyond saying they could be "eligible for consideration" for such help in the future.

Chief Ominayak and his team began to feel they had been used by a government more interested in getting re-elected than in doing justice. After all, the Lubicon were now negotiating the conditions on which they would permit other Canadians to make vast fortunes out of their lands, and they were being offered virtually nothing for that permission.

The negotiations began two weeks before the federal elections of November 15, and the fact that negotiations were under way enabled Mulroney and his ministers to go to the people, suggesting that they were ready and willing to deal justly with native people. They knew that the Lubicon's long struggle had elicited much sympathy and support from many people in Canada, who would approve of the idea that, at last, they were to be dealt with honestly.

Towards the end of January 1989, after six weeks of mostly fruitless talks, the Lubicon withdrew, unwilling to continue to be used as pawns in a federal public-relations game. The federal government then unleashed a nation-wide public-relations effort to make the Lubicon appear unreasonable.

But, the fact is that these talks foundered, as so many had done before, on a very fundamental disagreement between the native people and the federal government. The Lubicon believe they did not sign Treaty 8 in 1899, and that what they have been trying to negotiate is an agreement to share their land, based on their traditional use, occupancy, and ownership of it.

Ottawa has argued that the Lubicon signed the treaty, and that what they, the federal negotiators, have been trying to do was limited to redressing the government's failure to fulfil specific obligations undertaken in 1899.

Though from time to time agreement is reported to be close, at time of writing, in spite of the promising effort made by Chief Ominayak and Premier Getty in October 1988, it has so far been impossible to overcome this fundamental difference of viewpoint.

GITKSAN AND
WET'SUWET'EN

THE CONFRONTATION

September 16, 1988, Gitksan hereditary chiefs broadcast on BVLD Radio, Smithers, B.C., a clear warning to Westar, a major forest resource company, not to build a bridge across the Babine River at Sam Green Creek.

This is only one of many confrontations in recent years, and to understand the history of the chiefs' relationship with white people is to better appreciate their commitment to the blockade at Sam Green Creek.

As the chiefs prepared for the inevitable confrontation at the bridge site, their thoughts raced back over the years to the many times that government and industry had combined forces against their people, to the many years of unfulfilled election promises of provincial and federal candidates, and to the nearly thirty years of destruction of some of their territories through short-sighted logging practices. This time the chiefs had decided that no logging could take place in their territories on the north side of the Babine River, and they would make their stand at the proposed bridge site.

The barricades went up. The confrontation at Sam Green Creek began....

Unflinching Resistance to an Implacable Invader

N.J. Sterritt
President of Gitksan-Wet'suwet'en Tribal Council, 1981–7

Gitksan and Wet'suwet'en people experience history in cycles rather than as a straight line through time. Incidents from the past and from the future inform decisions made today. Thus it is with the Upper Skeena village of Gitwangak. In 1888, tension was high on the Skeena River in northwestern British Columbia. The Gitksan population in the area had been decimated in 1887 by a measles epidemic introduced by the white man, one of a series of diseases that has swept through the region during the past fifty years. It is the Gitksan and Wet'suwet'en worldview that deaths are not accidental and that they must be punished. Compensation must be given when a person dies.

An incident that occurred at the time of the measles epidemic illustrates how the whites who came among the Gitksan failed to appreciate that different laws and a different order already were in force.

The Gitksan chief Kamalmuk lost his sons to measles, and in fulfilment of the law of compensation he shot and killed Neetuh, a member of his clan, who favoured the whites, and therefore seemed to be responsible for the death of Kamalmuk's children.

Kamalmuk then paid the appropriate compensation to the Gisgaast clan, fulfilling the traditional requirements.

But the whites, ignorant and fearful of this Gitksan cosmology, nevertheless felt it was their duty to bring order to the area, so they sent in a provincial police party, who shot and killed Kamalmuk, otherwise known as Kitwancool Jim.

The Marshmallow War

One hundred years later, another drama unfolds at Antkii'is, an Eagle fishing site on the south bank of the Skeena River, opposite Gitwangak. This time it is fishing jurisdiction that is at stake. In mid-summer 1986, about three dozen Department of Fisheries and Oceans (DFO) and RCMP officers assembled about one mile south of Antkii'is. The DFO officers, armed with shotguns and flak jackets, and with helicopter backup, were preparing to invade the Gitksan fish camp at Antkii'is. About one hundred Gitksan and Wet'suwet'en and their supporters had anticipated the attack. They were led by two young leaders, Glen Williams and Don Ryan, both of whom are direct descendants of Kamalmuk (Kitwancool Jim) and his wife, Hanamuuk (Fanny Sunbeams).

This raid was just one of a series of armed DFO raids against the Gitksan and Wet'suwet'en and other native fishermen in British Columbia. The raids had grown in intensity over the previous ten years, with active resistance occurring throughout the province as frustration grew at the senseless application of DFO regulations against native people. At Antkii'is, the officers alleged that the Gitksan were fishing without DFO permits, and during a closure of the river. The Gitksan maintained, as they always have, that they owned the fish in the river, and had the authority and responsibility to harvest the fish.

This fishing site is owned by Gillawoo' of the Gitwangak Eagle Clan. The family has authorized construction of a smokehouse. Soon tents, a tipi, campers, and a cookshack fill the area.

The camp is carefully regulated, and the Gitksan and their supporters are well disciplined. Children and dogs of all shapes, sizes, and ages are caught up in the enthusiasm and the sense of adventure. Beautiful sockeye and spring-salmon are caught, smoked, jarred, and eaten fresh daily as hagwiljam (fish chowder) or fried or barbecued. The elders guide the young people. They entertain and instruct them with stories of the distant past, and of their own youth on the river and in the surrounding mountains, hunting mountain goats and picking huckleberries and blueberries. These are fond memories, and the young learn more of who they are and what it means to be a Gitksan or Wet'suwet'en person in this beautiful place. They even learn of the Skeena River Rebellion of 1888 from the elders.

At night there are strategy sessions. The young men plan how to deal with the DFO when they eventually raid the camp. For, despite the carnival atmosphere, this is serious business. 40 km (25 miles) to the northeast, another camp is being built on the Skeena River near Kispiox at Gwin 'Oop. A crew from this camp will go and help, and a joint strategy will be applied. The question on everyone's mind is how to respond effectively to the force of DFO. Of course, the media is asking the leaders this daily, always with leading questions, trying to put words in the mouths of the people to obtain a good headline. The issue is a national one now and has been brought to the attention of the prime minister.

Just after noon, on July 3, 1986, the Fisheries officers nervously move in with their walkie-talkies, cruisers, and full backup. They face a wall of fishermen and supporters at the entrance to the Antkii'is camp-site. Young men and elders, women and children refuse to allow the DFO access to the camp or to the net site on the river just below the camp. Glen Williams, as spokesman for the camp, insists that this is Gitksan land and that the DFO have no right to be there. Peter Woloshyn, a Fisheries officer representing the DFO, demands access to the fishing site, and attempts to break through the line of bodies. This procedure is repeated two more times, until it is obvious that the fishermen are not going to back down.

The officers decide for the time being to retreat to their vehicles nearby. Just as they open the doors to enter, the defenders of Antkii'is, men, women, and children alike, suddenly hurl their carefully hidden weapons at the officers.

The officers, anticipating the worst, duck and scramble to get out of the way and into the safety of their vehicles, until their panic leads to incredulity, and then smiles, and then laughter as they realize that they have been overcome by—marshmallows... and the Gitksan sense of humour. Woloshyn salutes with a V-for-victory sign and drives away with his men.

Battling the DFO

It was some ten years before the Antkii'is incident that the Gitksan and Wet'suwet'en began to learn how to deal with DFO's Indian strategy. On July 19, 1977, a Gitksan fisherman from Gitanmaax received a summons to appear in court for illegal sale of fish, pursuant to the Fisheries regulations. Later, some seventeen other Gitksan and Wet'suwet'en fishermen received similar charges. Most were mystified and did not know the basis for the charges. As each of the fishermen was later to learn, they were the victims of "Operation Round-up," a massive undercover operation designed by the DFO to enforce the Fisheries Act of Canada and to end the alleged illegal sale of salmon by native fishermen in B.C. The DFO chose to commence this operation on the Skeena River against Gitksan and Wet'suwet'en fishermen.

As the fishermen were charged, they turned to the Gitksan–Carrier Tribal Council (GCTC) for advice and assistance. This was just one of several coincidences that began to work in favour of the fishermen, for it also happened that a young lawyer, Stuart Rush, with experience in aboriginal law, was teaching part time at Northwest Community College, about 140 km (90 miles) away in Terrace. When he was told the nature of the charges, he recommended pleas of not guilty, and he agreed to take the cases on behalf of the fishermen.

Until this point, almost without exception, the DFO had found that charges laid against the Gitksan and Wet'suwet'en resulted in guilty pleas. The people simply wanted to avoid the hassle and expense of lengthy proceedings in a court that all too often in the past had found them guilty in any event. The reaction of the DFO officers in charge of this operation was consternation at the not-guilty pleas, and concern at the effective defence put up by the Tribal Council's lawyers. In the words of one of the officers, "We hit a brick wall [on this one]."

It was in the aftermath of the charges being laid and during the course of the court proceedings that the story behind the charges came out. The Operation Round-up plan went into effect at the beginning of the salmon season when Fisheries officers, posing as tourists, summer students, and Coca-Cola salespersons, approached Gitksan and Wet'suwet'en fishermen with offers to buy fish. Undoubtedly fish were sold. But the Gitksan and Wet'suwet'en defend the right to sell fish. Fish have provided an economic base for the people for centuries, and will continue to do so for centuries to come. However, this fact did not make it easier for the Fisheries officers to carry out their strategy. The majority of the fishermen are used to non-Indian people approaching them for fresh salmon. And others openly trade and barter in fresh salmon with non-Indians, satisfying mutual needs. The problem that the DFO faced was that these salmon were being offered as gifts. The people were prepared to give the "tourists" salmon. But, in order for the DFO to lay charges, money had to be exchanged, and for larger quantities of fish than the people were prepared to give away. The final day of court on Operation Round-up was July 19, 1978, exactly a year after the first charge was laid. Throughout that time only one charge was upheld by the Provincial Court, and that charge was acquitted on appeal at the County Court level in Prince Rupert.

This was an important series of victories for the Gitksan and Wet'suwet'en, who had maintained that the cases should never have gone to trial in the first place. The Tribal Council leaders felt strongly that if the DFO had concerns about the fishery, they should meet openly at the negotiating table with the people. It was the intention of the GCTC to commence a major study of the Gitksan and Wet'suwet'en fishery on the Skeena and Bulkley rivers and to assist the hereditary chiefs to reassert their authority over the fishery. The DFO personnel involved refused to co-operate with the attempt and proceeded to rewrite their regulations to eliminate "loopholes" in the act. In subsequent years, the DFO have become even more entrenched in their resistance to GCTC efforts to resolve Fisheries matters amicably. Charges were laid against the fishermen every year, even though the GCTC demonstrated its commitment to take action by undertaking a biological study, carried out by Fisheries biologist Mike Morrell, in the late summer of 1979.

Nevertheless, tensions continued to mount on the fishing sites. It became obvious that the DFO would continue to harass the fishermen until major changes occurred in the DFO attitude and their perception of their powers under the Fisheries Act. It was decided that other measures might cause the DFO to relax their increasingly aggressive approach. On the Tribal Council, we examined with our lawyers ways to approach the problem and determined that there are powers under the Indian Act that allow the development of by-laws that ensure that fur-bearing animals, fish, and other game on the reserve will be preserved, protected, and managed.

A Salmon-Fishing People

To understand fully the importance of salmon to the Gitksan and Wet'suwet'en one must go back in time. The Gitksan and Wet'suwet'en villages are all located at major fisheries. The canyons on the Skeena, Bulkley, and Babine rivers contain barriers and natural resting sites for the salmon. Here, for centuries, the people built elaborate weirs and baskets to capture the fish as they travelled each year to the spawning grounds at the heads of the rivers. When Europeans first arrived, they found thriving villages at each of the major canyons. As the fur trade developed, it relied on fish caught and smoked by the natives to supply the various trading posts throughout the west. The DFO Annual Report for 1878 estimated that 20,000 to 30,000 salmon were being sold annually to the Hudson's Bay Company post at Fort Babine by the natives. The people continued to provide salmon by trade and barter during the construction of the Collins Overland Telegraph line through Gitksan and Wet'suwet'en territories to Siberia. And a thriving trade was maintained by Skeena and Bulkley fishermen during the construction of the Grand Trunk Pacific Railway in the early twentieth century.

The significance of the village sites as fisheries was recognized when reserves were established beginning in the 1870s, and even today court victories are based on the fact that the reserves were established for the Gitksan and Wet'suwet'en because of the adjacent fisheries.

The first salmon cannery was built at the mouth of the Skeena in 1877, and soon eighteen canneries were operating. In contrast to the efficient and selective weirs and traps used by the Gitksan and Wet'suwet'en and their neighbours up-river, the coastal industry caught the salmon by pursuing the fish with hand-, sail-, and gas-powered boats and gill nets. Obviously, before long the barons of the commercial fishing industry would view the native fisheries near the spawning grounds as a threat to the thriving coastal fishery.

By 1881, fishery problems begin to occur between natives and the commercial interests on the Skeena, and in 1882 the Nishga complained of interference with their fishing by the canneries. In 1887, a delegation of chiefs travelled to Victoria with concerns about the effect the canneries were having on the aboriginal economy. By 1906, the DFO, with full support of the fishing industry, adopted a much more aggressive stance against the inland fishery. A Fisheries officer, Helge Helgeson, was dispatched to eliminate the weirs near the spawning grounds at the headwaters. He was ultimately honoured, not by the DFO, but by the cannery owners at the Skeenamouth, with a gold-headed cane and just over $600 for his efforts. It was during this period that the "food fishing" laws were developed that made it illegal for Indians to catch fish for other than food purposes. And it was these regulations that the DFO were attempting to enforce seventy years later with Operation Round-up. Between 1906 and 1977, everyone participated in the aboriginal economy, from farmers, to tourists, to the RCMP and a court clerk whose disappointment was expressed quietly during the year-long trials in 1977–8.

The present structure of the coastal salmon fishery makes no sense to the Gitksan and Wet'suwet'en. The argument that traps and weirs would destroy the salmon runs was the stated reason for the development of "food-fish"-only regulations at the turn of the century. A further argument, advanced more recently, is that the quality of fish caught up-river is unfit for commercial sale. These arguments are wrong. But more importantly, if attempts to enforce federal laws continue and if the DFO continues to harass native fishermen, the Gitksan and Wet'suwet'en will be deprived of a sound economic future based on an invaluable resource within their lands. Tests done by the GCTC and others have shown that fish caught in the inland rivers produce a quality product, whether canned, smoked, or fresh. Of course, the oil-rich coastal salmon is not to everyone's taste.

Also, at a time when the world's energy resources are diminishing, it makes little sense to expend millions of dollars in fuel, technology, and capital to indiscriminately harvest the salmon around the mouth of the major salmon-producing rivers and in the oceans. Gill nets and purse seines kill the fish and do not discriminate between strong and weak stocks. It requires very little in the way of capital, technology, or fuel to allow the salmon to swim up-stream to be selectively harvested undamaged in weirs and baskets. A further benefit to this process is the elimination of waste. By this method, one can catch and keep the strong salmon stocks and return those that are weak or endangered. In any event, an inland commercial operation would allow more Gitksan and Wet'suwet'en people to participate in the fishery than is possible under the current system of coastal canneries and fishery. Little capital is required, but federal and provincial attitudes would have to change.

The Gitksan and Wet'suwet'en Take Charge

By 1983 it was obvious that the DFO was redoubling its enforcement capability, rather than trying to work with native leaders. And the politicians lack the will for innovative change in the fishery. The Gitksan–Wet'suwet'en Tribal Council (GWTC, formerly GCTC) began to develop a set of by-laws for management of the fishery. As with every other initiative on behalf of the people's rights, this one was not to be without its difficulties. The first set of by-laws was comprehensive and included all of the lands of the Gitksan and Wet'suwet'en, not just the reserves under the Indian Act. These by-laws were disallowed by the assistant deputy minister of Indian Affairs. The GWTC appealed the decision and lost. However, the lawyer acting on behalf of the federal government in the appeal offered to assist the GWTC with a redraft of the by-laws that, in her opinion, would receive ministerial approval by the Department of Indian Affairs. This was not to be. The GWTC lawyers drafted and redrafted the by-laws for the next three years. Indian Affairs always found a reason to return the by-laws for another change, until the leaders of the GWTC and the bands involved in this effort, through frustration demanded that the department take the by-laws seriously.

By this time, other people had become interested in the by-laws. It seemed that Indian Affairs was vetting the by-laws through the DFO, and perhaps they, in turn, feeling threatened, sought political allies in the form of sports and commercial fishermen in B.C. In 1986, the Pacific Fishermen's Defence Alliance was formed specifically to discredit the GWTC fishing by-laws, and generally to advance the interests of sport and commercial fishermen over those of native fishermen everywhere in B.C. In the midst of what was rapidly becoming a volatile situation in B.C., then minister of Indian Affairs David Crombie sought a compromise with the GWTC.

The procedure is: the minister can actively disallow by-laws; however, if he does nothing for forty days, then the by-laws come into effect. But Crombie was prepared not to disallow the GWTC by-laws if the GWTC and member bands would agree not to implement the by-laws for two months so that a mutual agreement could be obtained between the sport, commercial, and Indian fishermen regarding an inland commercial fishery. This arrangement was acceptable to the GWTC and member bands. In spite of this, the Fishermen's Defence Alliance, two days before the scheduled implementation date, supported by the provincial government, and with federal financial assistance, sought and obtained a court order restraining the GWTC from implementing the by-laws. We intended to conduct a test fishery in 1986, but the government, by various means, denied us, and our test has yet to be carried out.

To add to our frustration, through government bungling in that same year, 1.5 million salmon in excess of spawning needs were allowed up the river. Our test would have required only 10,000 salmon, but we had to watch as these 1.5 million fish swam past us. The government's management of this was another fiasco: those 1.5 million salmon never made it to the spawning channels on Babine Lake. The DFO barricades were closed before them, and the fish were allowed to rot and die.

The Chiefs Sue British Columbia

On October 23, 1984, a Gitksan chief, Delgamuukw, Albert Tait, sang his Limx Oii, or sad song. The centuries of emotions embodied in the song set in motion one of the largest and most complex legal confrontations between aboriginal people and the Canadian government that this century is likely to witness. Beside Delgamuukw stood Gisday Wa, Alfred Joseph, a

Wet'suwet'en chief. Through these two hereditary chiefs, the Gitksan and Wet'suwet'en people served formal notice that they were suing the Province of British Columbia for title to 57,000 sq. km (22,000 square miles) of territory on the upper Skeena, Bulkley, and Nass rivers in northwestern British Columbia.

The Gitksan and Wet'suwet'en are two neighbouring, but separate native peoples. The Gitksan live on the Skeena River in five villages, and the Wet'suwet'en live in two villages on the Bulkley River. These people have a shared culture through inter-marriages and working together for centuries, yet retain different languages and societies. Linguistically, the Gitksan are more closely linked to the Nisga'a and the Tsimshian to the west, while the Wet'suwet'en are linked to the Dene, or Athapaskan-speaking peoples. Linguists consider the Wet'suwet'en unique among all Athapaskan-speaking peoples.

The Gitksan and Wet'suwet'en territories are situated some 640 km (400 miles) north of Vancouver, B.C., and they straddle the beautiful and rugged Skeena Mountains. For centuries, successive Gitksan and Wet'suwet'en leaders have defended the boundaries of their territories. Here, a complex system of ownership and jurisdiction has evolved, where the chiefs continually validate their rights and responsibilities to their people, their lands, and the resources contained within them. The Gitksan and Wet'suwet'en express their ownership and jurisdiction in many ways, but the most formal forum is the feast, which is sometimes referred to as a potlatch. Here Gitksan and Wet'suwet'en government occurs.

Since Europeans first came to the Upper Skeena in the early nineteenth century, the hereditary chiefs have continually tried to get the Crown to address the question of their land title. At the turn of the century, delegations of chiefs travelled to Victoria and Ottawa to appeal directly to the government. The hereditary chiefs took every opportunity to address government representatives, and to appeal for formal resolution of the refusal by European settlers to recognize the true owners of the land they lived on.

It was in the three decades after 1880 that the federal and provincial governments set up Indian reserves in British Columbia. However, by 1908, reserve allotments were halted by provincial protests, and efforts were made by the province to reduce the size of reserves, which led to the striking of a special federal-provincial commission. In 1912, Commissioner J. A. J. McKenna met with B.C. premier Richard McBride to settle the problems. The outcome of their meeting was the McKenna–McBride Agreement leading to a five-man Royal Commission on Indian Affairs. This commission toured the province for three years, commencing in 1913, and was mandated to set aside Indian reserves and to convey title of those reserves from the province to the Dominion.

The McKenna–McBride Commission came to the Skeena and Bulkley river areas in 1915. Here the commissioners were confounded in their efforts, for, without exception, the Gitksan leaders demanded that their ownership rights to land be dealt with. In each village, the commissioners left in frustration after trying to convince the chiefs that they should discuss reserve allocations without prejudice to their aboriginal title. The issue of aboriginal title continued to be raised by successive leaders and chiefs. Throughout that time the people have been incredibly patient and trusting, believing in the justice and goodwill of Canadian governments long after anyone could reasonably have expected them to. This is not surprising when the historical record is reviewed. Successive government representatives attempted to obtain the people's co-operation by holding out the carrot of another phantom process whereby the "land question" would be dealt with. The McKenna–McBride Commission was one of the first and best examples of this, but there were others. Not much has changed in seventy-six years. Today, Prime Minister Mulroney and some of the premiers are suggesting to present leaders that, if they endorse the Meech Lake accord, it will create an opportunity for renewed First Ministers' conferences on aboriginal rights.

An Unjustified Optimism

It was a sense of optimism that carried the Gitksan and Wet'suwet'en into the 1970s. In 1973, the chiefs increased their efforts to achieve resolution of their land title. The *Calder* case, in which the Nisga'as' pursuit of a declaration of aboriginal land rights ended in a split decision at the Supreme Court of Canada, resulted in the federal government developing a policy of land-claims negotiations. The James Bay Cree had just finished litigating and negotiating their land claim with Quebec, and the Council of Yukon Indians had started negotiating with the federal government. Set against this scenario of optimism, a new provincial government program, the Northwest Development Plan, under NDP premier Dave Barrett, was set to be implemented. This economic-development program targeted on the considerable resources of the northwestern part of British Columbia and, in particular, those of the Gitksan and Wet'suwet'en.

The Gitksan and Wet'suwet'en ideas of development are tied to their laws and their ways of managing the land. They are therefore more than externally conceived economic developments through megaprojects or clear-cut logging. Progress is more than high wages from a single resource economy. For decades the resources of the Gitksan and Wet'suwet'en territories have been the object of resource-development schemes conceived in the boardrooms of Vancouver, Toronto, Montreal, and New York, or in the corridors of government in Victoria or Ottawa. The people know that they own and govern their land, and that they are responsible for it. Progress, for the people, means caring for the land and its resources so that the land is there for future generations of all peoples to enjoy. The people will share their land, but they must ensure that there is something worthwhile to share. And they will use all legal and political means at their disposal to defend their land.

William Brown, a Hudson's Bay Company employee, was one of the first Europeans to travel into the Gitksan and Wet'suwet'en territories. In 1826 he travelled west from Fort Kilmaurs on Babine Lake to the large Gitksan village of Kisgagaas near the mouth of the Babine River, where he met the hereditary chiefs Niigyap, Wiiminosik, and Gwoimt. His records document that the Hudson's Bay Company was receiving direct competition from the Gitksan, Wet'suwet'en, and the coastal peoples, who acquired furs and traded directly to the coastal fur buyers. Earlier, in 1821, Peter Ogden had travelled on behalf of the Hudson's Bay Company to Hotset, or Moricetown as it is known today, on the Bulkley River. He referred to the Wet'suwet'en chiefs of the day as "men of property," and recognized that the chiefs managed and regulated access to their resources through a land-tenure system.

Contrast Peter Ogden and William Brown's first observations in the 1820s with those of Joseph Trutch, governor of the colony, forty years later: "Indians have really no right to the lands they claim, nor are they of any actual value or utility to them, and I cannot see why they should...retain these lands to the prejudice of the general interest of the colony or be allowed to make a market of them either to government or individuals."

By the turn of the century, it was obvious to the Gitksan and Wet'suwet'en that their efforts to communicate openly and directly to representatives of the governments were being ignored. Nevertheless, they continued into the twentieth century with petitions to the government, which went unread, and delegations to Ottawa and Victoria, which were ignored. Such efforts were met by enforcement in 1918 of a prohibition against the potlatch, and with federal legislation in 1927 making it illegal to raise money to advance a land claim. Gitksan and Wet'suwet'en feasts did not stop, and many people were arrested and jailed. It was during these years that the Oakalla Penitentiary in New Westminster, B.C., became known on the Skeena as the "Kitwancool Reserve" because of the number of Kitwancool Gitksan jailed for holding feasts and for removing surveyors' stakes as the government attempted to lay out the Kitwancool reserves.

At the same time, the Wet'suwet'en were blatantly dispossessed of their prime agricultural lands in the valley bottoms. With a life that spans nearly a century, Johnny David, Maxlaxlex, almost in an understatement, described his experience in 1908 in his commission evidence in the Delgamuukw trial: "In the area of North Bulkley my father had a big smokehouse and when he died the white people burnt it down and they kicked me off the land. My dad died in 1908 and must have been around 30 or 40, and I got a letter from Mr. Loring, who was the Indian agent at Hagwilget. I received a letter from him telling me to get off the land and he was going to give me acreage in Hagwilget, which he never did."

There are other examples of deceit by the commissioners, Indian agents, and priests and of Wet'suwet'en dispossession. But the real problem lay in the attitudes of white settlers and their government representatives. The hearings demonstrate that the commissioners more often than not deceived the people by promising that the land question would be dealt with fairly by the governments at a future date if only the people would address the question of how much reserve land they wanted now. The following discussion between William Holland, a Gitksan chief from Gitwangak, and the chairman of the commission at Hazelton in 1915 is typical of many of the meetings in the Skeena area:

> *William Holland*: The Chief wants me to speak for him...we just want one thing and that is to get back our land again — the land was here before we were here and we want to get it back — all the land along the Skeena River.
>
> *The Chairman*: Some of the Indians, and those who are supporting your claim, thought at one time that if you applied to us for certain lands and we gave them to you that you were, to some extent, giving up some of your privileges; that if you accepted those lands you would not have the further rights to take this matter up in the Courts, but a further Order-in-Council was passed expressly stating that this would not affect you in the least.

The Gitksan and the Wet'suwet'en people were opposed to reserves. They were clear in their opposition to the commission, and the message was received and ignored; for example, in Hagwilget, a chief said, "If you want to help us there is only three things we want and that's the first thing just people dead. It's just the same thing as tying them up and letting them die."

The commissioner replied: "You mean that to restrict or confine the Indians to their Reserves, you mean that is killing you." The chief's answer was yes.

At the same time, a Gitksan, Roy Wesley, told the commission:

> I wish to tell you that this Reserve that you have just spoken about is something that we don't wish for…this country originally belonged to our ancestors — we were placed here originally by God, and it is only quite recently that the government has sent men out here to measure this land immediately around us, we were not notified of it when they did. Then the Provincial Government came in and sold the remaining land immediately around us…and what we most strenuously object to is that you insist upon us having this Reserve.

The Gitksan and Wetsuweten chiefs in their 1984 land-claims case, were not surprised when the Province of British Columbia filed its Statement of Defence, contradicting the oft-repeated assurances of the McKenna–McBride commissioners that the Gitksan and Wet'suwet'en would not jeopardize future efforts to resolve their aboriginal title by participating in the commission hearings on reserve allocations.

Surviving the Depression

The depression came to the Gitksan and Wet'suwet'en territories in the 1930s. Those settlers who relied on the wage economy, farming, mining, and logging, and who carried debts, were most affected. There were lines of people seeking assistance in Hazelton. Those who relied on the local resources, such as fish, berries, trapping, and hunting, suffered least. The Gitksan and Wet'suwet'en were not affected at all. In fact, it was the native economy that shored up those non-Indians who were affected by the depression. Gitksan and Wet'suwet'en people, in particular, provided them with fish and berries.

Thus, despite one hundred years of European presence in the territories, the strength of Gitksan and Wet'suwet'en political, economic, and social institutions persisted. The Gitksan and Wet'suwet'en remained economically independent despite legislation enacted more than fifty years earlier designed to "colonize" the people through assimilation and denial of their rights and responsibilities. The people have remained strong and independent because their basic economic unit, the House (a historic and biologically related kinship unit), has remained intact.

For thousands of years the House has been the key to survival for the Gitksan and Wet'suwet'en people. The Gitksan and Wet'suwet'en people would survive even during adversity as long as the people's economic activities within their lands and resources could accommodate the House. Little did the people realize that the final thrust of efforts to colonize them and their territories would soon strike at the core of the House. There have been many attacks on the House over the years, ranging from forcible separation of children and parents through residential schools, to attempts to confine the people within reserves established around the villages and fishing sites of the people. Undeniably these and other acts of assimilation by the governments had an impact on the social and political life of the people. However, because of the nature of economic activity at the time, such as trapping, fishing, small-scale logging, prospecting, and packing, which were all conducive to the viability of the House, the people remained strong and resilient.

The end of the Second World War marked the beginning of the final attack on the economic well-being of the Gitksan and Wet'suwet'en people. Learning from their war-time co-operation, industry and government moved to integrate their activities to accelerate economic activity. Large Crown corporations were formed and, in the resource sector, licensing arrangements were changed to favour big business over local operators. In B.C.'s forest industry, this change was heralded by the introduction of the Tree Farm Licences (TFLs). The possession of the TFL allowed a corporation to control, develop, and harvest vast areas of forest land in B.C. TFL #1 was issued to Columbia Cellulose in 1948 and included the forests of the Skeena and Nass rivers centred on the Terrace area. By the end of the 1950s most of the Indian-owned logging operations in the Skeena-Bulkley area had been taken up by the larger logging companies who were contracting to Columbia Cellulose.

At the same time, the Department of Indian Affairs began to adopt a welfare approach with the people. The older people scorned welfare, and refused to accept the offers. But the growing lack of economic opportunities and changing attitudes of an increasing number of students who had been through the "residential" school system led to more and more of the younger people accepting financial support and welfare when the need arose.

The Impact of Clear-cut Logging

The impact of capital-intensive clear-cut logging on the communities of Northwestern British Columbia was dramatic. It had its effect on everyone. On the one hand, some stood to gain, at least in the short term, in a boom-and-bust economy. On the other hand, many stood to lose over the long term. Not only native communities are affected. The municipality of Terrace is a community that thrived as the centre of logging activity in the Northwest during the 1950s and 1960s. But, as the forests closer to Terrace were harvested, and as lumber markets fluctuated wildly in the 1970s, Terrace was the first to suffer. It is still not the thriving community it was in the earlier years of logging. But many of those who came to Terrace because it was a place to make a quick buck moved on to follow the big money elsewhere. It is those who would like to make Terrace their home that have a stake in its future.

This is the dilemma facing the Gitksan and Wet'suwet'en people. Not only is the Northwest our past, it is also our future. We are committed to the wise and long-term use of our lands and resources.

The village of Kitsegukla is a community that has been hard hit by the combined political, social, and economic forces of government and industry over the years. In the early 1970s, unemployment in the village ranged between 65 and 90 per cent, depending on the season. A 12 to 15 per cent unemployment rate anywhere else in Canada is considered a national disgrace. The prolonged effect of such forces can have negative social and economic effects on a community. This was the case for Kitsegukla by 1975. During the 1950s, many hereditary chiefs and their House members had hand- and horse-logged the Kitsegukla Valley in a moderately successful way. Clear-cut logging came to the valley in the 1960s and largely displaced the logging activity that formed part of the economy of the Kitsegukla people.

By 1975, the people had had enough. Logging plans indicated that the Kitsegukla Valley was to be logged more intensively than before, and loggers working on behalf of Rim Forest Products and B.C. Timber (formerly Columbia Cellulose) were set to move into the valley. By virtue of its location near the entrance to the valley, all of this was to happen almost on the doorsteps of the people of Kitsegukla.

The people barricaded the only entrance to the valley. It is their valley and their resources, and it is they who should benefit through the harvesting of the valley's resources. The people were determined to stop the logging by others, and to take over their valley and do all the logging, on their terms, themselves. There was a stand-off at the barricade for nearly two weeks. Ray Jones, president of the Tribal Council and a leader in the

Kitsegukla community, negotiated on behalf of the chiefs and villagers. The owner of Rim Forest Products, from Vancouver, negotiated on behalf of the company. While the objective of the village had been to participate in a range of logging activities, from felling the trees to processing the wood in a sawmill, the negotiations resulted in the village acquiring five logging trucks to haul the trees from log dump to sawmill. The Department of Indian Affairs eventually found some of the money necessary to acquire the trucks, and the balance was guaranteed through the band's capital-fund account held by Indian Affairs in Ottawa. This was a solution favoured by everyone. The barricades came down. Logging by the company began in earnest while the community began the long process of negotiating with department staff for the monies required, and those politicians who did get involved moved on to other more pressing concerns. Eventually, in about two years, five brand-new trucks were delivered to the village. And the village was in the logging business. Or was it?

The difficulty with this solution to the Kitsegukla problem is that it did not deal with the real issues in the community. First of all, five trucks require only five drivers, or ten if double shifts are worked. Second, banks expect to receive regular payments on loans as large as those for the five trucks; and third, people on welfare don't walk out the door and into ten-hour-a-day, five- and six-day-a-week jobs. So, who got the jobs? Generally speaking, those who already had truck-driving jobs, not necessarily from the community, and who were able to provide reasonable assurance to the board of directors that the bank payments would be made.

Eventually, the trucking company folded. There was a little loss of pride when the company folded, but that's probably the only loss, since by itself, the trucking solution could not solve the problems faced by the community. This is only one of many examples where Gitksan and Wet'suwet'en problems have not been solved by outside forces.

The Chiefs Assert Their Authority

The logging practices that concerned the Kitsegukla chiefs in 1975 have not improved. The pace of logging has accelerated. Logging and lumber production are important to the economy of the Gitksan and Wet'suwet'en territories. Participants in the forest economy include those who are attracted to the area for work, members of pioneer families who settled in the area years earlier, and Gitksan and Wet'suwet'en people. As mentioned above, the latter two classes of people have a particular stake in the future of the area. They are concerned about the environment and about their children's future life-style.

In 1984, the Gitksan and Wet'suwet'en hereditary chiefs sued the province on the basis of their ownership of and jurisdiction over their territories. At the same time, the Tribal Council, at the request of the chiefs, served notice by letter to all logging companies in the territory, and the Ministry of Forests, of this fact. They also advised the logging companies that current logging plans were not likely to be affected, but efforts by the companies to enter previously unlogged areas would be opposed by the chiefs. With two exceptions, the logging companies and the Ministry of Forests ignored this notice.

Westar, the current successor to Columbia Cellulose, is a major logging company in northwestern B.C. It has operations in Hazelton and other parts of the province. Many of the smaller companies that formerly operated in the area have either been consolidated or subcontracted by Westar, which holds much of the licensed timber in the Hazelton area and develops its logging plans and road infrastructure well in advance of entering an area to log. Westar holds a licence through the provincial Forest Act to harvest a vast, pristine area north of the Babine River, at its confluence with the Skeena, and planned to gain access by bridging the Babine here. Logging was to commence in the Shedin Valley at Sam Green Creek, near the ancient Gitksan villages of Kisgagaas and Anlagasimdeek, in 1991. The hereditary Gitksan chiefs who own this area decided that this could not happen.

An exchange between William Jackson, a Kisgagaas chief, and Commissioner MacDowall, of the McKenna–McBride Commission, in 1915 was prophetic of events to occur at Sam Green Creek in the 1980s:

William Jackson: We are asking to get back the land of our grandfathers — we want our places, and we want our places to be free as they were before; as our fathers had a free living in their own land, we want to be the same way. Where we catch fish, where we hunt and where we get berries, we want to use it as our fathers did. God gave us this land where we were brought up, and it was free. There was no bothering us and we want the land just as it was before the white men came into this country.

MacDowell: William Jackson and Indians of the Kisigas Tribe — you need not speak to us about holding this land the same as your grandfathers did — the world moves along, and you in your lifetime must move with it — It is for the sake of your grandchildren that we are here; to preserve something for them. The world will be different for your grandchildren than what it is today, and if you think of them at all you should select a piece of land for them — if you are not willing to do that, we might as well not talk to you at all.

Jackson: What is moving this world?

MacDowell: You will have to go to a wiser lot of men than the Kuldoes to find that out — but you will have to move with the world. If you don't you will be wiped out.

Jackson: Who gave us the land — it was God. We heard it and all we know is that you people are taking away our land — our own.

MacDowell: We are sorry that you have not seen fit to answer our questions, and all that remains to be done is to wish you Good-Bye.

Perhaps it was just farewell, and not good-bye, that Commissioner MacDowell bade the Kisgagaas people in 1915. Almost seventy-five years later the descendants of William Jackson and other Kisgagaas chiefs were asserting their authority and responsibilities over their lands north of Sam Green Creek, or Xsi Adee'a as it is known in Gitksan. It forms part of the boundary between the territories of Miluulak (Frog or Lax Seel Clan) and Wiigyet (Fireweed or Giskaast Clan), two chiefs from Kisgagaas. William Jackson was Gisgaast. Robert Jackson, a member of the House of Miluulak, is a descendant of William Jackson's wife. Ralph Mitchell and Elsie Morrison are both Gisgaast and descendants of William Jackson. Also involved were Gwoimt, Kathleen Wale, and her son Fred, descendants of the Lax Gibuu (or Wolf) Chief, Gwoimt, who met fur-trader William Brown in 1826 close to the Sam Green site. They and other Gitksan and Wet'suwet'en chiefs and supporters set up camp on the south bank of the Babine River, opposite the mouth of Sam Green Creek. The Gitksan and Wet'suwet'en people intended to stop the building of the bridge. The Babine River at Sam Green Creek has become, in part, a symbol, and the people will not let the river be crossed.

The confrontation at Sam Green Creek really began the previous spring at Pinenut Creek, which flows west through the territory of Kispiox hereditary chiefs into the Skeena River about 23 km (14 miles) north of the village of Hazelton. The valley bottom here is forested with jackpine and is a favoured wood-cutting and deer-hunting area. The area was first logged, by hand, in the 1940s, when it supported a mixed economy of logging, trapping, and hunting. Now much of the area is bare from the clear-cut logging that commenced in the 1960s. The hereditary chiefs do not want the Skeena north of Pinenut Creek to be subjected to similar waste and destruction. They are committed to action.

The road block at Pinenut Creek was set up in spring 1988. But Westar had anticipated this. In April, Westar had obtained an ex-parte injunction (without representation by the chiefs) prohibiting the hereditary chiefs from blockading road-building and logging activities up the Skeena to the south side of the

Babine River. This was a setback, and the means by which the injunction was obtained convinced the chiefs and younger leaders that the courts would continue to favour Westar's interests over theirs.

The Westar road continued up the east side of the Skeena River in 1988. It had been roughed out to the south bank of the Babine River at Sam Green Creek based on an "authority to construct a bridge" issued by the B.C. Ministry of Forests on September 8, 1988. But the Gitksan and Wet'suwet'en disappointment had given way to solemn resolve. In August 1988, a camp was built similar to the ones built at Antkii'is and Gwin 'Oop two years earlier. The Babine River joins the Skeena River near here, and the sockeye salmon and steelhead trout, on their way from the coast to the Babine spawning grounds, provide fresh fish daily for elders and young people.

A smokehouse was built for curing the salmon, and a root cellar for storage of vegetables and berries. A grizzly bear wandered through camp early one morning, reminding the three dozen occupants that, despite the road, this is still a wilderness area, and the bear's presence heightened the sense of excitement at the blockade. A barricade is built across the logging road near the proposed bridge site. At this point, all were prepared to halt Westar's march towards Sam Green Creek and the untouched Shedin watershed.

Buoyed by their earlier victory, Westar proceeded on the premise that they would obtain an injunction to bridge the Babine and log the Shedin watershed as a matter of course. The marshalling of several RCMP officers near the camp lent support to Westar's confidence, and recognition of the chiefs' determination.

On September 16, the chiefs had warned Westar not to proceed with the bridge by public notice over BVLD Radio in Smithers, reinforcing their May 1988 letter, which had conveyed the same message. The chiefs and their leaders reminded Westar that they would obstruct their workers and not allow bridge construction to take place. Ignoring the chiefs' warnings, on September 29 Westar's general manager of Northwest Operations, Keith Spencer, proceeded to the bridge site with the intention of re-establishing survey sites for the bridge footings.

An Echo from the Past

It was then that the confrontation occurred. The sense of futility and frustration of William Jackson before the Reserve Commission in 1915 was now echoed as expressions of political will and authority in the statements of his grandchildren to Westar officials at the Sam Green camp. This was no ordinary confrontation, for behind Westar and its wealth of lawyers and financial resources stood the full co-operation and support of the provincial government lawyers who have been working on the Delgamuukw case. There was little doubt in anyone's mind that this confrontation would shift, in part, from the camp at the Babine River to the courtrooms of Vancouver.

For the chiefs, this was a political confrontation. And they remained vigilant at the Babine camp while the Westar injunction was responded to by the chiefs' own counter-injunction. The chiefs knew that their last resort was to stand firm at the end of the road. But they and their young House members also knew that they should draw upon the wisdom and patience of William Jackson and others like him by forcing government and industry to obey their own laws. And so this became both a political and a legal confrontation.

In October 1988, the chiefs scored a political and legal victory when they won an injunction preventing Westar from crossing the Babine to log the Shedin watershed. And later, in spring 1989, the chiefs also won Westar's appeal of their injunction in the Appeal Court of B.C. The chiefs' lawyers drew heavily upon the evidence presented in the Delgamuukw case. Similarly, in addition to the technical aspects of logging and road construction, Westar drew heavily upon the work and advice of the provincial lawyers in Delgamuukw to frame their evidence. Two Appeal Court judges found in favour of the chiefs, while one found against them. The victory is tied to the outcome of the major court action in the land-claims case. If the chiefs win in Delgamuukw, they will win the injunction.

These two injunctions represent an important victory for the Gitksan and Wet'suwet'en people. The events at Sam Green Creek demonstrate that the evidence of the elders and the principled courage of the younger chiefs can produce real progress on aboriginal title. William Jackson's wisdom, which escaped the notice of insensitive commissioners in 1915, was not wasted on his children and grandchildren.

The Need to Educate the White Man

The ghost of the former governor of the colony of B.C., Joseph Trutch, continues to materialize through the statements of today's B.C. politicians. Thus, it was possible for Allan Williams, the attorney general of the newly elected Socred government, to say in 1975: "Just because a bunch of Indians wandered up and down the Rocky Mountain trench for a few hundred years, doesn't mean they own it."

In nearly two hundred years of contact, the Gitksan and Wet'suwet'en people have learned far more about the white man than white men have learned of the Gitksan and Wet'suwet'en. The statement above conveys both ignorance and contempt for the original people of B.C. The responsibility for bridging this cultural ignorance lies partly with the Gitksan and Wet'suwet'en, and they have made serious efforts to do so. But an equal and perhaps greater responsibility lies with non-Indian society and its leaders. Sam Green Creek, Antkii'is, and Kitsegukla are just a few of the recent examples of how the people's responsibilities for their land are being translated into action.

The chiefs have strong imperatives for immediate action. On each visit to their territories they see the accelerating rate of clear-cut logging, the widespread use of chemical pesticides on farms and forests, the water pollution from open-pit mines, and are well aware of the threat posed by hydro-electric dams on their salmon rivers. At the same time, their exercise of jurisdiction on the territory and at the river fishing sites faces mounting harassment from Fisheries officers and conservation officers. Most compelling of all, the chiefs are anxious to ensure that, in future, their children and grandchildren are not consumed by alcohol, drugs, violence, family breakdown and the whole host of social ills that afflict societies denied self-determination and thus self-respect.

The need for immediate action has not blinded the chiefs to the need for thoughtful implementation. Long before European colonization, the Gitksan and Wet'suwet'en social and economic systems were interwoven with those of the peoples around us through family ties and shared histories. Although each society was distinct, they shared a common view of how the world worked. Our oral histories record a dynamic culture with numerous migrations throughout the territory. Each migrant group was expected to understand and obey the laws of those who had arrived previously and each added important new elements to the society and the culture. With this history in mind, we have watched with interest the emergence of Canadian society over the past hundred years and have found it wanting. Not only does it disrespect the society of the people originally here but it forcibly prevents the chiefs from obeying their own laws. They realize that a future based on our own laws and institutions will necessitate informed negotiations with the non-Indian people around and among us. Who the chiefs will negotiate with and the framework for those discussions have not been determined. That will, in part, be moulded by the ultimate decision on the Delgamuukw court action and in part by the extent of de-facto assumption of jurisdiction by the chiefs.

There is continued tension on the Skeena and Bulkley rivers. It is difficult to know what the short-term outcome of this struggle will be. If the history of the last two hundred years is any indication, the Gitksan and Wet'suwet'en people will continue to have a difficult struggle. But if the history of the last ten thousand years is considered, then bet on those whose weapons include honesty, integrity, patience, and determination.

EPILOGUE

The Solutions We Favour for Change

Georges Erasmus
National Chief, Assembly of First Nations

The story told in this book — whether about the past or the present — is not a particularly cheerful one. Our people have lived through a grim history, characterized by the cultural arrogance of those who came to us from across the water, their relentless grab for our land, and the repeated betrayal of the promises they made to us.

Nevertheless we cannot afford to be pessimistic. Our people have retained, with what many observers have described as extraordinary tenacity, the central core of their beliefs, values, and cultures. We have no doubt about our continued survival, far into the future. We have always been here. We are not going anywhere. And the Canadian political system eventually will have to treat us as a permanent, and important, part of this country.

We believe that solutions to our many problems lie at hand. Unfortunately, governments have so far been reluctant to adopt the solutions we have suggested, but we intend to persist, and are confident that eventually they will see reason and meet with us in negotiations towards a new relationship.

In these final words I want to outline briefly the major solutions we propose.

1. Our Place in the Constitution

I described in the Introduction the callous way in which we have been shut out of the Canadian constitutional process, but what is now clear is that if we are to get major changes quickly (and we need them quickly) this process must be reopened for aboriginal people.

Changes must be made in the Meech Lake accord to establish that First Nations and aboriginal peoples are a founding people, a major part of the cultural fabric of Canada, and that we are distinct. This is important to us to ensure that our rights — already recognized and affirmed in the constitution — are protected against whatever legislation is enacted to emphasize the place of the English and the French as the dominant peoples of modern Canada.

The constitutional process, once reopened, would have to recognize very clearly the inherent right of self-determination of First Nations and aboriginal peoples so that native people can get on with governing themselves.

As part of this recasting of the accord, the formula for changes in the status of the Northwest Territories (the only area of the country where we are a majority) should revert to its pre-patriation status: that is, such a change should require the approval of only the federal government, and not, as now proposed, that of all the provinces.

2. Treaties and Treaty Rights

Another process that should be gotten underway immediately is the implementation of the treaties. There are three main areas of contention.

First is the matter of treaty interpretation. It is common practice that agreements and treaties between parties are not to be interpreted unilaterally or with prejudice to one of the parties, and yet this is exactly what Canada has done with our treaties. There are existing rules for treaty interpretation laid down by the Supreme Court of Canada, but the federal government still sees fit to ignore them. Equity and justice require that Canada agree to sit down with the First Nations directly affected, and come to agreement on this matter of how the treaties will apply today, and in the future.

Second is the issue of treaty implementation. Many of the provisions of the treaties have never been properly fulfilled. For example, many communities in the prairie provinces are still awaiting their land entitlements, more than a hundred years after their treaties were signed. Their prospects for developing viable economies, and for providing adequate shelter for their citizens, have been severely compromised because they do not have access to the lands due to them. Agreements were reached in both Saskatchewan and Manitoba between the federal government, the Indian Nations, and the provinces, regarding the land quantum formula to be used, but these agreements were unilaterally scuttled by the current Conservative government.

These communities must have an adequate land base, and it must, at the very least, be derived from 1976 population figures (as reflected in the "Saskatchewan formula"). At the same time, we believe that there is a need to revisit the whole matter of land, and that current population figures are a legitimate starting-point for these discussions. There is also a host of other matters related to the non-implementation of treaty provisions on the part of Canada, particularly in the areas of hunting, fishing, health, shelter, and economic development. And yet we have no opportunity, as First Nations, to discuss these matters with Canada. This needs to change.

Third is the matter of who has responsibility for fulfilling the terms of the treaties. Many of the treaties were signed before the "provinces" existed, and yet, today, First Nations are told that their rights and entitlements have been superseded by provincial authority, and that the federal government can do little to assist in obtaining recognition of First Nations' rights in these areas. This is particularly true of the so-called pre-confederation treaties, which cover much of the Maritimes, Quebec, Ontario, and some of British Columbia.

Many of these treaties do not even deal with the matter of sharing lands and resources, but rather with trade and alliance. And yet, today, these First Nations are told that their rights to the land and its resources have somehow been "superseded" by law. In our view it is both unconscionable and patently racist that the land rights of aboriginal people can be dismissed with such nebulous and opportunistic arguments. The federal government has an obligation to deal with this matter, and to bring the provinces into line in areas where there are jurisdictional overlaps. We cannot sit back and continue to let the federal and provincial governments pass the buck while our communities suffer. There must be a commitment that the other existing levels of government begin to deal with us responsibly.

In general, we look to a change in the federal government's attitude towards our treaties. Our treaties are the same as those signed in the United States, where the courts have recognized that the treaties did not extinguish all aspects of First Nation sovereignty. The U.S. government and the fifty states have learned to live with this legal interpretation of the meaning of the treaties, and have dealt with First Nations on that basis.

In Canada, too, we should have a political process that recognizes that the treaties signed between Britain, the United States, and Canada did not extinguish our sovereignty. The U.S. system places more emphasis on the courts than does ours: we say, let's use the political forum to solve this problem and implement First Nations' self-government immediately.

There is one other important, needed change: a place has to be made within the present legal system for the concept of aboriginal title. As we have argued this case, we have encountered resistance because there is no neat niche for it within the British legal concepts of land-holdings. What we need is a revision of these concepts to take account of a land-tenure system that existed before Crown title.

3. Non-Treaty Areas

The federal government's policy on comprehensive land claims in the many areas of the country in which treaties were never signed should be changed in several ways.

First, negotiations on self-government must take place as part of the land-claims process, and should be given constitutional protection. We believe the negotiations of land claims must extend to jurisdiction over that land.

Second, the recommendations of the study by the task force on comprehensive claims policy (outlined in more detail in the Introduction) should be implemented. These recommendations provide very real alternatives to extinguishment, and, on the basis of this enlightened policy, we could speed up a land-claims process that, at the present rate of progress, will take more than a hundred years to resolve all outstanding claims.

Third, the number of land claims being negotiated should be greatly increased, in our view at least tripled, from six at any one time (the government's present limit) to fifteen or eighteen. More than one First Nation could be represented at the negotiating table. In most cases, fundamental questions could be negotiated jointly, with more specific aspects being fine-tuned in separate talks. This was the method used in the James Bay negotiations, where Cree and Inuit were dealt with together, yet separately for specific matters. Such joint negotiations would greatly speed up what is currently a long and laborious process.

4. Education

We urge that a major study on native education, which the Assembly of First Nations has recently completed, should be fully implemented by the federal government. A first step would be immediate recognition that First Nations have jurisdiction over their own education, and that it is not a provincial responsibility.

We believe that education should be recognized as a treaty right, and that the funding needed to develop a native-education system at least equal to that of Canadians should be made available. To do that, of course, would require special funding to enable our people to catch up to the general standards of Canadians in a number of areas (including such things as the literacy rate and the ratio of graduate students and practising professionals to the general population), with special provision for development and protection of First Nations languages and cultures.

To this end we also urge creation of an aboriginal languages institute, with an endowment of at least $100 million, to fund community-controlled and -initiated language programs. The model for such a government-sponsored program exists in the Maori Language Nests developed in Aoteoroa (New Zealand), where the object is to bring Maori children to proficiency in their own language before they enter school.

5. Justice

The recommendations made by the Native Law section of the Canadian Bar Association for major changes to make the Canadian justice system much more sensitive to aboriginal needs should be implemented, but, more than that, a separate native justice system should be recognized and created right across the country, as part of First Nations' self-government. Already some First Nations, such as Saddle Lake in Alberta, and Akwesasne in Ontario and Quebec, have begun to move in that direction, having established their own tribal courts and their own legal code. These tribal courts differ from the Canadian justice system in that they mediate and conciliate between parties, rather than forcing confrontation between adversaries.

6. Self-Government

Finally, the central need if we are to reverse the trend that maintains so many of our communities in poverty and alienation, is the attainment of our right to govern ourselves.

There has to be a very genuine shift in the attitude of Canadians on this question. In our view, the provincial and federal governments should recognize and support the concept that aboriginal people will govern themselves, and do everything in their power to move in that direction. This is not impossible, as I pointed out earlier: it is already the common practice of the U.S. government, and there is no reason it could not become so in Canada.

This would mean, specifically, that federal/provincial programs would accept aboriginal governments as similar in status to the provinces, so that, in future, federal funding of programs for native people would no longer go through the provinces, but would go directly from the federal government to the First Nations themselves.

To this end there would be bilateral First Nations/federal arrangements in a whole range of services — child care, family services, education, environment, and many others for which the federal government now doles out money to the provinces, who then pass it on to First Nations communities, after taking a healthy slice of it for administration. Such a changed system would be a saving to the country, and would ensure that more money goes to where it is intended, and most needed.

This may appear to be a formidable list of changes, both in attitude and policies, that we are demanding of Canadians. We are, however, becoming a little tired of hearing the repeated expressions of shame and dismay over the "national tragedy" of Canada's treatment of its native people. It is time to move to action.

We do not believe any thoughtful Canadian can be happy with the present situation. Change is needed, and it is needed quickly. We cannot afford to lose another generation of our children to alienation, low self-esteem, glue-sniffing, alcohol, suicide, and the many other horrors that afflict so many of our communities.

We wish to fulfil that vision of a better Canada with which this book opens. We realize all people, within and without Canada, are bound together in a complex, rapidly changing world. We think our traditions and the cultures we have inherited have much to say that is of value to others as we all try to deal with the forces of change.

We know from bitter experience that others do not know what is best for us. We are engaged in a fight we will never give up, a fight to implement the policies we know will help us lift ourselves above our present problems. We hope for and welcome the support of other people in Canada in that struggle.